GERMAN MEN OF LETTERS

Twelve Literary Essays

Alex Natan, Senior History Master at King's School, Worcester, is also England correspondent to Continental newspapers, periodicals and broadcasting stations. He is the author of

Neues Deutschland (Oxford)
Great Britain Today (Munich)

and other books on Art and Sport.

GERMAN
MEN OF LETTERS

Twelve Literary Essays

edited by
ALEX NATAN

OSWALD WOLFF (PUBLISHERS) LIMITED
London, W.1
1961

FIRST PUBLISHED IN SEPTEMBER 1961
© 1961 OSWALD WOLFF (PUBLISHERS) LTD

MADE AND PRINTED IN GREAT BRITAIN BY
THE GARDEN CITY PRESS LIMITED
LETCHWORTH, HERTFORDSHIRE

CONTENTS

PREFACE

A collection of essays on the literature of a foreign country, as distinct from a history of literature, usually has some central theme to justify its existence. Writers follow up certain streams of consciousness, are attracted by particular moods which recur from time to time, or compare a literary movement with its corresponding period in the literature of other countries. The main purpose of this book is to fill existing gaps in contemporary English writing on German literature.

Interest in German life and letters has been steadily increasing since the end of the war. Knowledge of the classical poets and writers alone has become inadequate for the accurate assessment of the character of a country which baffles the student by its sphinx-like traits and the apparent inconsistency of its various moods and tempers. Goethe laid bare the conflict of the two souls which supposedly rend every German's heart. His dichotomic lines, "Himmelhoch jauchzend, zu Tode betrübt," embrace the whole range of emotions, that enigmatic variation between extremes of opinion, action and condition which has determined in the past and still determines the fate of Germany, thereby touching the heart chord of European existence. To understand the complex nature and reactions of a German, a closer and more detailed knowledge of his literature is essential. Certain questions are posed by a close inquiry into the main streams of German literature in the nineteenth century; the answers are sure to create a desire for a closer acquaintance with some poets not so well known or entirely overlooked in this country.

When faced with a selection of authors about whom relatively little has been written in English, I was surprised how limited the material is to which a student has access. The final choice of the authors presented in this book was a very personal one. When making my decision I discarded any rational method of selection but yielded to certain memories of my formative years. When Eichendorff could transport me, when Hebbel excited me beyond any previous experience, when Storm made me first aware of the sadness that is life, and Fontane's "Effi Briest" moved me to tears of pity and compassion, a deep devotion to poetry was planted which has never died. Again and again I have tried out these writings on my pupils and have always found their response spontaneous and gratifying because the message they contain has brought a startlingly new revelation of poetic powers to young English readers. This collection of essays may follow an utilitarian purpose, but the thoughtful reader will notice a perceptible link between the chosen authors. I hope it will also shed a different light on those two souls which, in more than one respect, have caused the Germany of today to become a house divided against itself.

ALEX NATAN

INTRODUCTION

by ALEX NATAN

Just as Winckelmann had become a slave to an "idée fixe"—that noble simplicity and serene grandeur furnish an absolute symbol for justifying Greek art as the perfect form of expression for human emotions—so *Johann Friedrich Herder* became the servant of another "passion maîtresse." Herder's rejection of any absolute norm in aesthetic values, and his emphatic defence of their relative aspects as one among many forms of poetry and art, attracted my interest when I came upon two German opinions about Herder diametrically opposed to each other. The one claimed Herder as a precursor of German nationalism and anti-Semitism—"ein Prophet wahrhaft völkischen Bewusstseins"[1]—while Karl-Gustav Gerold wrote in a recent German appreciation of Herder: "Aber die Hingabe und Kraft, die Herder daran wandte, den Kosmos als Gestalt zu erkennen und den Menschen zum 'Humanus' zu bilden, gibt unserem Ringen nach einer neuen Humanitas und nach einer ganzheitlichen Weltschau Ansporn und Zuspruch."[2]

As a young man Herder had taken ship from Riga to Western Europe. He kept a diary of this voyage which reveals the quintessence of his life. The open sea became a symbol of a daring journey into life. He yearned to get rid of the fetters of a traditional education in order to find a natural life, to escape from the fossilized prejudices of his time and to aim at true humanity. Herder's intellectual development displayed a Protean nature which made him into a true "Praeceptor Germaniae." He absorbed rationalism, sentimentality and classicism before embracing the universality of romanticism. His place as an influential promoter of Germany's classic age is unassailable, for without his revolutionary manifesto *Von Deutscher Art und Kunst* the Sturm und Drang movement might have taken a different course altogether. Without his friendship, Goethe might have written poems and dramas different from *Götz*, *Werther* and *Faust*. Without Herder's collection of folksongs, the romantic anthology *Des Knaben Wunderhorn* might never have appeared. "Herder was the wind which set the waves in motion, wild and turbulent in the Storm and Stress, stirring the depth of Goethe's soul, acting as a favourable gale to German romanticism." Herder was the fertile, even restless instigator of the angry young men of his own time, whom he urged to rebel against convention and meaningless codes of behaviour, against repression and a tradition allegedly alien to the German character. In Herder Rousseau found his German mirror.

His studies of Shakespeare and "Ossian" are of permanent value because they led Herder to an analytical differentiation between genuine, original poetry and the derivative, intellectual writings of the later epochs of a doomed civilization. His pantheistic philosophy may be outdated, but his conception of the meaning and aims of language even today make fascinating reading. His immortal fame, however, rests with his *Ideen zur Philosophie der Geschichte der Menschheit*, of which Alfred Weber, Herder's descendant as "Kulturphilosoph," wrote: "Wer dieses Buch liest und von dem Atem, der hier weht, sich nicht berührt fühlt, wer nicht fühlt, hier ist eine tiefere Sicht des Menschen . . . in eine bereits innerlich wahre Form gebracht, der weiss wohl selbst noch nichts von jener Tiefenschau des Menschen, die dieser deutsche Jahrhundertausgang mit dem Ausdruck Menschlichkeit benannte." [3]

No Teutomaniac has the slightest justification in claiming Herder as one of the founding fathers of his racial psycho-pathology merely because he has made false capital of the mythology which Herder gave new life. Herder was an outstanding humanist, of whom the American Professor Robert Clark writes in his recent book on Herder: "For better or for worse, Herder's thought transcends German national culture." Herder's epitaph in the Town Church of Weimar—"Licht, Liebe, Leben"—is the noblest tribute posterity has paid to his genius.

In the preface to his novel *Vittoria Accorombona, Ludwig Tieck* writes in July 1840: "Diese Vittoria Accorombona wird, so hofft der Dichter, die Herzen der reinen und starken Gemüter für sich gewinnen und so die Verleumdung des alten englischen Tragikers verdunkeln, dessen poetischer Wert von manchen neueren Kritikern viel zu hoch angeschlagen ist." [4] The English dramatist mentioned here is John Webster whom Ludwig Tieck accuses of having falsified the cloak and dagger story of the Venetian beauty Vittoria Corombona in his play *The White Devil*. While Webster's stark tragedy has stood the test of time very well, Ludwig Tieck's "rectified" novel is as forgotten today as its author is overlooked, in spite of his literary work having extended to forty volumes.

A reason may be seen in the fact that Tieck was not so much a poet as a potent stimulator who played a similar role in the *Romantic movement* to that of Herder's in the *Sturm und Drang*.

Not without justification, Tieck has been mockingly called the "Impresario" of the Romantics; for his gifts were many-sided. Certainly he was critical and sensible enough not to approve completely of all the extravagances which the Romantic movement was capable of displaying. After Goethe's death Tieck became the rallying-point of German literature. He lived to the ripe old age of eighty years, by which time the classical and the romantic periods had long ago become historical movements. It was his young friend Heinrich Wackenroder, a poet in his own right, who had died in his 25th year, who first interested Tieck in the romantically distorted images of mediaeval German chivalry. Both young writers had collaborated in the *Herzensergiessungen eines kunstliebenden Klosterbruders*, an early attempt at discarding the classical, Mediterranean ideas of art in favour of a nebulous Germanic-Gothic conception: "Nicht bloss unter italienischem Himmel, unter majestätischen Kuppeln und korinthischen Säulen, auch unter Spitzgewölben, krausverzierten Gebäuden und gotischen Türmen wächst wahre Kunst hervor." [5]

As a collector and narrator of German fairy-tales, dug out from old chap-books, Tieck became the precursor of the brothers Grimm. The genre of the fairy-tale allowed Tieck to indulge in the fantastic world of mediaeval sagas and dreams. His "Künstlerroman," *Franz Sternbald's Wanderungen*, a memorial to his dead friend Wackenroder, depicts faithfully the artistic atmosphere of Nürnberg at the time of Albrecht Dürer. Tieck attempts to show a young artist's apprenticeship to life through the medium of the arts. To him the artist is a genius particularly blessed by God. The parallel to Goethe's novel, *Wilhelm Meisters Lehrjahre*, is obvious, but the Olympian of Weimar was not at all flattered by this imitation. He mocked at Tieck by brushing aside his effusive theorizing about principles of art as "Sternbaldisieren." This "Erziehungsroman" is, on the whole, an unhappy attempt by Tieck to dabble in a genre which is essentially German in conception and treatment.

The drama was the weakest form of romantic expression. But Tieck's play *Genoveva* not only became the model of the elder Romantic movement but also exercised a considerable influence on Schiller's *Jungfrau von Orleans*. His better known fairy-tale, *Der Gestiefelte Kater*, permits Tieck a significant blending of the miraculous with reality. It is still an enchanting play of Romantic irony, which furnished the story for the English Christmas pantomime *Puss in Boots*. In Tieck's play animals suddenly assume human speech, a favourite device of many German romanticists, which enabled them to zig-zag along the undefined frontiers between "sein und nicht-sein". The versatility of Tieck, who tried his hand at every genre in literature, is also displayed in his story *Der Blonde Eckbert*, an incredibly blood-thirsty affair anticipating the almost magnetic attraction of the bizarre, of the ghoulish, of the uncanny and of all those psycho-pathological traits E. T. E. Hoffmann was to revel in at a later stage. Tieck remained an unceasing experimenter, of never failing interest and, for this reason, should be rescued from oblivion. In his poetic moments of near-greatness he was able to write genuinely romantic verses:

> "Mondbeglänzte Zaubernacht,
> Die den Sinn gefangen hält,
> Wundervolle Märchenwelt,
> Steig auf in der alten Pracht." [6]

" . . . dann erlebte man jene Abende, im Wiesental, beim Schein des verzauberten Mondes, beim Klange der Klampfe, beim Singen alter deutscher Volkslieder. Die Jungen, sentimental und romantisch wie nur deutsche Jungen in dieser Stimmung sein können, werden fast eins mit dieser Natur, und diese Natur ist deutscheste Natur, es ist ein inniges Kommunizieren mit dem deutschen Mutterboden." (Alfons Rosenberg) This description of the German Youth movement, written in 1960, recalls faithfully the mood which a reading of *Joseph von Eichendorff's* poetry produces: the irrational, emotional search for the "Blaue Blume" of metaphysical experience.

In spring 1851 Bismarck reported to his wife from Berlin: "Eichendorff . . . weisst Du, dass der Mann noch lebt? Wohnt hier im Kadettenkorps bei seinem Schwiegersohn, der dort Lehrer und Offizier ist. Lass es Deiner Begeisterung keinen Abbruch tun, dass er . . . Geheimer Regierungsrat ist." [11] The world seemed to have forgotten the poet who was then only sixty-three years old. Bismarck's remarks unconsciously contained the full bitterness of Eichendorff's life: isolation and uprooting. The poet who wrote of his native Silesian homeland found himself homeless early in his life; the defender of the "alten, schönen Zeit" had to feel the chill of a world which, for many years, appeared to him cold and "gemeinheitsselig". [12] The quintessence of German romantic poetry cannot be studied better than in Eichendorff's verses and unfinished novels. They contain all the ingredients which give German poetry its outstanding incandescence—the magic sesame of "Sehnsucht" and the striving for an unobtainable happiness denied to the denizen of a realistic workaday world. This never died in Germany and furnishes a basic key for the understanding of the best in the German Youth movement, as the above quotation aptly shows.

The wanderlust which embraces the limitless sky, the driving clouds and the mysterious stars is a lasting feature of Eichendorff's verses. Even if Brentano-Arnim's collection of folk songs acted as a "blessing fairy," Eichendorff's lyrical confessions remain poetry of a very personal experience—profound, intimate, lovable. The mysterious rustling of the dense forests of his Silesian youth accompanied the poet on his life's long journey. With a simple diction, accessible to everybody, Eichendorff unveils the unending wealth and secrets of Nature. Often it seems as if the wonders of Nature raise their voices to dissolve every sympathetic soul in melodious harmony. And yet, in spite of all his longings for the unattainable, Eichendorff's poems radiate a superb inner balance, a soothing calm and the knowledge that God runs the world in the best possible way:

> "O wunderbares tiefes Schweigen,
> Wie einsam ist's noch auf der Welt!
> Die Wälder nur sich leise neigen,
> Als ging der Herr durchs stille Feld." [13]

His unfinished novel, *Aus dem Leben eines Taugenichts*, reflects the magic, irresponsible glory of German Romanticism, unrivalled in the field of emotional fiction. The movement was drawing to its close and Eichendorff's fragment was a wonderful swan song. Wanderlust and uncontrollable yearning for all sensuous experience; sultry summer nights re-echoing the murmuring sound of fountains; innocent girls dancing and playing under the linden tree; restless students and crumbling moss-grown ruins and palaces in the moonlight; gardens and disguised countesses; happiness, love and foolishness: thus the poet and dreamer Eichendorff sees the world. But this story of delightful make-believe displays also an almost inaudible undertone of irony and mockery—a certain detachment which will come to full maturity in Thomas Mann.

Eichendorff's life was long, and towards the end of it he was aware of the threat which the awakening sciences held for his imagery and intentions. He was convinced that they would destroy belief and morals, the keynotes of that humbleness which the poet so revered. In his last years he realized, with the clearness of a seer, how the boundless energy of the new exploring human spirit would create a new world, which would find it difficult to appreciate the subtle melody of romantic abandon.

Impressions which a child retains from listening to poetry read to him may often linger on through life and determine many a predilection. Poems from *Heidebilder* filled me with fear because of the pagan spirit of moor and mist which never lost its ultimate terror; they stimulated a longing for such a landscape, so eerie and alien to a town-dweller.

Annette von Droste-Hülshoff is Germany's greatest poetess, very likely her only important woman writer, as German literature is curiously devoid of feminine talent of the first magnitude, with the exception perhaps of Ricarda Huch. All the major works of Annette von Droste were written within the compass of two years, when she, a lonely, sick and middle-aged spinster, was in love with a precocious seventeen-year-old boy, inferior to her in every respect. "My talent has grown and died with my love of you. What I am I have become through you and for your sake." These parting words of the poetess would lead one to expect a writer of the self-dramatizing qualities of a George Sand. But Annette von Droste was quite the opposite of such an extrovert mannerist. She was timid, reticent and usually the prisoner of a nervous uneasiness, partly born of ancestral pride and prejudice.

Annette von Droste stands aside from the main current of German literature. It has been occasionally pointed out that she is much more akin to the English Lake poets than to her own romantic contemporaries. She is sundered from the Lake poets, however, by her consciousness of the evil as well as the good that lies in nature, and by her awareness of the same dichotomy in her own soul. Her deep-seated religious beliefs helped her to overcome the corrosive resignation and vagrant restlessness which prevented poets like von Platen and Lenau from reaching greatness, though they had much in common with Annette von Droste. Her premature birth and subsequent frail health destroyed any hope of fulfilling herself as a woman and mother. She mastered these denials of basic human needs by becoming deeply devoted to the German landscape and by regaining her inner equilibrium in her unwavering faith in the Catholic Church. Successfully her inner tensions are played out against the endless moors of Westphalia and the lakescape of the Bodensee, and by expressing the pious longing of the simple people living in those regions. Her carefully sifted work contains ballads, lyrical poetry and many religious songs. Apart from an almost second-sight into natural phenomena, the form of her poetry is decisively influenced by her wide knowledge of the world, unusual for any woman of her time; by her mastery of several foreign languages; and by her devotion to history, music and even the natural sciences. Her best religious poems, in *Das Geistliche Jahr*, a cycle celebrating the festivals of the Church, uncover her hard, inner struggle for mercy and redemption. Her lyrical efforts to portray the phenomena of Nature achieve far more than a mere impressionistic reproduction of nuances of colour, or a naturalistic depiction of the microcosmic life in forests and fen country. Beyond the visible images one perceives an intuitive understanding of the mystery of the life force itself. In some of her poetry the awareness of demonic forces is felt with the sensitivity of a Geiger-counter. Subconscious memories emerge to torment the poetess, and passions suddenly sweep away all self-restraint. What does Man really know of the bottomless abyss of his soul, out of which Fate grows?

An answer is provided in her story *Die Judenbuche*, for which she has written a remarkable introduction. There is hardly a story in German literature which manages with such masterly skill a description of the psychology of evil through completely un-psychological means. It is the technique of Annette von Droste to narrate only the bare facts and to leave to the intuition of the reader the fathoming of the psychological dénouement. This is a story with a criminal background, set in the grey mists and dark forests of her native Westphalia. Uncanny forces are at work to give a sinister interpretation to accident, heredity and landscape, from which the story emerges. Just as her poetry only touches upon the intense emotions of her own spiritual experience, the mood of *Die Judenbuche* remains always hidden under the haze of a "clair obscur." The art of Annette von Droste lies in her particular gift of providing a framework of absorbing lyrical impressions, painted with delicate pastel colours, and leaving effect and evaluation to the perception of the reader.

All great drama is, in essence, great theatre too. Three of *Franz Grillparzer's* twelve dramas, all of them in verse, must rank as masterpieces of their kind, though none of them has ever been performed professionally in England. Twice since the end of the war I had a chance of seeing the famous Burgtheater of Vienna perform plays by Grillparzer and was struck how brilliant they are in conception, how eternal in their message, how grandiose through their magnificent acting parts, and how absorbing through their modern application.

With Grillparzer the "grand siècle" of German literature reaches its end, as the Austrian poet combines, for the last time, the best elements of classical and romantic experience. There is a splendour of feeling and a clarity of thought which ennoble his plays. But already a dark premonition is perceptibly dawning that a future will see ruthless ambition and a striving for power and glory dominating Man and thus robbing him of the peace of his soul. One of Grillparzer's biographers thinks that happiness requires

courage. "Grillparzer did not have the courage to be happy."
As the poet is afraid of losing everything, he recognizes the tragical
threat to Man in the self-disintegration of his Ego.

> "Und die Grösse ist gefährlich
> Und der Ruhm ein leeres Spiel:
> Was er gibt, sind nicht'ge Schatten,
> Was er nimmt, es ist so viel!" [14]

Grillparzer is closely connected with the old tradition of the
Viennese theatre and its delight in plays of metamorphosis and
magic (Zauberspiele). The mimic and scenic art of the popular
Viennese stage evolved a bewitching combination of local buffoon-
ery and the highly developed form of enunciation which the classical
German theatre had produced. It was finally Vienna, through its
treacherous, ironic attitude to life which smothered the poet like
the tentacular arms of a hothouse plant. Not without deeper
significance, the Vienna of Grillparzer was called a "Capua des
Geistes." Though Goethe and Schiller were his paragons, it is the
melancholic passivity of Vienna which seeps through all his work.
In his autobiographical story *Der Arme Spielmann*, Grillparzer
emphasizes the nature and the confines of that irresponsibility which
is so typical of the city which is neither German nor Romanic
nor Slav, and yet embraces significant traits of all three.

In his dramas the characters, like puppets, are dragged by
invisible forces to their perdition. With passionate fervour and
searing abandon Grillparzer yields to the magnetic forces of life
which catch him inescapably in their vortex only to wash him
ashore disappointed and heart-broken. This conflict between a lust
for life and bottomless despair; between passion and resignation;
between the lack of conscience as an active factor and a conscience
suffering in paralysed passivity; between the longing for happiness
and the complicated tasks of an artist; are the ever-recurring
themes of Grillparzer's dramas. It is always a basic pessimism
which conditions the dichotomic conflicts of his plays.

Like so many great German poets, Grillparzer is fascinated by the
close affinity of love and death, by a superb fulfilment of life and
by lethal blindness. To appreciate the greatness of Grillparzer
a knowledge of the defunct Austrian monarchy is essential. Its
deceptive charm, its elegiac disposition, its retentiveness of inner
freedom through the resignation of all outward glory, explain much
about a world which died an almost baroque death. Byron, who had
heard of young Grillparzer, noted in his diary:

> "Read the Italian translation of the German Grillparzer—
> a devil of a name, to be sure, for posterity. But they must learn to

pronounce it. What with all the allowance for a translation ... the tragedy of Sappho is superb and sublime! There is no denying it. The man has done a great thing in writing that play. And who is he? I know him not; but ages will."

Ages have ...

In the year following *Friedrich Hebbel's* death one of Germany's leading literary periodicals published an obituary which, in spite of much appreciation, called the playwright "einen dramatischen Charlatan par excellence." This proof of the narrow-mindedness of Hebbel's contemporaries is only surpassed by a Norwegian newspaper of the same year which decried Henrik Ibsen, then writing *The Pretenders*, as "als Dramatiker eine grosse Null." [15] This rejection of Hebbel, who, in more than one respect, was a spiritual father of Ibsen, is not surprising, because he had given new forms, new depths and new awareness to the realistic drama. His self-torturing insistence on a search for the ultimate meaning of existence and for the deepest significance of ideas shocked his contemporaries.

After a life of misery and distress Hebbel had reached the conclusion that Kant's belief, that Man is only responsible to God and to his own conscience, must be discarded. For Hebbel all life is tragic and, therefore, Man will only be guilty as long as he is active and encounters forces stronger than himself. Hebbel, a great psychologist by intuition, is particularly interested in the decisive turning-points of History or of any individual life, when Man is forced to sacrifice himself to forces which guarantee a further evolution of the human race, a better crystallization of its ethical duties, and a new nobility of the heart. To a historian Hebbel's intuition is of absorbing interest, since he anticipated the modern biographical approach in his application of psychological methods.

Hebbel's dramas are interpretations of ideas, and are not conditioned by facts or circumstances. His themes are character studies, and he eschews any pragmatical empiricism. They are without time and within time, and deal with problems of lasting validity; with the individual in his struggle between "seinem persönlichen und dem allgemeinen Weltwillen"; with the relationship between the individual and the community, between man and wife; and with Man in face of eternity. It is this Faustian struggle against metaphysical forces which is largely responsible for Hebbel being nearly unknown in Britain. If my information is correct, no play by Hebbel has ever been publicly performed in England.

In some of his tragedies Hebbel is attracted by the potent forces of love, the ultimate necessity which holds the world together. The love of the individual man for his fellow-man, or of man for woman, must be founded on reciprocal respect and mutual confidence. Thereby the inner and true meaning of existence is underlined: participation in that creative process which must be daily renewed to keep the world turning.

Most of his plays belong to the modern theatre of Western Europe. The final words of *Maria Magdalene*—"Ich verstehe die Welt nicht mehr"[16] could bring down the curtain on many contemporary plays. To understand this tormented poet one should read Hebbel's diaries, a monologue of epic qualities. The fundamental ideas of his creative mind pave fresh ways to a new conception of drama: how Man is enchained by the restless process of evolution; how the great individualist becomes isolated, through his very individuality and the boundlessness of his ambition, from the main streams of conscience; how he pays for his guilt through his final understanding of the meaning of life. German interpreters of Hebbel have seen in this brooding dreamer for whom all experience became tragical judgment, a dangerous rival to Shakespeare as a tragic poet, without, of course, touching the creative genius of Shakespeare, who remains a unique, universal phenomenon. But here is a yardstick with which to gauge and measure Hebbel's importance: his conception of tragedy points a way to reach beyond Shakespeare, for the first time in the history of European drama.

When I was a schoolboy my form master used to read *Theodor Storm's* short story, *Pole Poppenspäler*, to us before we broke up for the Christmas holidays. I still read this story at regular intervals, as well as many others which Theodor Storm wrote, for their spell has never been broken. They are Novellen reaching the same high standard as those of Kleist and Thomas Mann. Fascinating as I find the landscape of these stories in itself, its main attraction for me lies in its function as a superb framework for the events portrayed. It is the realism of Storm's work, and in particular the defeatist outlook on life and a certain, always recurring, pessimism, which leaves such an unforgettable impression on the reader's mind. All these prose stories possess lyrical qualities, which are only surpassed by Storm's poems; the poet himself ranked these highest among his many achievements, but they are hardly known in this country.

Storm's life and work is deeply influenced by his devotion to his native country, sea-girt Holstein, which, with its seascape of ocean, fenland and "Geest"[17] acts as a perfect foil for Storm's stories.

They are played out against the treeless expanse of a land which Time has passed by. Along hedges and ditches Storm introduces his readers to sleeping villages and into dreaming old houses, where the atmosphere of years gone-by hovers about like the smell of the rotten wood doomed to destruction, as indeed so many of the inmates are doomed to perdition. On the tables of the peasant cottages and patrician town mansions lie old chronicles; the poet skims their pages, his interest is caught by an occurrence long since past, and suddenly the past changes into the present. The basic melodies of Storm's poems and short stories consist of an awareness that life is not eternal, and is lost to anybody unable to hold it. Storm does not believe in an after-life or in redemption, for he has stressed his atheism more than once. For him enthusiasm and beauty perish just as incomprehensibly as human love and hatred. All his characters are steeped in an almost nihilistic acceptance of their fate, and the shades of the past arise from tormenting memories. A deep-seated urge to fathom the brittle existence of Man has turned the poet into a superb narrator.

The characters reflect the harsh, lonely landscape, where heath and moor stretch to the far horizon. A wan light, often eerie and ominous, illuminates it. Seldom described but ever present is the North Sea, which more than once takes on itself the function of an ogre in a fairy tale. Such a landscape can be very quiet but within lurk strange, hidden dangers, reminding us of the way in which Pan frightened Greek shepherds in the still noon-haze of Arcadia. Since death is ever present, Storm describes the world not as it is but as it appears to him in the distortion of a dream or as a mirror of memory. The mood of these stories is always sensitive. A predilection is shown for weak-willed, if not completely spiritless characters; some of them are on the verge of sentimentality and nearly all of them display helpless resignation to the fate meted out to them. They suffer from loneliness, immured in their complex inner life, or try to escape from reality into the past. A means to such an escape is a preoccupation with music—Storm himself used to compose and conduct choirs, and the musical vibration of his style gives its own attraction to his "Novellen." Since nearly all the stories lack a firm frame they often become dreams in prose, nocturnes in the twilight between truth and fiction. They rarely conclude with a "happy ending."

Personal grief and unhappiness are reflected in Storm's later, more mature works, the tones of which are darker, cloudier and often starkly tragic. His concentration on the narrow confines of his home country; his preoccupation with the family as a psychological problem; his undying fascination with the secret of life and death and his rejection of every heroic attitude, make the poet's loneliness understandable in a way that is sometimes terrifying. "Wenn wir uns recht besinnen, so lebt doch die Menschenkreatur jede für sich, in fürchterlicher Einsamkeit. Ein verlorener Punkt in dem unvermessenen und unverstandenen Raum." [18] When reading his poetry one is struck by the anticipation of later impressionism and by the poet's deep understanding of the whims of his fellow-men. Are not the following lines a revelation of what many of us feel in the vortex of our days?

> "Und war es auch ein grosser Schmerz,
> Und wär's vielleicht gar eine Sünde,
> Wenn es noch einmal vor dir stünde,
> Du tätst es noch einmal, mein Herz." [19]

While the great novelists of the nineteenth century triumphantly succeeded in probing, describing and analysing "la comédie humaine" of France and England, Italy and Russia, *Gottfried Keller* was content to write novels and stories reflecting the life of the Swiss bourgeoisie at home and abroad. About him Ricarda Huch wrote: "Im Leben eines jeden Mannes gibt es ein wesentliches Problem, das ihn vom keimenden Bewusstsein an bis zum Ende begleitet: das Verhältnis des Einzelnen zum Ganzen in immer weiteren Kreisen; bei jedem aber stellt es sich nach seinen individuellen Verhältnissen in verschiedener Weise dar. Gottfried Keller hatte vorzüglich drei Aufgaben vom Schicksal zu lösen bekommen: die Beziehung des Sohnes zu seiner verwitweten Mutter, die Beziehung des schweizerischen Mannes zu seinem Volke, und zwar besonders zu seinem Heimatkanton, und die Beziehung des Schweizers, eigentlich des Deutsch-Schweizers, zum Grossen Kanton, zu Deutschland." [20] It is, however, important to understand that Keller thought of his contemporary Germany as "ein Zerrbild der Kultur," from which he had twice escaped. He was "ein enttäuschter 48er," an idealist who had seen his political dreams perish during the abortive revolution of 1848.

In the history of German prose Keller stands at the turning point between romantic illusions and a healthy appreciation of reality. For him God is not the mysterious ruler of the Beyond but identical with a robust worldliness. A well-to-do and sheltered bourgeoisie provided the canvas for Keller's display of his views and thoughts on politics, morals and local parochialism (Kantönligeist).

Keller never loses his way in narrow-mindedness or petty squabbles but succeeds in passing over the frontiers of national limitation into the realm of human freedom and free humanity.

Keller's sympathies are usually with the humble and efficient middle-classes, but he becomes pitiless when dealing with the manipulations and self-satisfaction of a money-spinning plutocracy. His objectivity never panders to a relativism which forgives everything because it understands everything. Keller's confession to a full enjoyment of life is coupled with a responsibility for giving life a moral meaning, of improving on it, and with that equanimity of amused observation which enables him "ruhig zu bleiben im Gemüt, was auch die Ergebnisse des Nachdenkens und des Forschens sein mögen." [21]

His autobiographical novel, *Der Grüne Heinrich*, ein "Erziehungsroman" *par excellence*, renders an account of how Keller managed to rid himself of all irrational moods, of all romantic and aimless fancies, and of how he came down to the active life of a good and humane citizen. Out of tender love for his Switzerland, the model country for a democratic bourgeoisie, and with a certain ironical detachment, Keller's collections of stories were born, a vastly entertaining mirror of his own times. Keller caught his fellow-men in their own web, usually a web of boundless optimism which was apt to simplify life far too much, only to become intoxicated afterwards with the spectre of Progress. Within the narrow framework of a Swiss setting Keller pours scorn profusely and trenchantly on the spirit of Philistinism, on the conceit of "diese kleinbürgerliche Gemütssphäre." [22] Keller is a teller of tales who understands the frailty of a human heart and the pitfalls of a human life. He is so eminently readable because a rich vein of humour relieves the tension at the right moment.

Keller's masterly command of words; his humility; his scintillating "impersonal" style; his decisiveness and firmness in handling his material; most of all his talent for bringing out the simplest feelings of the common people in a warm and clear light, make Keller's popularity understandable. He has been a "wahrer Volksdichter." Nietzsche's pronouncement is perhaps the most suitable explanation for my predilection for this teller of superb tales: "Ausgereifte Geister lieben die Wahrheit auch in dem, wo sie schlicht und einfach erscheint . . . weil sie gemerkt haben, dass die Wahrheit das Höchste an Geist, was sie besitzen, mit der Miene der Einfalt zu sagen pflegt." [23]

The middle of the nineteenth century witnessed in Switzerland a splendid cultural flowering in science, art and literature. Basel, where the mytho-maniac painter Arnold Böcklin was born, became the centre of activity of the social historian J. J. Backofen, the brilliant interpreter of the part matriarchy has played in history, and of Jakob Burckhardt, the eminent art historian. At a later date Friedrich Nietzsche was to join Basel's élite. In Zürich lived the two most important Swiss poets, Gottfried Keller and *Conrad Ferdinand Meyer*. In retrospect both writers appear as "verkörperte Gegensätze des höchsten Grades," to apply Schiller's classical, aesthetic distinction. Both poets offer fascinating contrasts.

Conrad Ferdinand Meyer took most of his working material for his stories, ballads and his poetry from history, preferably from the Renaissance. Its great protagonists provided superb canvases, on which he could paint allegories of human values, positive and negative. Meyer was a most sensitive writer. Born into a patrician family of ancient lineage, he remained a romantic aristocrat in his innermost heart. Being an ailing neuropath throughout his life, Meyer never ceased longing for virility and soundness of mind and body. Suffering from the immediacy of life, he strove for detachment and aloofness. As the bourgeois stability of his own times seemed uneventful, if not boring to him, the poet yearned for the epoch of great and heroic figures, which the Renaissance had produced. He was subconsciously convinced that a coming age would demand men of strong will, of nobility, of immense courage to scale alone the heights. Not for nothing was Meyer a contemporary of Nietzsche. He, too, believed in supermen.

To fathom the complex psyche of C. F. Meyer it is necessary to know the pathological inheritance with which both parents had burdened the poet, and which contributed so much to the nervous breakdowns marring the poet's life. Moreover, Meyer suffered from the delusion of Calvinistic damnation, believing that he was to be excluded from the blessings of predestination and condemned never to achieve his salvation. Only at a later stage, after having read Pascal's *Pensées*, did Meyer find consolation in the belief that he could become eligible for God's mercy, if he would only live the life of a good man. His journeys to Paris and Italy awakened a lively sense of form and beauty, which the influence of Jakob Burckhardt considerably increased. The reading of Burckhardts's *Kultur der Renaissance in Italien* brought Meyer into direct contact with this fascinating phase of cultural development. Only late in life he found the courage to put pen to paper and to publish its results. Within twenty years Meyer wrote the best of his works, an effort which completely exhausted his energy. A high-strung morbidity put the poet under the care of an alienist. When he was released, C. F. Meyer was a spent force, a giant volcano which had ceased erupting. All his stories reflect an uncontrollable yearning for an heroic affirmation of life and for the freedom to be an untrammelled master of his own destiny. Carried away by the splendour and beauty of his Machiavellian characters, Meyer was at the same time gripped by a most sensitive moral conscience concerning the amorality of his creations. Those were the conflicts in his soul which brought him to the verge of madness. The poet attempted the solution by presenting them as a mirror of a historical past. Thus Meyer became the champion and master of the historical "Novelle." All questions and all doubts which tied Meyer to his heroes, his love for those grandiose personalities over whom a curse of History held sway, his loneliness, his challenge to fate, all have combined in inducing the poet to express himself in the medium of the "Novelle." Here he displays in symbols what his soul veiled in suffering silence. The essential subject-matter of the struggle between law and passion, between worldliness and devout submission, between politics and God's service, between might and justice, is largely identical with the contrast between men of extrovert-southern disposition and men of an introvert-northern character, between Romanic and Germanic nature, between Renaissance and Reformation.

C. F. Meyer's verses evoke dying anguish and new lust for life. Their fall is like heavy brocade in a robe of many folds, reflects plastic vigour, is perfect in form and steeped in the esoteric and darker sides of life. Intoxicated by his yearning for perfect beauty, the poet became a hedonist among poets of the German tongue. Experience serves him as poetic symbols. His symbols, however, are disguises for images, in which Meyer banishes the ordeal of enduring a terrible reality.

C. F. Meyer fell a noble victim to his obsession with men and ideas whose dwelling-place was in the beyond of good and evil. When finally the ethical conscience triumphed in the artist over his aesthetic abandon, it was too late. Meyer's life as a poet had run its course long before Death terminated it.

In his excellent book about *The German Novel* Roy Pascal analysed the reasons why this genre of writing has been prevented from scaling the heights of world literature. Pascal makes the interesting point that every German novelist has lived the sheltered life of a "bon bourgeois," whose prosperity has not allowed him to probe the depths of human misery and emotions, as great writers like Balzac, Dickens or Dostoevsky were able to do. A case in point is *Theodor Fontane*, who began to write novels when he was approaching his sixtieth year, when he had reached full maturity and an inner balance which permitted him that detachment which may ultimately have proved a bar to real greatness. Fontane began as a journalist, wrote poetry and spent some time in England where he came under the influence of Sir Walter Scott's "Minstrelsy." The result can be read in Fontane's collection of ballads, which much enriched this type of German literature.

Fontane's fame, however, rests on those novels which depict Berlin and Prussian society in the nineteenth century. This is a world dominated by the military caste in which the civil service and an old established bourgeoisie played only minor, though not unimportant, parts. The novelist describes vividly the "nouveaux riches" of the "Gründerjahre" as well as the sharp-witted lower classes. Fontane's force is that of a great raconteur who, as a regular visitor to the Berlin salons, views their varied occupants with the eye of an acute and intelligent observer. He shows us how and why conflicts of human nature may arise from a shallow social life, though he resists the temptation of being carried away by the wealth of his sociological investigations. Fontane always tells his tales sombrely and realistically, just as his great contemporary, Leopold von Ranke, advised historians to write their accounts: to depict events as they really happened. Fontane's style is witty, ironical and eminently intelligent. He refrains from pathos and stops on the threshold which leads to the most intimate relationships of his fellow-men.

Fontane's detachment permits him a certain amount of scepticism, but allows him simultaneously a disposition to remain good-natured and to show always the better sides of his characters. The wisdom of his own rich life is reflected in his aperçus and epigrams, random notes which, like lightning, shed suddenly a brilliant light on a situation. He is master of the conversation, a superb artist of the dialogue and causerie—probably the result of his French origin—which makes the reading of his letters so delightful. In spite of his predilection for ironic nuances and sardonical asides, Fontane will never lose himself in details. In a letter, written to Ernst Bertram, Thomas Mann posed the question many years ago, whether Fontane could be called a Romanticist. "Im deutschen Sinne gewiss nicht. Seine Romantik ist romanischer Herkunft." [24]

I must confess that *Effi Briest*, once described as a German *Madame Bovary*, seems to me one of the best German novels prior to those of Thomas Mann. This novel is a masterly work of art, which shows Fontane's epic genius. Here the author reveals his deep knowledge of the vagaries of the human heart. With his acute gift for social observation, Fontane tells a realistic story, set in the framework of a society displaying clear signs of brittleness and decay, anticipating the atmosphere of the *Buddenbrooks*. The world of the bourgeoisie

approaches its end. All social taboos have become questionable, all
human relations doubtful, all values ripe for reassessment. In
Effi Briest Fontane portrays the Prussian society which was to perish
in 1914. Here in this novel he reaches a greatness which often
reminds the reader of what is best in Trollope. It is masterly how the
author handles its characters, socially penned into tight compart-
ments of age, rank and sex, yet full-blooded enough to suffer their
fate, each in his or her appointed way. Fontane refuses to take sides.
He will only observe and convey his realistic impressions. He will
not judge; perhaps he is unable to do so, for reasons Roy Pascal
has mentioned. Fontane thinks any social comment of psychological
analysis is beyond the powers of a confessed Positivist. He never
answers the question of guilt. Effi Briest's father comments on the
moving fate of his daughter with a gesture of resignation and with
the telling words: "Schuld? Das ist ein *zu* weites Feld!" [25] All
Fontane can do, is to shrug his shoulders and murmur:

> "Halte dich still, halte dich stumm . . .
>   nur nicht forschen, warum? warum?" [26]

A hundred years after Winckelmann had set up his aesthetic
images of ancient Greek art which were destined to wreak much
havoc in German literature, a poet was born to smash the idols of
the Hellenic mystagogues, though, in the end, he found his way
back, not to the serenity of the Mediterranean, but to the plain
horrors of the tragedy in the House of Atreus.

Gerhart Hauptmann's rise to fame—he won the Nobel Prize and
Oxford made him an honorary doctor as early as 1905—coincided
with the provocative imperialism of the Wilhelminian empire, with
the industrialization of Germany, and with the predominance of a
materialistic conception of life. Mechanical machinery replaced
manual labour. Great cities sprang up to house, in squalid slums,
the amorphous mass of workers. The scientific-technological
advancement enriched the bourgeoisie enormously, while the
formation of Socialist parties and the birth of a determined class-
consciousness presaged the inescapable changes in Germany's social
and political structure. It was a time without any pronounced
social conscience, full of shallow pleasures and cultural platitudes.
Life in Germany became an ever-widening chasm of social contrasts
and a challenge to the younger generation, a challenge to which
they were eagerly responding through the artistic medium of the
Naturalist movement.

This new "Sturm und Drang," which arose in the Germany of the
eighties and nineties, became a strong protest against her prevalent

Zeitgeist, against all the illusions in which most classes seemed to be tightly wrapped. The social, individualistic, dissecting and stirring analysis of foreign writing which penetrated the last recesses of the human psyche produced a new method of observation. It lent its own voice to planned economy and science, for it too strove for truth. This new method cut up life in innumerable squares and sensed precisely causes and effects of human behaviour. In Germany Naturalism remained a transitory phase, as it seemed doubtful whether an impressionistic observation of facts alone was literature at all, and not merely social propaganda.

Naturalistic writers such as Kretzer, the Hart brothers, Holz, Conrad and Schlaf are forgotten today. Only Gerhart Hauptmann proved a giant amidst a multitude of dwarfs—a true poet, whose considerable work spanned more than eighty years. His plays written during his naturalistic phase stood the test of time and are in the repertoire of most German theatres of today. His first drama, *Vor Sonnenaufgang*, possesses only historical importance, whereas *Die Weber* presents a compassionate comment on the social evils at the beginning of the industrial revolution. *Fuhrmann Henschel* and *Rose Bernd* are dramas of long sufferings, showing a deep insight into the limitations of a suffering human soul. *Der Biberpelz* is one of the few German comedies ever written, a social-critical satire on Wilhelminian society.

In Hauptmann's naturalistic plays man suffers and is tormented by his innate weakness in facing his fate. He becomes the victim of his impulses and of social conditions, and must forsake his freedom in order to live in a soul-destroying treadmill from which he can only escape through the despair of self-immolation. All the characters of Hauptmann's plays are incapable of forging their own destiny. They are misunderstood and yearn for a life of freedom and health, and yet never possess the will to realize their longings.

Foreign criticism has never dealt very fairly with Gerhart Hauptmann whose success outside Germany was limited, though he had come to be recognized as the legitimate successor to Hebbel. His critics have maintained that Hauptmann never discovered his true self but instead experimented and applied his great talents to all the styles and forms of expression current during the long spell of his life. The answer to the many complex questions as to Hauptmann's literary value may be seen in the fact that the poet was concerned less with problems than with characters. He possessed the outstanding gift of re-creating them into full-blooded human beings with whom we may have rubbed shoulders in reality. This protean talent of Hauptmann is the outcome of his religious scruples and metaphysical reasonings. These were of the highest emotive kind, a combination of deep love and social pity for every human creature. To understand the depth and width of his compassion Gerhart Hauptmann's plays deserve a hearing either through the media of broadcasting and television, or on the legitimate stage.

With Herder's death in 1803, Germany's classical period reached its apogee. It is perhaps fitting to conclude this collection of essays with *Hugo von Hofmannsthal* who, in more than one respect, played out the century in a mellow and melancholy mood, no longer certain of established values. His friend and mentor, Hermann Bahr, once jokingly blamed the poet for not having died before his coming of age, for "dann wäre er die schönste Gestalt der Weltliteratur geworden." [27] What the Austrian poet wrote before the turn of the century contained his best literary work—work which was never completed but abruptly terminated by his accidental death; it has come down to us as a noble fragment.

Unlike his contemporaries, Rainer Maria Rilke and Stefan George, whose equal he certainly was, Hofmannsthal disdained to be an evangelist of a new style or a preacher of an obsolete tradition. His art was conservative. It aimed at preserving and rejuvenating all that was grand in European heritage. Hofmannsthal lived consciously in the euphoria of a dying Europe, in a time of the devaluation of all values, without being deceived, however, by its passing character. "Sind wir nicht am ärmsten, wo wir am gesichertsten, am reichsten, wo wir am gefährdetsten sind . . . kommt es nicht darauf an, immer aufs Neue die Gefährdung aufzusuchen?" [28] With Hofmannsthal a baroque blending of "mediaeval morality, Mediterranean form, oriental dream, Mozartian rococo and the mellow abundance of the Renaissance" ends a century which had experimented with every mood of literature.

While still a schoolboy Hofmannsthal came to full maturity as a poet. His remarkable command of language and imagery enabled him to reach perfection in feeling and thought. "Denn dieser junge Mensch schreibt Verse, die solange leben werden wie die deutsche Sprache, Verse, die wie im Traum eingegeben scheinen, scheinbar ohne Körper und ohne Schwere, aber zugleich von einer Süssigkeit und Reife, deren man die deutsche Sprache vorher nicht für mächtig gehalten hätte. Ein solches Wesen erschien der junge Dichter: ganz aus Geist und Ahnung gewebt, ganz aus Traum und Rausch genährt, ein Ariel, der mit den Füssen die Erde kaum zu streifen schien." [29] (R. Alewyn.)

In his important speech of 1907, "Der Dichter und diese Zeit," Hofmannsthal questioned the function and position of a poet in modern times: "Die Verworrenheit und die Vielfältigkeit der Zeit gestattet es dem Dichter nicht mehr, in einer der grossen mythischen Formen, als Priester, Seher oder Prophet dem Zeitalter gegenüber-zutreten. Wie die dichterische Substanz kollektiv, so ist der Dichter anonym geworden. Jeder hat am Dichterischen teil, der Dichter an Jedem. Das Inkognito ist sein Lebensform." [30] The poet calls himself "der lautlose Bruder aller Dinge," [31] and his time unusual: "Die Zeit ist sonderbar, Und sonderbare Kinder hat sie: uns!" [32]

When Arthur Schnitzler published his play *Anatol*, Hofmannsthal wrote a prologue, the quintessence of which is reflected in his own complete work and in the attitude of a generation which was to perish in 1914:

> "Also spielen wir Theater,
> spielen unsre eigenen Stücke.
> Frühgereift und zart und traurig,
> die Komödie unsrer Seele,
> unsres Fühlens Heut und Gestern,
> böser Dinge hübsche Formel,
> glatte Worte, bunte Bilder,
> halbes, heimliches Empfinden,
> Agonien, Episoden. . . ." [33]

While Herder was an inspiring interpreter who optimistically believed in a new golden age, Hugo von Hofmannsthal looked upon himself as a preserver of the values of the past, which the new century was about to corrupt and to corrode, and as a defender of its potent qualities against this "waste of substance."

From Herder to Hofmannsthal: a hundred years of German prose, verse and drama. Points of orientation to fathom the ambivalence of the German character and to understand much that is noble and much that remains questionable in its history, political and literary.

> "Wie's dich auch aufzuhorchen treibt,
> Das Dunkel, das Rätsel, die Frage bleibt." [34]

TRANSLATIONS

1. A prophet of genuine racial consciousness.
2. But the devotion and the energy, which Herder spent on recognizing the universe as part of a morphology and in educating Man to become "humanus," lend encouragement to our striving after a new "humanitas" and after a total conception of the world.
3. Whoever while reading this book, is not touched by the wind which breathes here, whoever does not feel that a deeper insight of Man has here

already achieved a profoundly true shape, does not know anything of that deep perception of Man, which the end of this German century called humanity.

4. It is the poet's hope that his *Vittoria Accorombona* will conquer the hearts of all pure and strong minds, in order thereby to obscure the defamation of the old English tragic poet, whose poetic fame is far too highly estimated by many modern critics.

5. Not only does true art live under an Italian sky, under majestic domes and Corinthian columns, but also under pointed arches, tangled edifices and Gothic towers.

6. Moon-lit magic night,
   Captivates the mind,
   Wondrous fairy-sight,
   Rise in ancient state.

7. Who are just as profound as they are clear and active.

8. It is not enough for a deeply-penetrating mind merely to build worlds:
   But a loving heart satisfies the striving spirit.

9. It is night: all playing fountains become clearer.
   And my soul too is a playing fountain.
   It is night. Only now all songs of lovers stir.
   And my soul too is the song of a lover.

10. . . . and then the experience of those evenings, in the meadows, under the light of a magic moon, at the sound of the guitar, singing ancient German folk-songs. Youth, sentimental and romantic as only German youth can be in such a mood, almost dissolve into this Nature, and this Nature is a most German Nature, it is an intimate communion with the German native soil.

11. Eichendorff . . . do you realize that this man is still alive? He lives here in the cadet corps with his son-in-law who is a teacher and an officer. Don't let the fact that he is a privy councillor detract you from your enthusiasm.

12. Prone to baseness.

13. O wondrous deep silence,
    How lonesome this world still is!
    Only the woods bow quietly,
    As if God walked through a peaceful field.

14. And greatness is perilous,
    And renown a hollow game;
    All that it gives is worthless shadows,
    What it takes away is so much!

15. As a dramatist a mere nonentity.

16. I do not understand the world any longer.

17. Geest: high and dry land of North German coastal region.

18. If we reflect rightly, every human creature lives for himself, in appalling loneliness.

19. Even if it meant much anguish,
    Even if perhaps it was a sin,
    If, once again, it would appear,
    Once again, you would do the same, dear heart.

20. There is one essential problem in the life of every man, which accompanies him from nascent consciousness to the end: the relation of the individual with the whole in ever widening circles; according to his own individual circumstances it presents itself differently in every single case. Fate predestined Gottfried Keller to solve predominantly three problems: the relation of the son with his widowed mother, the relation of the Swiss with his people, in particular with his native canton, and the relation of the Swiss, really of the German Swiss, with the greater canton: with Germany.

21. To keep his mind in peace, whatever the results of reflection and exploration may be.

22. Mentality of petty bourgeoisie.

23. Mature minds love truth even in plainness and simplicity . . . because they have noticed that truth is wont to express the maximum of spirit, which they possess, with the air of innocence.

24. Certainly not in the German sense. His romanticism is of Romanic origin.

25. Guilt? That is too wide a field.

26. Keep quiet, be silent . . .
    Do not ask, why? why?

27. . . . then he would have become the noblest figure in world literature.

28. Aren't we poorest when feeling safest, richest when most imperilled? . . . isn't it just the point to search out peril every time?

29. For this young man writes verses which will be alive as long as the German tongue is alive. They seem inspired by a dream, apparently without substance and without weight, and, at the same time, emit a sweetness and maturity, of which nobody would have thought the German language to be capable. 'As such a being the young poet appeared: wholly woven from spirituality and premonition, wholly nurtured from dream and intoxication, an Ariel, who hardly seemed to touch the earth with his feet.'

30. The confusion and the diversity of our times no longer permits the poet to face his age in one of the great mythical shapes, as priest, seer or prophet. As the poetical substance has been collective, the poet has become anonymous. Everyone participates in poetry, the poet in everybody. The incognito is his form of life.

31. The mute brother of all things.

32. The time is uncommon and has uncommon children: us.

33. This is how we act our parts out,
    Acting plays of our own making,
    Early, ripe and sad and tender,
    The commedia of our spirit,
    What we feel as time slips by us,
    Ugly facts in pretty guises,
    Smooth-tongued speeches, coloured pictures,
    Half-felt feelings senses in secret,
    Agonies and episodes. . . .
                    (Translated by John Bednall)

34. However much urge drives you to take notice;
    the mystery, the puzzle, the question remain.

Johann Gottfried Herder

Johann Gottfried Herder

by AUGUST CLOSS

ON 25 August 1744, Johann Gottfried Herder was born in the little East Prussian town of Mohrungen, the son of a sexton and teacher. After an unhappy childhood he went to the University of Königsberg in order to study medicine but his deep religious feeling and inclination towards the study of classical and modern authors made him soon give up medicine for theology. Immanuel Kant (1724–1804), who lectured on astronomy and philosophy at the University, exercised a decisive influence on young Herder and made him acquainted with Rousseau's doctrine of the nature of man. In later life, however, the philosophy and criticism of Kant became the objects of fierce attack by Herder who also came under the spell of Johann Georg Hamann (1730–88), like Kant a son of Königsberg. This so-called "Magus im Norden" challenged the supremacy of reason in the age of enlightenment. He to whom poetry was the mother-tongue of mankind, drew Herder's attention to the Bible, to Shakespeare and to *Ossian* and taught him English. With Hamann's help and recommendation Herder became a teacher at the Cathedral School (Domschule) in Riga in 1764, and about three years later, owing to his inborn powers of preaching, a special post as Prediger was created for him at Riga.

In 1767, anonymously, appeared his *Fragmente über die neuere deutsche Literatur* which constitutes an important document of the new era of German Storm and Stress and which amongst others inspired the poets of the so-called *Göttinger-Hain-Bund* (set up in 1772). These writers worshipped Klopstock as their idol and enthusiastically celebrated the virtues of Nature, friendship, originality and Volksdichtung. In a similar way, Herder praises the utterances of the poetic genius and condemns the restrictions laid down by the narrow interpretations of reason. Moreover, in true poetry he wants to hear not only the personality of the creator but also the voice of the whole nation, and again and again, in his earlier as well as later writings, he tries to understand and explain every great work of art through an interpretation of the climate, the age and religion and culture in which the poet lived and worked. His predilection for mythology and for the old resources of German poetry is a consistent development of such an approach which rejected any slavish imitation of foreign, literary models.

Herder stayed in Riga until 1769 when his *Kritische Wälder* appeared, i.e. before his journey to the West of Germany where he met Matthias Claudius and Lessing and (in Darmstadt) his future wife Karoline Flachsland. He then went farther on to Holland and France. In the above work he deals particularly with Lessing's famous treatise: *"Laokoon: oder über die Grenzen der Mahlerey und Poesie* (1766). For Lessing, succession in time is the sphere of the poet, as a picture of simultaneous scenes in space is that of the painter and sculptor:

"Körperliche Schönheit entspringt aus der übereinstimmenden Wirkung mannigfaltiger Teile, die sich auf einmal übersehen lassen. Sie erfordert also, dass diese Teile nebeneinander liegen müssen; und da Dinge, deren Teile nebeneinander liegen, der eigentliche Gegenstand der Malerei sind, so kann sie, und nur sie allein, körperliche Schönheit nachahmen.

"Der Dichter, der die Elemente der Schönheit nur nacheinander zeigen könnte, enthält sich daher der Schilderung körperlicher Schönheit, als Schönheit, gänzlich. Er fühlt es, dass diese Elemente, nacheinander geordnet, unmöglich die Wirkung haben können, die sie, nebeneinander geordnet, haben; dass der konzentrierende Blick, den wir nach ihrer Enumeration auf sie zugleich zurück senden wollen, uns doch kein übereinstimmendes Bild gewährt; dass es über die menschliche Einbildung geht, sich vorzustellen, was dieser Mund, und diese Nase, und diese Augen zusammen für einen Effekt haben, wenn man sich nicht aus der Natur oder Kunst einer ähnlichen Komposition solcher Teile erinnern kann. . . .

"Ein anderer Weg, auf welchem die Poesie die Kunst in Schilderung körperlicher Schönheit wiederum einholt, ist dieser, dass sie Schönheit in Reiz verwandelt. Reiz ist Schönheit in Bewegung, und ebendarum dem Maler weniger bequem als dem Dichter. Der Maler kann die Bewegung nur erraten lassen, in der That aber sind seine Figuren ohne Bewegung. Folglich wird der Reiz bei ihm zur Grimasse. Aber in der Poesie bleibt er, was er ist; ein transitorisches Schönes, das wir wiederholt zu sehen wünschen. Es kommt und geht; und da wir uns überhaupt einer Bewegung leichter und lebhafter erinnern können, als blosser Formen oder Farben, so muss der Reiz in dem nämlichen Verhältnisse stärker auf uns wirken als die Schönheit." [1]

Herder rejects Lessing's arguments that poetry represents thoughts, images and actions "in a sequence of time" and sculpture or painting a picture "in space" where the scenes have a simultaneous character. He thus again destroys the boundaries of the respective arts, which Lessing in opposition to Horace's "Ut pictura poesis" had so brilliantly established.

In his first *Wäldchen* which is devoted to Lessing's work Herder tries to achieve a balance between the author of *Laokoon* and Winckelmann. His main objection to Lessing's thesis lies in his belief that poetry and painting or sculpture are really not comparable, as they are subject to essentially different laws, e.g. the law of successiveness (sequence of time) is not the essential criterion of poetry, because the Zeitfolge is but a *conditio sine qua non*, a necessary and arbitrary limitation imposed on poetry: cf. Herder, I. para. 16, l.c.: "Die Zeichen der Malerei sind *natürlich* ... Die Zeichen der Poesie sind *willkührlich*." Energy, not the law of successiveness, creates the essential quality of poetry. Successiveness is common to speech in general as well as to poetry: "Diese *Kraft* ist das Wesen der Poesie, nicht aber das Coexistente, oder die Succession ... Wenn ihn (the poet) seine *Kraft* verlässt, wenn er mit seinen Vorstellungen unabhängig von seinen Tönen die Seele nicht *täuschen* kann: ja, dann geht der Poet verlohren, dann bleibt nichts als ein Wortmaler, als ein symbolischer Namenerklärer" ...

It is this *Kraft* or magic power which bestows life on poetry and which is the centre from which the creative activity emanates.

It was a stroke of luck for Herder as well as for German literature as a whole that he surrendered his position as a travelling-tutor and companion to the young prince of Holstein-Eutin when he was at Strassburg where he had to undergo an eye operation. Herder's *Journal meiner Reise im Jahre 1769*, though not published in his lifetime, is a self-revealing diary of a tortured, Faustian character and at the same time an important document of the rising Sturm und Drang movement in Germany. Goethe, who studied law at the University from April 1770 to summer 1771, met him there and received from him important artistic and philosophic suggestions at a most vulnerable and at the same time creative period in his early development. Above all Goethe learned to admire Shakespeare through Herder's eyes.

Whilst in Strassburg Herder wrote the much discussed treatise: *Abhandlung über den Ursprung der Sprache* which is still often referred to by comparative philologists and literary critics and for which he was awarded a prize by the Berlin Academy of Sciences in 1772.

Herder sees the origin of language in "Besonnenheit" (recollection and reflexion) which is the creator of the human word: "Dies Erste Merkmal der Besinnung war Wort der Seele! ... Als nacktes, instinktloses Thier betrachtet, ist der Mensch das elendeste der Wesen" . . . As we shall see, in his *Ideen* (II) Herder follows up this very theme with special reference to language and culture. Language is to him, as it is to Hamann, the key to the understanding of man, but Hamann (see J. C. O'Flaherty, l.c.) severely criticized Herder's theory of the origin of language, because Herder seemed to oversimplify the issues. Abstract language, according to Hamann, can never precede natural language which has a "bipolar nature"; it is reflective (besonnen) as well as perceptive; it translates thoughts into words, things into names; "Reden ist übersetzen . . . Gedanken in Worte, Sachen in Namen, Bilder in Zeichen . . . Poesie ist eine Nachahmung der schönen Natur . . . Die Natur wirkt durch Sinne und Leidenschaften" (Hamann: *"Aestetica in nuce,"* 1762).

In the meantime Herder had become Hofprediger in Bückeburg (1771–6). His literary achievements were crowned by his editorship (with Goethe and Möser) of the world-famous essays: *Von deutscher Art und Kunst* (1773) which are the artistic declaration of "Sturm und Drang" in German literature. Two of these contributions are from his own rhapsodic pen: *Auszug ans einem Briefwechsel über Ossian und die Lieder alter Völker* and *Shakespear (sic)*. Herder contrasts natural art, "Naturdichtung" and poetic artistry, "Kunstdichtung." The former is directed to the people, the latter to the intellectuals mainly; the former is naive, popular and fresh, the latter intelligible only to a limited circle of initiated readers. Accordingly, Ossian and Shakespeare and the Volkslieder belong to "Naturdichtung" which is not concerned with rigid rules such as those of dramatic unity. When turning to Shakespeare he breaks out into words of lyrical enthusiasm: "Eine Welt dramatischer Geschichte, so tief und gross wie die Natur . . . Hier ist kein Dichter! ist Schöpfer! ist Geschichte der Welt! . . . Nimm dieser Pflanze ihren Boden, Saft und Kraft, und pflanze sie in die Luft: nimmdiesem Menschen Ort, Zeit, individuelle Bestandheit—du hast ihm Othem und Seele genommen, und ist ein Bild vom Geschöpf . . ." [2]

In his *Älteste Urkunde des Menschengeschlechts* (1774) Herder interprets the Bible as an expression of national poetry of highest order, an art which was rooted in the spirit of Old Israel. His later work *Vom Geiste der ebräischen Poesie* (1782–3) develops those ideas in further detail.

The first section of this book on Hebrew poetry is composed in dialogue form. The author praises the wealth of Hebraistic idioms, synonyms and images of light and sunrise, etc. At the same time he explains its lack of hymns to the sun and other celestial bodies as owing to the poets' fear of idolatrous worship amongst the Jews. A number of judiciously chosen quotations illustrate the vividly expounded interpretation and analysis. The second section is mainly concerned with questions of the origin and character of Hebrew songs. Its beginning is traced back to common roots, both divine and profane. In the poetic word, emotion and image are combined. The outward perceptions press themselves upon the creative soul, whose inner vision condenses them to their final poetic expression. Herder emphasizes the fact that most of the great Hebrew poets were holy men, prophets or distinguished leaders, such as Moses and David, in whose *Psalms* the religiously inspired poetry of his country found its individual artistic culmination. Again and again Herder refers the reader to contemporary writing, particularly to that of Klopstock, "der uns Deutschen zuerst den wahren Ton des Ebräischen Psalms näher gebracht hat."

In 1776 the Duke Karl August at Goethe's recommendation made Herder chief pastor (Oberpfarrer) and Generalsuperintendent at Weimar where he spent his life as Court preacher, pedagogue and author until his death on 18 December 1803. During these vital years of creativity Herder's great works were published: 1778–9 *Volkslieder*, 1782–3 *Vom Geiste der ebräischen Poesie*, 1784–91 *Ideen zur Philosophie der Geschichte der Menschheit*, 1793–7 *Briefe zur Beförderung der Humanität*, 1795–6 *Terpsichore*, and finally the *Cid*—translation, complete edition not until 1805, i.e. two years after his death.

The collection *Volkslieder* (second edition entitled *Stimmen der Völker in Liedern* (1807), reflects Herder's love of "popular" poetry and admiration of Bishop Thomas Percy's anthology of English and Scottish ballads: *Reliques of ancient English poetry* (1765), which caused a literary sensation in Germany and had its marked impact on poets such as Bürger and above all on the German Romantics who, in their turn, influenced Walter Scott, Rossetti and others. The very term "Volkslied" goes back to Herder whose selection contained amongst other jewels poems such as *Heidenröslein, Edward, Ännchen von Tharau, Nordische Lieder, Lieder der Wilden*, etc. Herder's *Ideen* (as they are usually called) are a colossal torso revealing the historical development of the human race towards the noble goal of humanism (*Humanität*). Before, however, dealing with his views in that gigantic work about the landscape, religion, custom, art, law, science, the physical and spiritual aspects of a culture and their mutual interrelationships, a further glance at Herder's biography will be welcome.

In the summer of 1788 he accompanied the Dowager-Duchess Amalie to Rome and Naples. There he looked at art with eyes different from those of Goethe who travelled to Italy (September 1786–

June 1788) as a creative artist. Herder was, in contrast, essentially a moralist and preacher whose ideal was less the work of art than the guidance of mankind towards humanism. His speeches were renowned for their simplicity and humane approach. He preferred to "talk" rather than to preach; cf. Herder's own epigram: *Der rauschende Strom*: "Wollt ihr den Strom der Rede, dieweil er rauschet, vertrocknen? Lasst ihn. Wenn er nur rauscht, ist er am wenigsten tief." There should indeed be a place of honour for Herder in the history of the art of rhetoric. Even Schiller, who thought "good sermons" an impossibility, was profoundly impressed by a Herder sermon. It was considered proper manners in Weimar to hear Herder's orations.

In the years 1783–93 Herder remained closely connected with Goethe. When, however, Goethe and Schiller (in 1794) became friends, Herder gradually had to drop out of the triumvirate. Goethe's interests were at that time absorbed in studies of botany and optics. Moreover, there were other reasons for Herder's estrangement from Goethe. In particular Goethe's liberal-conservative attitude in politics was not always acceptable to the liberal author of the *Ideen*.

In this greatest of Herder's works a divine order is seen in mankind's historical development: "Der Gott, den ich in der Geschichte suche, muss derselbe sein, der in der Natur ist." His belief in Christianity is not so much based on the miracle but on the miraculous, not so much on certain events but on what those events mean to us and demand from us. It is a religion without dogma in a way similar to that of Novalis in *Die Christenheit oder Europa* (1799), but Herder would not have approved of the view that religion was a matter of merely private concern—Religion als Privatsache—as expounded by the Romantics, particularly by Friedrich Schleiermacher in his Reden *Über die Religion* (1799) and in *Monologe* (1800). According to Herder, Christianity is the revelation for all times and all nations leading ultimately to Humanism (*Humanität*). Whereas, particularly nowadays, man seems to be the victim of chance, time and decay, Herder believes in the words by Persius: "Quem te Deus esse jussit et humana qua parte locatus es in re disce." [3]

In Section I of the *Ideen* man is shown as the microcosm in the macrocosm of our universe. The earth is the stage of human history. Many cosmic catastrophes had to precede man's own development. Nature remains eternally young, even if awe-inspiring disasters such as the earthquake of Lisbon (1755) threaten our existence. Cf. Goethe about that event:

"But an extraordinary event, affecting the whole world, deeply disturbed the boy's peace of mind, for the first time. On the 1st of

November 1755, the earthquake at Lisbon occurred, and spread a mighty terror over the world, long accustomed to peace and quiet. A great and magnificent capital, at the same time a trading and maritime city, is smitten, without warning, by a most fearful calamity. The earth trembles and totters, the sea rages, ships are dashed together, houses collapse, churches and towers on the top of them, the royal palace is in part swallowed by the waters, the cleft earth seems to vomit flames, since smoke and fire are seen everywhere amid the ruins. Sixty thousand persons, a moment before in ease and comfort, are annihilated at once, and he is to be deemed most fortunate who was not allowed time for thought or consciousness of the disaster. . . ."

". . . God, the Creator and Preserver of Heaven and Earth, whom the explanation of the first article of the creed represented as so wise and benignant, had, by giving both the just and the unjust a prey to the same destruction, not manifested Himself, by any means, in a fatherly character . . ." (*Poetry and Truth* I, 1, revised translation by Minna Steele Smith, London, 1908.)

To the question: "Where is man's home?" Herder replies: "Here, where you stand." This also implies that he rejects any artistic predominance such as the "absolute" classical ideal, because there is *no* absolute standard of art and culture. Everyone loves *his* custom, *his* family, *his* home, *his* landscape—not because they are better or the best but because in them he finds and realizes his own Self, whether in the hot South or in the harsh North. Everything on earth is purposeful, even the length of the days, of the seasons and of the ages. Everywhere moderation rules. Man, for instance, has neither the muscular might nor the powerful senses of the animals. But he walks upright; he is endowed with the faculty of reasoning; he is balanced between delicate health and at the same time tough endurance; above all he is creative. The human language is the means of achieving culture and art. He can subject his instincts to the commands of reason. Man can decide freely. Work becomes difficult only when performed merely by the human body without the spirit's inclination. Finally, man can conquer bodily illness through the power of his spirit. A number of related meditations appeared in Schiller's poem "*Die Künstler*" (1788–9) in which the idea of the artist as the *total* man is the leading theme in the sense of Hamann and Herder.

Section II of the *Ideen* deals with the traditions and government of single nations. Man is "not created for the state." Religion, not the state, is the oldest tradition of man on earth, who is given the divine gift of language leading us to culture and lawfulness; cf. Herder's saying: "A nation has no idea if it has no word for it. The most

vivid conception remains vague feeling until it is incorporated in
man's memory by the word . . ." We are here reminded of the doctrine of language amongst the German Romantics and, in our time
of Stefan George's lapidary sentence: "Kein ding sei wo das wort
gebricht" ("*Das neue Reich*"). [4]

It is, according to Herder, man's word which makes him human.
It controls his emotions, it perpetuates the memory of the hero
through poetry, it creates traditions, laws, science and art, it
fastens the bonds of love; it preserves the works of the genius (Homer,
Ossian), it renews the past and connects the first with the last
thinking man on earth.

The monumental witnesses of human civilization, especially that
of the Greeks, are invoked in Section III of the *Ideen*. Again and
again he lays emphasis on the individual process of the development
of a culture under the special conditions of time, region, spiritual
and physical climate, circumstances and particular events. There is
and can be no Homer in the East. The Greeks by virtue of their
characteristic genius, nature and landscape, were able to create an
art which is unique in its grace and strength, beauty and control.
Later on, in the essay *Iduna* Herder also turns to Northern
mythology for inspiration, and thus Iduna, the apple of rejuvenation,
became the apple of discord between him and Schiller. But Herder
was quite consistent in his theory about art in discarding any
absolute, classical criterion and by advocating an artistic expression
which is rooted in a nation's individual characteristics. As already
mentioned, he thereby paved the way to the Romantics (e.g. W.
Schlegel) who like Herder broke the prerogative of classicism over
other cultures.

At the conclusion of the *Ideen*, Herder's stress on ethical questions
become strongly marked. It was this moralizing tendency which
alienated also the Romantics from him. The purpose of all our
human progress, was according to him, the realization of "Humanität" which through Jesus Christ had been bestowed upon us, i.e.
genuine brotherly love, human responsibility and dignity, a
community of men without the necessity of the worldly arm of
force. Herder's vast panorama of European civilization breaks off
with the Middle Ages.

Iduna displeased Schiller who had invited Herder to contribute
to the *Horen*, but who at that time believed in a timeless, classical
ideal and who rejected Herder's defence of a "national" expression
of art. Yet fundamentally both authors had much in common: both
endeavoured to raise individual man to a higher spiritual level;
both recognized in Greek art a maximum of artistic achievement, both
were, in contrast to Goethe, moralists, but in Schiller's view the

way to freedom and the wholeness of Man led through the aesthetic experience of beauty, cf. Schiller's twenty-third letter *On the aesthetic education of man* (1794–5): "There is no other way to make the sensuous man rational than by first making him aesthetic . . ." and the twenty-second letter (l.c.): ". . . the wholeness of Man is affected by the form alone, and only individual powers by the content . . . only from the form is true aesthetic freedom to be expected. Therefore, the real artistic secret of the master consists in his *annihilating the material by means of the form* . . ." (trans. by R. Snell, London, 1954).

Moreover Schiller's views on *Wilhelm Meisters Lehrjahre* (1795–6) proved that he was essentially nearer to Goethe than Herder, who felt repelled by the "dubious" character of the actress Philine. Thus Herder felt more and more isolated and withdrew from the society of his former disciple into the vastness of his philosophical and historical vision.

The key-note of his *Ideen*, that a Divine Will guided us to *Humanität* is also expressed in Herder's conversations about *Gott* (1787), a treatise which shows influences from Spinoza's concept of "deus sive natura," Shaftesbury's idea of a harmonious universe and Leibniz's belief in the goodness of the Creator, the freedom of man, and the compatibility of faith and reason: "la conformité de la foi avec la raison." The infinite is contained in the smallest as well as in the biggest. The universe is an organism which is subjected to the eternal law of continuous change: there is attraction and repulsion, friendship and antagonism, a constant variation of give and take. We are reminded here of Goethe's concept of "systole and diastole." Herder symbolically describes the divine source of all existence by the use of the tree-image: "God is the eternal root of the immeasurable tree of life which is winding itself through the universe."

The *Zerstreute Blätter* (1785–97) are a collection of some of Herder's own writings, translations and essays about literature, containing amongst them also the *Blumen aus der griechischen Anthologie*. Herder, in contrast to Lessing and his love of the Roman epigrams of Martial, refers the readers to Greek epigrammatic style, i.e. he prefers a more poetic mode of expression to witty bareness and intellectual points. In most recent years Stefan George's *Tafeln* again seem to tend rather towards Lessing's than Herder's style of epigrams.

Part of the *Zerstreute Blätter* are the *Paramythien*, Greek fables about the echo, the dying swan, the sphinx, etc.; and the *Blätter der Vorzeit und Jüdische Fabeln* and *Blumen aus morgenländischen Dichtern*. All these publications added to Herder's influence on the

German Romantics and above all on Rückert who enlarged the sphere of literary motifs by translations from Indian, Persian and Arabic poetry. Herder, like the Romantics, and to some extent Goethe, also favoured "*Legenden*," yet Schiller was right in criticizing Herder's moralizing tone and lack of true naiveté in the legends: cf. "Das Teufelchen mit dem verbrannten Daum," Cäcilia," "Die wiedergefundene Tochter" (probably based on the Vitae Patr. or Acta S.S. about Saint Euphrosyne). Not until Gottfried Keller (in his *Sieben Legenden*) did the art of legend-writing find a true master of visual immediacy and poetic imagination.

The *Briefe zur Beförderung der Humanität* (1793–7) continue the *Ideen* and depict progress as well as regression of Humanism at Herder's own age, i.e. the time of Frederick the Great, Maria Theresia and Joseph II. Although according to Herder, poetry is a public not at all a merely private concern, its ultimate goal does not lie in the spirit of his time but in that of Humanism, because Man is not born for the state—on the contrary, the state is made for Man. Under the impact of Winckelmann's concept of Greek sculpture Herder again praises Classic art as one of the great "schools of Humanism." Yet he adds that even the Greeks had not comprehended the whole range of artistic imagination, e.g. Mary, the Holy Virgin, as the ideal image of chastity, loveliness, motherly-love and innocence. Anticipating Novalis's view of a united Christian Europe, Herder longs for the time when nations will speak the language of *one* religion, *one* heart and *one* mind.

Terpsichore (1795–6) deals with lyrical utterances as the core of all poetic expression. By "Terpsichore" he obviously means the muse of lyrical poetry, not the muse of dancing. Poetry as e.g. that of the seventeenth-century Latin poet and Jesuit Jacob Balde, pronounces powerful convictions, sublime thought and golden wisdom. The poet speaks as the inspired prophet who sings the praise of the Creator. Lyric verse is indeed the flower of our human voice, "the most perfect expression of emotion or vision in most beautiful sounds," where ear and eye unite, the eye shaping the images in a simultaneous vision, the ear comprehending all its movements in succession.

When in this connection Herder talks of "the ear of the eye" and "the eye of the ear" he intentionally mixes up the senses and foreshadows the use of "synaesthesia" by German Romantics, e.g. Tieck, F. Schlegel, Brentano, etc., for whom image and music, space (eye) and time (ear), found a unity in the lyrical word. Thus in many respects Herder was a precursor of later literary movements, though he at the same time remained the spokesman of unchangeable truths. Shelley's words about the unacknowledged legislators or

Grillparzer's meditations at the grave of Beethoven (1827) would and could also have been Herder's views on the creative artist. Any purely formal artistry is devalued as rootless art. Any nation, without the power and gift of song, lacks, according to him, character.

In the epilogue to the third volume of *Terpsichore*, Herder deals with the problem of translation and originality. This chapter is, unfortunately, much too much neglected by modern critics. Herder does not "translate"; he "rejuvenates" the text, following its spirit rather than its actual sounds and images, e.g. in the case of Jacob Balde he does not "beautify" the original but he removes some stains from its beauty; he places the poetry into its own historical time; he follows as conscientiously as possible its metre and rhythm, but he avoids any impression which might sound alien to the German ear.

Apart from the above aspects of criticism in literature Herder's thoughts and theories also influenced Slav philosophy and even politics. Professor A. Gillies in his *Herder* (Modern Language Studies, 1945) devotes a fascinating chapter on Masaryk, the philosopher and President of the Czechoslovakian State, who hailed Herder as the father of the Slav Renaissance. Panslavism of the nineteenth century (e.g. that of Šafařik and Kollár) owes much to Herder's conception of language and nations and humanism as expressed in the *Ideen*, etc. President T. G. Masaryk, too, saw in Herder's ideal a valuable counterforce against determinism, scepsis and the corroding effects of irony. Like Herder, Masaryk believed in the integration of Nationalism and Internationalism, and in the cultivation of "Total Man," the whole man in every sphere of life. Nationalism must not be debunked; it is a "fact of nature"; but it must be guided intelligently. Only then can nationalism and cosmopolitanism be reconciled, and then nations will understand and recognize the character of other nations and other customs.

It is, moreover, significant that Herder's late antagonism to Kant is shared by Masaryk who attacks the "excessive intellectualism" of Kant as something dangerous, leading men to the overweening pride of an intellectual superman. It ends in the extreme subjectivity or "aristocratic idealism" of a Fichte and a Schelling, and finally nihilism. To Masaryk, Herder was the heir of the pre-reformer Hus (1369–1415) and of the pedagogue Comenius (1592–1670), whilst modern Panslavism could also find inspiration in the author of the *Ideen*.

Herder's last and important poetic work is *Der Cid. Nach spanischen Romanzen besungen*, based on a French prose-version of the Spanish romances about Cid's fight against the Moors in the eleventh century and also on some original Spanish romances

which enabled him to become acquainted with their characteristic
metre of four rimeless trochaics:

> "Trauernd tief sass Don Diego,
> Wohl war keiner je so traurig;
> Gramvoll dacht' er Tag' und Nächte
> Nur an seines Hauses Schmach" . . .

The following chronological table will illustrate the literary
situation in Germany shortly before and after the death of Herder:

1798–1800:	*Das Athenäum*
1799	Schiller: *Die Piccolomini*; *Wallensteins Tod*; F. Schlegel: *Lucinde*; Schiller settles in Weimar.
1800	Novalis: *Hymnen an die Nacht*; Schiller: *Maria Stuart*; Schleiermacher: *Monologe*; L. Richter: *Titan*.
1801	Schiller: *Die Jungfrau von Orleans*; C. M. Brentano: *Godwi*; Dorothea Schlegel: *Florentin*; death of Novalis
1802	Novalis, *Heinrich von Ofterdingen*
1803	Schiller: *Die Braut von Messina*; Goethe: *Die natürliche Tochter*; J. B. Hebel: *Allemannische Gedichte*; H. v. Kleist: *Die Familie Schroffenstein*; Herder: *Cid* (complete ed. 1805); death of Gleim, Klopstock and Herder
1804	Schiller: *Wilhelm Tell*; Tieck: *Kaiser Oktavianus*; death of Kant
1805	Goethe: *Winckelmann;* edition of the first volume of *Des Knaben Wunderhorn* by Arnim and Brentano; death of Schiller.

Herder's last years of life were overshadowed by loneliness and
disappointment. At his death in 1803 he was not quite sixty years old.
In the same year Klopstock died, aged nearly eighty, and also
Gleim, aged nearly eighty-four. It was at the dawn of the new
century when German Romanticism had been born of Classicism
and was still coexistent with it.

Herder was not only one of the most powerful pioneers of Storm
and Stress and Romanticism but also a universal thinker, a creative
translator and above all a decisive stimulus to the young Goethe.
It is not surprising that Mephistopheles in *Faust*, in part at
least, betrays Herder's own features. He deepened if not awakened
Goethe's love of the Volkslied, of *Ossian* and Shakespeare; he
again and again pointed to the roots of one's own culture, language
and surroundings. Moreover, his concept of nationalism and
"Humanity" as expounded in the *Ideen* not only found response

in his own time but also fertilized modern ideas about the development of nations. His work, as we have seen, lives on into the present age.

Herder's view of life is essentially an optimistic one, as he, in spite of the tragedies in world-history, passionately believes in the power of Good in men to overcome evil. No man, according to his message can live for himself alone—he must dedicate his whole life to mankind.

TRANSLATIONS

1. "Physical beauty arises from the harmonious effect of manifold parts that can be taken in at one view. It demands also that these parts shall subsist side by side; and as things whose parts subsist side by side are the proper subject of painting, so it, and it alone, can imitate physical beauty. The poet, who can only show the elements of beauty one after another, in succession, does on that very account forbear altogether the description of physical beauty, as beauty. He recognizes that those elements, arranged in succession, cannot possibly have the effect which they have when placed side by side; that the concentrating gaze which we would direct upon them immediately after their enumeration still affords us no harmonious picture; that it passes the human imagination to represent to itself what kind of effect this mouth, and this nose, and these eyes together have if one cannot recall from nature or art a similar composition of such features (Chapter XX).

"Another way in which poetry in its turn overtakes art in delineation of physical beauty is by transmuting beauty into charm. Charm is beauty in motion, and just for that reason less suitable to the painter than to the poet. The painter can only help us to guess the motion, but in fact his figures are motionless. Consequently grace with him is turned into grimace. But in poetry it remains what it is—a transitory beauty which we want to see again and again. It comes and goes; and as we can generally recall a movement more easily and more vividly than mere forms and colours, charm can in such a case work more powerfully on us than beauty." Chapter XXI; trans. by W. A. Steel, London, 1959.

2. A universe of dramatic history, as great and deep as Nature . . . Here is no poet, here is a creator, is history of the world . . . Take from this plant its soil, sap and strength, and plant it in the air: take from this man space, time, individual reality—you will have taken away his very breath and soul" . . .

3. "Whatever God destined you to be, know the place allotted to you amongst men."

4. "Let nothing that cannot be expressed, exist."

BIBLIOGRAPHY

HERDER, JOHANN GOTTFRIED: *Sämtliche Werke*, ed. by B. Suphan. 33 vols. Berlin, 1877–1913.

HERDER, JOHANN GOTTFRIED: *Journal meiner Reise im Jahre 1769*, ed. by A. Gillies. Blackwell's German Texts, 1947.

HERDER, JOHANN GOTTFRIED: *Von Deutscher Art und Kunst*, ed. by E. Purdie. Oxford, 1924.

CLARK, R. T. *Herder. His Life and Thought*. University of California Press, 1955.

CLOSS, A. *The Genius of the German Lyric*. 2nd ed. appearing shortly. London.

CLOSS, A. *Die neuere deutsche Lyrik vom Barock bis zur Gegenwart*, pp. 134–7, in W. Stammler's "Deutsche Philogie im Aufriss," 2nd revised and enlarged ed., II. 1960. Berlin.

CLOSS, A. *Die Wurzeln der Romantik bei Herder*, Mod. Lang. Quarterly. Seattle, 1941, II.

GILLIES, A. *Herder*. Oxford, Blackwell's "Modern Language Studies." 1945.

HAYM, R. *Herder*. 2 vols. (Biography). Berlin, 1880–5.

KÜHNEMANN, R. *Herder*. Munich, 1927.

MASARYK, T. G. *The Making of a State*. London, 1925.

McEACHRAN, F. *The Life and Philosophy of Herder*. Oxford, 1939.

O'FLAHERTY, J. C. *Unity and Language: A study in the philosophy of Johann Georg Hamann*, with an introductory note by Walter Lowrie. University of North Carolina Studies in the Germanic Languages and Literatures, 1952.

ROBERTSON, J. G. *Genesis of Romantic Theory*. Cambridge, 1923.

SMITH, R. G. *J. G. Hamann: 1730–1788*. London, 1960.

TRONCHON, H. *Allemagne-France-Angleterre. Le jeune Edgar Quinet*. Paris, 1937.

WALZEL, O. *Das Prometheussymbol von Shaftesbury zu Goethe*. Munich, 1932.

Ludwig Tieck

Ludwig Tieck

by JAMES TRAINER

THE literary reputation of Ludwig Tieck in the mid-twentieth century falls far short of that envisaged for him by Coleridge in 1817 when he wrote to Southey: "As a poet, critic and moralist, he stands (in reputation) next to Goethe (and I believe that this reputation will be fame)." In his own day Tieck's high status was acquired in great measure through his involvement in the movements and counter-movements, the fashions and factions of an experimental period in German Literature. As these issues have lost in relevance, so Tieck's prestige has gone into such gradual decline that even his more individual contributions and achievements have become obscured. From our perspective in time we can see that his chief influence has been indirect, as innovator and pioneer whose total impact on the history of German Literature has been greater than the sum quality of his individual works.

From his earliest boyhood days Tieck evinced a passion for books which was never to desert him, and for this reason he knew no greater ambition than to become the creator of such books, a professional writer. His earliest attempts were undistinguished and ponderous imitations which served chiefly to attract the attentions of two of his Berlin schoolteachers, Rambach and Bernhardi, who enlisted their promising pupil to complete various projects of which they themselves had grown tired. It was therefore to the sensational adventure story of *Mathias Klostermayer* and to the completion of a trivial novel with the unpromising title *Die eiserne Maske. Eine schottische Geschichte* that Tieck's first creative effort was directed. To his childhood appetite for reading, always ravenous rather than discriminating, came this second period of enforced preoccupation with the ghost-and-horror stories currently popular, and all the products of his adolescent years have to be considered against the background of these unfavourable circumstances. *Alla-Moddin* (1790), a three-act play embodying the anti-Jesuit feelings of the time but utterly void of characterization or dramatic tension; *Almansur* (1790), an idyll with distinct echoes of *Werther* and Ossian, telling of the youthful hero's withdrawal from the world to the life of a recluse; *Abdallah* (1792), a vicious tale of conflicting passions, likewise set in the Orient and again centred round the torments of youth in a hostile world; these three works, although of little artistic merit in themselves, contain in embryo the Tieck of maturity, imitative yet strongly imaginative, pretentious yet probing after truth, formless yet concentrated, remote yet highly personal. For all their bombast and rant they were at least records of the melancholic depressions and gloomy introspections of their author. And already within them lay the dormant seeds of his Romanticism.

In the process of gradual transformation to this Romanticism no single element was more decisive than the unstable temperament of the man himself. In early life, reliving what he had read in horror novels, he held long vigils in dark churchyards in the attempt to conjure up the spirits of the dead; he claimed to have experienced hallucinations in various forms which made him fear for his future sanity, and as a student in Halle he once fell into a feverish coma after an all-night reading of *Der Genius* by Grosse. This intense engrossment in supernatural phenomena found a violent expression in the descents of Abdallah into the underworld and in the horrific images of *Karl von Berneck* (1795), yet in its more refined form it provided the salient individual characteristic of Tieck's Romanticism, the awareness of the close relationship between the supernatural (das Wunderbare) and the commonplace (das Alltägliche). In sharp distinction to the intellectualism of a now moribund Enlightenment, Tieck made a genuine appeal to the irrational, the sincere belief, in the words of Uhland, that "das Unendliche umgibt den Menschen, das Geheimnis der Gottheit und der Welt." It was for this reason that from the wide range of literary forms to which he turned his hand, he achieved his greatest success with the *Märchen*, in which the realms of the real and the supernatural become fused until they are barely distinguishable.

Tieck's propensity for the supernatural was early encouraged by what he found in Shakespeare. While still at school he had acquired a copy of Eschenburg's translation of *Hamlet*, and to that moment we can trace the beginning of his life-long enthusiasm for Shakespeare and the Elizabethan stage. In later years he carried out extensive research into the genesis of the plays, supervised the translation of nineteen of them by his daughter Dorothea and Count Baudissin, and planned (but never completed) a *magnum opus* which was to have presented the results of this industry. But what first attracted him to Shakespeare may be gathered from a letter to Wackenroder written in 1792: "Auch für das Fürchterliche, Schauerliche, Angsterregende sind die Seelen sehr verschieden gestimmt; als ich den Shakespeare zum erstenmal flüchtig durchlas, erschien mir alles in einem düsteren, fürchterlichen Lichte, über alles Angenehme hatte ich hinweggelesen . . ." [1] It was the frightening and the gloomy that he found so arresting, and it is not without significance that the two Shakespearean works which most influenced his youthful dramas were *Hamlet* and *Macbeth* with their predominant ghost themes.

In 1796, by which time he had come to a deeper appreciation of the poetic content of these tragedies, he published his first critical essay, in which he examined Shakespeare's supernatural techniques and thereby unconsciously formulated what was to become his own method. This essay, "Shakespeares Behandlung des Wunderbaren," came to the conclusion that the plausibility of Shakespeare's ghost scenes lay in the creation of the necessary illusion before the action involving the marvellous had ever begun. In this way there could be no abrupt hiatus between natural and supernatural, the spectator was gradually prepared for the participation of the spirits and his tendency to rationalize was overcome before it had even begun to operate. "Denn eben darin besteht der Probirstein des echten Genies, dass er für jede verwegene Fiktion, für jede ungewöhnliche Vorstellungsart schon im voraus die Täuschung des Zuschauers zu gewinnen weiss." [2] The fact that Tieck genuinely accepted the existence of phenomena classifiable as supernatural contributed greatly to their convincing portrayal, since the principle of universal demonism which represented every object as "possessed" was eminently suited to the creation of the illusion. Once that is established we have reached an understanding not only of his technique of the supernatural but also of the nature of his belief in it. This consisted in replacing the subjective distinction between real and marvellous with the belief that the two differ only in the degree of frequency, that any event normally accepted as supernatural would, with constant repetition, come to be regarded as everyday, and conversely, that most things which we consider everyday are in fact miracles stripped of their wonder by recurrence. Tieck's romantic demonism was therefore aimed at establishing through the medium of the empirical world the existence of a higher order. To the man who is conscious of the presence of this force in his daily surroundings its appearance in less usual forms will not entail any loss of logical sequence. Tieck is never explicit whether the hallucination is a subjective phenomenon in the mind of the beholder or whether it is meant to be generally perceptible. But the fundamental issue is that for the victim of the apparition it is a reality in the same sense as any other object. If what he sees at this moment is not real, then for him there can be no reality—the natural and the supernatural fall together, for they are one and the same. The world is too full of unknowns for its mystery to be solved like a simple equation, and on this argument Tieck based the incoherent world of his *Märchen* where it is equally vain to inquire after the "whence" or the "whither." In *Der blonde Eckbert* (1796) this was skilfully accomplished by the introduction of a succession of characters, that is real people, who are finally revealed as the assumed forms of the same person, that is supernatural metamorphosis. What Eckbert had imagined to be an intimate conversation with a close friend had in fact been a confession of guilt to a higher being. He learns that his wife Bertha was in reality his sister and at one blow he feels his whole existence to be shrouded in uncertainty and confusion, "er konnte sich nicht aus dem Rätsel heraus finden, ob er jetzt träume, oder ehemals von seinem Weibe Bertha geträumt habe; das Wunderbarste vermischte sich mit dem Gewöhnlihsten . . ." (3)

In the cultivation of this sense of bewilderment an important role was assigned to nature, for the transition from one realm to the other was most adroitly achieved by a sudden change from a familiar to an unknown landscape. Two specific backgrounds, mountains and woods, were favoured for this purpose as being the most suited to the creation of uncanny atmosphere. This originated undoubtedly in the common situations of the popular adventure novels which associated mountains and woods with fear because it was in such solitary regions that bandits and marauders were most likely to be encountered. Tieck removed the bandits and replaced them with demonic forces whose power was the more formidable for being intangible and unpredictable. In the case of Bertha the fear of mountains was instinctive and associated with the word itself: ". . . das blosse Wort Gebirge, wenn ich davon hatte reden hören, war meinem kindischen Ohr ein fürchterlicher Ton gewesen." (4) In *Der Runenberg* Christian's father ascribed a magnetic power to the mountains, the mere sight of which could lure the unwary to destruction, and warned his son "vor dem Anblicke des Gebirges." Nature was not merely the inanimate background to the events about to take place but was itself possessed and liable to intervene decisively in the fate of the hero. Sunshine and thunderstorms were no longer symbols of Divine favour and Divine wrath, rather the pleasure and peace of a harmonious natural scene would inculcate into the hero the knowledge that the powers of evil were lulling him into a false sense of well-being that his disenchantment might ultimately be the greater. A similar awareness of impending horror was experienced in the silence of the woods, the *Waldeinsamkeit* of *Der blonde Eckbert*, in which man is alone and therefore thrown upon his own resources in the conflict between human and natural, intellectual and demonic. Its magical association is implied in the changing refrains sung by the bird, first when it is taken away by Bertha on her escape from the old woman's cottage, "Waldeinsamkeit, wie liegst du weit!", and in the note of joy when it is finally restored to its original surroundings:

> "Waldeinsamkeit
> Mich wieder freut,
> Mir geschieht kein Leid,
> Hier wohnt kein Neid,
> Von neuem mich freut
> Waldeinsamkeit." [5]

The peculiar effect of Tieck's romantic *Märchen* derived, therefore, from the identification of certain real milieux with their latent supernatural potentialities, and so long as his efforts were being harnessed to the creation of that effect this formula was reapplied. *Der Runenberg*, which alternates similarly between the planes of the real and imaginary, contains the identical components in the opening sentence, where we find Christian sitting "im innersten Gebirge ..., indem das Rauschen der Gewässer und des Waldes in der Einsamkeit tönte." [6] To reach the magic region of the *Runenberg* he too must pass through lonely woods and mountain clefts, from which he emerges in that state of bewilderment which seems inevitably to foreshadow eventual madness, "das Seltsamste und das Gewöhnliche war so in einander vermischt, dass er es unmöglich sondern konnte." [7] Franz Sternbald "felt a strange uneasiness when he looked towards the wood," and Ludwig Wandel (in *Die Freunde*, 1797) noticed that his melancholy deserted him as he left the shadows of the forest: "Er schritt aus seiner Schwermut heraus, so wie er aus dem Schatten des Waldes trat: denn oft sind die Gemälde in uns nur Wiederscheine von den äussern Gegenständen." [8] In this statement the relationship of man to nature is more clearly established. The dark and formidable wood impresses its sinister mood upon the mind of the wanderer to create a sense of anxiety which disappears only when the impression is removed. In this way nature was able to influence the course of events by affecting the disposition of the participants and by subduing them through its ubiquity. And through this universality nature was raised in the *Märchen* from the status of an accessory to a position of prime importance.

Tieck's study of Shakespeare had served to make him aware of music as a further "mechanical device" for the preparation of supernatural adventure and the registration of emotional climax, and as a result his own work became markedly aural in appeal. He illustrated his point that "die Phantasie wird durch Töne schon im voraus bestochen und der strengere Verstand eingeschläfert" by reference to the musical interpolations in *The Tempest*. But in the case of the almost tone-deaf Tieck the music itself was less significant than the fact of its unknown provenance, and in the process of assimilation into his "possessed" world of total animation, "music" came to be replaced by "sound." Since every object exists, it requires a means of communication, its own "sound," for the discerning observer is affected as much by what he hears as by what he sees. In natural descriptions these sounds remained predominantly musical, the evocative horn, the shawm and harp, or more vaguely, sung refrains, sighs and whispers, producing what Thalmann calls the "Musikalität des Daseins," an important element in the Romanticist's synaesthetic world of sight, sound and smell.

These romantic *Märchen* of Tieck exemplify his willingness to break new ground and prepare the way for greater men who were to follow. His inconsistency in this genre, particularly the unhappy relapses into black magic realism represented by *Liebeszauber* (1811) and *Der Pokal* (1811), was due to lack of perspective and lack of intellectual stamina alike, but through the simplicity of their presentation and their powerful insistence on the irrational, his *Märchen* were influential in the revival of this literary form.

On the other hand Tieck's essays in the genre of the dramatic *Märchen*-comedy survive chiefly as curios of their own age, saturated as they are with personal and topical allusions too obscure to be relevant to later generations. In *Der gestiefelte Kater* (1797) satire has almost completely ousted the fairy-tale element still discernible in the dramatization of *Ritter Blaubart* (1796). Not content with the primary illusion of the actor-audience relationship, Tieck brought the whole world of the theatre on to the stage in *Der gestiefelte Kater*, so that we hear the complaints of the spectators and the apologies of the author, we listen to a formal disputation on the merits of the play being performed and, when the curtain rises prematurely at the beginning of Act Three, we catch a glimpse of the chaotic conditions behind the scenes. This method of "Romantic Irony," in which the actor, by speaking intermittently out of character, asserts his real existence as distinct from his existence within an artificial role, is meant to reflect the Romanticist's view of himself contained within a world which he is constantly striving to transcend.

In applying the Aristophanic method of ironic comedy to the familiar tale of *Puss in Boots* Tieck sought to expose the debasement of the contemporary theatre by the cloying sentimentality of its authors encouraged by the servile flattery of the critics. But it was not towards Böttiger, Kotzebue and Iffland alone that his attacks were directed. The dissatisfaction of the audience in the play represented the false values of the "enlightened" theatre-going public, while the inefficiency of the technicians and scene-shifters was a protest against the elaborate décors and mechanical contrivances of the fashionable productions. This spirited assault upon theatrical authority presents Tieck to us in a new light, as the writer of tendentious comedy far removed from the suggestive mystery of *Der blonde Eckbert*. A closer analysis of the play will reveal, however, that here again there are two distinct planes of exposition. The task of satirizing the theatre in the guise of a fairy tale was accomplished, in broad terms, by assigning to the actual stage the elements of phantasy, the quest of Hinze to win for his master the hand of the princess, while in the auditorium the reality of artistic controversy was being debated with vigour. Amid the clamour of the aggrieved spectators for good taste, morality and secret societies, with the rapturous Bötticher firmly gagged to subdue his enthusiasm, the author emerges in the epilogue to explain that the purpose of his play has been, "Sie alle in die entfernten Empfindungen Ihrer Kinderjahre zurück zu versetzen." [9] This was Tieck's restatement of his own belief in the supremacy of imagination and the unreliability of intellect, and it marks the line of progress from *Der blonde Eckbert*.

Encouraged by the favourable reception of *Der gestiefelte Kater* Tieck persevered in the completion of two further works in similar vein, *Die verkehrte Welt*, which was to be the cause of the inevitable breach with Nicolai, and *Prinz Zerbino oder die Reise nach dem guten Geschmack*, a verbose inflation of the anti-rationalism of his original comedy.

The products of Tieck's early creative life were characterized in general by an undisciplined facility in expression and a pessimistic introspection in content. When required to concern himself with tasks whose only attraction was financial, such as the continuation of the series of *Straussfedern* for the publisher Nicolai, his verbal dexterity made it possible for him to satisfy his master without undue mental exertion to himself. Yet such a deeply felt work as his tale *Abdallah* with its macabre imagery and horrific language was likewise doomed to artistic failure by the sordid monotony of the narrative. The advocacy of that moderation and restraint which tempered Tieck's extravagance and permitted his advancement to the Romanticism of *Franz Sternbalds Wanderungen* was the contribution of Wilhelm Heinrich Wackenroder.

The record of the intimate friendship which existed between them, formed when they had been schoolfellows in Berlin, is contained in the exchange of letters which took place when Tieck had gone to study at the University of Halle in 1792. Scattered among their discussions of *Die Räuber*, *Werther* and *Ardinghello*

we find Wackenroder's encouragement to his friend to complete
his projected tragedy on Ann Boleyn, to treat his art less lightly
and to sacrifice quality to nothing. In 1793 Wackenroder accompanied Tieck when he went to continue his studies in Erlangen,
and in the hours which they spent together exploring the art
treasures of Nürnberg and Bamberg and wandering through the
woods of Franconia in sight of ruins and castles which reminded
them so strongly of mediaeval splendour, they discovered a world
whose warmth and colour was in stark contrast with the cold
rationalism of their native Prussia. It was the rediscovery of a
romantic mediaeval world whose art had been inspired by its religion, and as a consequence, in the literary collaboration of Tieck
and Wackenroder which followed, art emerged once more as an
essentially religious phenomenon. This enthusiasm was quickened
in the following years by further journeys, pilgrimages one might
say, to Pommersfelden, Wolfenbüttel and Dresden where they added
to their knowledge of the German tradition an appreciation of the
Italian art of the Renaissance. The result was *Herzensergiessungen
eines kunstliebenden Klosterbruders* (1797), a series of short essays and
verses on mediaeval art, written mainly by Wackenroder with some
contributions from Tieck. Among these was a letter from "a young
German painter in Rome to his friend in Nürnberg," in which he
described his conversion to Catholicism under the impact of a
service he had attended in St. Peter's Church. The story of this young
painter Tieck and Wackenroder proposed to expand at some future
date into the form of a novel, but on Wackenroder's death in
February 1798 Tieck undertook to write the novel alone. It appeared in incomplete form that same year as *Franz Sternbalds
Wanderungen, eine altdeutsche Geschichte*, a fragmentary monument to
Tieck's unfulfilled potential.

The first important novel in imitation of Goethe's *Wilhelm
Meister, Sternbald* is the account of a painter's progress in the search
for a remote artistic ideal. In the first Book Franz, an apprentice
of Albrecht Dürer, takes leave of his friend Sebastian and sets out
from Nürnberg on his journey to the Netherlands and Italy. His
sole assets are a selfless devotion to his art and a childlike religious
faith, and with these he resists the early temptations to abandon
his mission and pursue wealth and comfort instead. This insistence
on the simplicity of childhood as the most desirable human state
we have already met in Tieck and it is one of the most common
motifs throughout his entire work. It is used as the symbol of a
happiness no longer attainable, the antithesis of the forward-looking
"Beyond" to which man's attention is directed in his years of reason.
There can be no greater proof of Franz's initial high determination

than his parting promise to Sebastian that, despite the world's sophistication and allure, "I shall always remain a child." Before he has even reached the Rhine, however, his singleness of purpose has been compromised in his fleeting encounter with a mysterious girl whom he comes to identify more and more with the abstract ideal for which he is searching. His last letter to Sebastian before leaving German soil reveals the mood of growing restlessness to which he has fallen prey and suggests that Franz may be more vulnerable before the world than he had considered possible.

Already in the second Book one feels Tieck's command of his material beginning to slacken. On his arrival in the Netherlands Franz is warmly received by Lucas van Leyden and the narrative is retarded by the first of the many discussions which make up such a large part of the novel and are really vehicles for the author's own thoughts on mediaeval art, the work of Dürer and the vocation of the artist. In this connection he is concerned as much with the poet as with the painter, for each, he maintains, is possessed by the same "rolling stream" of dreams and fancies from which he draws his inspiration. Dürer's unexpected arrival from Nürnberg is introduced to widen the scope of this debate and in the contrasting portraits which Tieck presents of the two great men and their relationship to their work, the story acquires momentarily an historical dimension which is sadly absent from the novel as a whole. But on the arrival of Rudolph Florestan, a gay young man whom Franz falls in with en route for Antwerp, a new note of worldly pleasure is struck. Florestan tells a story similar in outline to the circumstances of the mysterious girl's meeting with Franz, and from its happy outcome the latter is encouraged in the belief that sometime in the future he will be united with her again. By now his horizons are blurred indeed, and it seems incongruous that he should wish to continue his journey to Italy with a fellow whose interests are so far removed from his own. The role which Florestan now assumes as companion to Sternbald is indicative of two things: that far from finding its true fulfilment on the journey, Franz's character will decline into some form of denial of his existence as an artist and, following from this, that the thread of the novel in its original conception has slipped from Tieck's grasp to become rather a love and adventure story.

This tendency is confirmed by the events of Book Three. Florestan tells "amusing stories" as they go, he laughs at Franz's timidity and indecision and diverts his interest from the aesthetic to the mundane. For his part Franz upbraids his friend for his frivolity and sensuality but he is too irresolute a character to tear himself away from the evil influence once it has been recognized. With the loss of Franz's strength of will the effective simplicity of the opening scenes of the novel is lost in the complex of mystery and recognition which comes to dominate. By chance the travellers come across a beautiful Countess with her hunting party and they are invited to her castle where Franz is to paint her portrait. On arrival there her court poet is discovered to be a relative of Florestan; a picture which they see at her castle strongly resembles a man in monk's cowl whom they had recently met; they come across the man on a later occasion and learn that his name is Roderigo and that he is the vanished lover for whom the Countess is pining; on a visit to a hermit artist, Anselm, they find a painting of the girl who has so captured Franz's heart, only to be informed that she is the sister of the Countess and has been dead for nine months. It is true that long passages are still devoted to the discussion of art but as they are no longer fundamental to the existence of the hero their effect is artificial and contrived. The pious artist of the *Herzensergiessungen* has been superseded in Tieck's mind by the more vital figure of Wilhelm Meister and the incompatibility of the resultant hybrid character with the idealistic and spiritual world in which he was moving led to the impasse in which the work was eventually abandoned. In the final Book Tieck's handling of his hero appears more arbitrary than ever. His licentious behaviour in Florence is quickly forgotten when he reaches Rome where he is inspired by a new devotion to his art. He finds the girl of his desires and from the name Marie we gather that this is the same girl of whom Ludovico had earlier spoken so eloquently. With their meeting the novel breaks off abruptly and Tieck, despite his good intentions, found himself unable ever to recapture the mood in which it could be completed.

Sternbald owes its historical importance as the prototype of Romantic prose to its evocation of atmosphere. Franz is conscious of the ability of nature to impress itself upon the spirit of man through any of the senses, but chiefly through those of sight and sound. For that reason he is constantly conditioned by the brightness or darkness around him, by gloomy association of apparently unrelated circumstances, by recollection, longing and presentiment. He is consequently at the mercy of every passing whim, yearning for whatever is inaccessible and the restless victim of his own instability. All the way from Nürnberg to Italy the background remains as static as a stage-set with no description of specific country or people. Instead we have only a natural scene which is universal in its anonymity and the alternating melancholy or joy of Sternbald. This refusal to concede anything to the historical or geographical setting of a novel precisely defined both in time and place, emphasizes the subjectivity of its composition. The artist's desire to live his life on an idealistic plane away from the seducing influences of material prosperity or family responsibility resolves itself into gradual acceptance of integration in an unsympathetic society. As we know from Tieck's later notes on the proposed ending of the book, this was to have been the solution for Franz Sternbald, as it was for Tieck. His later objection to Sir Walter Scott's manipulation of historical fact, together with his own realistic treatment of similar themes in the *Novellen* of the Dresden years, mark his ultimate abandonment of an outworn ideal. The unconvincing representation of Franz as the central figure in the novel is closely bound up with the successful cultivation of the moods of visual and aural delight. Because Tieck regards the progress of his hero in emotional and idealistic terms, Sternbald at no time assumes the dimensions of a flesh-and-blood human being. He is fundamentally the embodiment of the artistic spirit of his author and his actions and reactions are for that reason presented invariably as the registration of subjective feeling. Seen in this light of spiritual autobiography Sternbald's position between the restlessness of *William Lovell* and the reflection of *Der junge Tischlermeister* explains the importance of Tieck's phase of pure Romanticism in his own development. To an age of sophistication *Sternbald* will make little appeal, but its appearance in the same year that Friedrich Schlegel put forward his theory of Romanticism in the *Athenäum* shows how well it was suited to the spirit of its time.

Tieck's identification of himself with that movement is implied in the title *Romantische Dichtungen* which he gave to the two volumes he published in 1799–1800. Among the new works contained in the second volume was his first venture in the form of the Romantic grand drama, the tragedy *Leben und Tod der heiligen Genoveva*. In form, it tends, with uneven success, towards the *Universalpoesie* spoken of in Schlegel's theory, while its content reflects the pseudo-catholic mysticism into which the author had plunged under the force of the emotional and intellectual experiences of those eventful years—the death of Wackenroder, the discovery of Jakob Böhme, the friendship of Novalis. The background is no longer the artistic age of Dürer but the religious age of the crusaders with its saints and miracles, and the poetic method consists, in Tieck's own words, in the creation of an atmosphere of the "childlike, playful aspect of religion." The artificiality of the mediaeval world which he has constructed derives from this attitude of playfulness, for it portrays the sentimentalized form of piety in which he would have liked to believe, rather than his true state of mind at the time. One feels that for Tieck, like so many of his characters, the reality lay in the yearning itself, and that the attractions of Catholicism would have been lost had he ever embraced the faith.

In the introduction to his Collected Works, Tieck is explicit about the attraction of the material and his enthusiasm for it. Basically it is the intermingling of sharply contrasting human emotions, a formula which he applied at least as early as *Abdallah* with its conflict of love and parricide. In *Genoveva* solitary nature, feelings of devotion and the miraculous were to be opposed in epic form to lively passion and everyday reality. But in practice the dramatic element was stifled by lengthy lyrical effusions which loosen the construction of the play by delaying the action, and by the subjective treatment of the heroine. Genoveva's role is one of passivity symbolic of humility and devotion and therefore too ethereal to sustain a drama of such proportion. If it can still be praised for its general poetic quality, and the sustaining of its peculiar tone of dignity, it must be conceded that these were not the qualities for which Tieck was really striving. *Genoveva* was conceived on a grand scale in which an amorphous "universality" outweighed considerations of time and space. The ambitious plans for *Phantasus* (3 vols., 1812–17) were a further manifestation of the same penchant for the grandiose.

Phantasus was intended to comprise fifty works—an introductory poem followed by seven readings of complete stories and dramas by a group of seven people—the whole to be unified into a novel by the discussions and intrigues of the participants. In this way Tieck hoped to assemble a selection of his scattered writings (several in revised form) augmented by an equal number of new ones. Barely two cycles of readings were actually accomplished, including the new *Märchen Liebeszauber*, *Die Elfen* and *Der Pokal*, the fairy-tale drama of Tom Thumb, *Leben und Taten des kleinen Thomas, genannt Däumchen* and *Fortunat*, the third of his grand dramas, consisting of a prologue and two sections each of five acts. *Phantasus* is an important milestone in Tieck's career, for it shows just how far he had begun to move away from the Romantic method and points the way to the realism of the later *Novellen*. Although the *Märchen* are still dominated by that characteristic fusion of the real and the supernatural, it is striking that it is no longer the idealized reality of *Der blonde Eckbert* in which the supernatural was tacitly accepted as an integral part, but the physical realism in which supernatural phenomena are recognized as abnormal. Most revealing of all, however, is the tone of the *Rahmenerzählung*. The exchange of opinions on subjects ranging from European literature through landscape architecture to the evils of tobacco, the anecdotes, the sparkle and wit, this is the cultured salon conversation which

Tieck had known in Jena and in Ziebingen and in which he so excelled. Köpke tells of the speculation among Tieck's friends as to the true personages concealed behind the names of Manfred, Lothar, Friedrich and the rest, and of his explanation that they personify various facets of their creator's personality. These dialogues are thus to be considered as an extended soliloquy in which we are acquainted with Tieck's own views on the questions which interested him. For the first time the writer of maturity discards his Romantic mask and shows himself to us as he really is.

This kind of didactic narrative set in a realistic environment is the common characteristic of the numerous *Novellen* of the Dresden period of 1819–42. Dismayed by the superficiality of the contemporary literature which, having arisen partly in imitation of himself, now debased the elements of fear and mystery to crude sensation, he engaged vigorously in bouts of polemic and dialectic far removed from the irrationality of his earlier years. This reversal was, however, less complete than seems at first apparent, since it affected the form and emphasis more than the ideal. There had, after all, been moments of realism in his contributions to the *Straussfedern* and more than one critic has recognized the moral justification of Eckbert's death in *Der blonde Eckbert*. Similarly, many of the later *Novellen* rely for their *Wendepunkt* on the familiar revelation of the miraculous amidst the commonplace. The abstract void has been replaced by reality, dramatic pretension by fluent narrative, but precisely because Tieck's belief in the supernatural extended to the real world it could never be abandoned. His definition of the *Novelle* shows that for him the distinguishing feature of that genre was "dass sie einen grossen oder kleinen Vorfall ins hellste Licht stelle, der, so leicht er sich ereignen kann, doch wunderbar, vielleicht einzig ist. Diese Wendung der Geschichte . . . wird sich der Phantasie des Lesers um so fester einprägen, als die Sache, selbst im Wunderbaren, unter anderen Umständen wieder alltäglich sein könnte." [10] But having once accepted the validity of programme literature, his incursions into the fields of social and artistic criticism refused to be restricted by the demands of theory. Consequently much of his narrative prose, particularly the longer histories such as *Der Aufruhr in den Cevennen*, *Der wiederkehrende griechische Kaiser* and the autobiographical *Der junge Tischlermeister* is not classifiable as *novellistisch* even by his own definition. Along with his underrated Renaissance novel *Vittoria Accorombona* (1840) they should perhaps be numbered among his abortive attempts to produce a masterpiece of wide authority. As it was he counteracted the insipidity of the current fashion by developing the artistic *Novelle* which has survived the ages of realism and naturalism as the medium for German narrative writing. His output of almost forty *Novellen* in nineteen years witnesses in the diversity of subject matter and the mixture of irony and wit, terror and humour to the versatility that was at all times his merit and his undoing. There can be no doubt that the social prestige which Tieck enjoyed in Dresden and the uncritical praise of his coterie there encouraged him to sacrifice artistic merit to the more immediate approval of his own age. His inability to curb his dire prolixity and shape his material into some more compact form, his commitment to feuds which were in truth beneath him, his lack of mental discipline—all this has robbed the *Novellen* of that timelessness which is the mark of the great writer. In a circle which looked to him for entertainment and amusement he found an outlet for the creative instinct which never deserted him. But the contested issues of his youth seemed remote and the men who had most stimulated his intellect were dead. If only the energy which was expended on the *Novellen* had been directed by a Novalis or a Solger to some less ephemeral purpose their impact would have been more considerable.

None of them has proved more durable than *Des Lebens Überfluss* (1839), the story of a young married couple estranged from their parents and left without resources whose mutual love and devotion bring them to accept the "notgedrungene Philosophie der Armut" that most of life's apparent necessities are dispensable superfluities. To avoid detection they remain within their first-floor room and as winter draws on they can keep their fire going only by using the stairs for fuel. When they have cut themselves off from all outside contact by this means the expected tragedy is averted by the arrival of a friend who brings them news of their parents' forgiveness. The narrative is skilfully presented. Tieck begins with a description of the scenes of tumult in the street on a cold day in February. This is really the final episode in the story, the discovery of the missing stairway, and he then goes back in time to unfold the sequence of events leading up to this. We are informed of incidents which had taken place prior to their withdrawal to this room by means of readings from Heinrich's diary which in their comment upon topics of wider interest allow Tieck scope for his critical wit. The *Novelle* is thus concerned with the revelation of willing sacrifice of rank and possessions to an idyllic penury lived in a secluded fairy world which is dependent for its continuance upon the removal of the only link with the outside world. "Wir leben," says Clara, "ein Märchen, leben so wunderlich, wie es nur in der Tausend und einen Nacht geschildert werden kann."[11] It is an existence without "life's superfluities"—money, comfort, abundance—sustained rather by the abstract qualities of love, cheerfulness and imagination, and for that reason it is incompatible with the world of reality. Their return to a less ideal plane is therefore accompanied by the symbols of prosperity which Vandelmeer brings to them as their private realm is about to be invaded. Their unsuspected wealth and the forgiveness of aristocratic parents replace the vanished stair and give them a means of access into the world. And perhaps *Des Lebens Überfluss* owes its prominence among the products of Tieck's later realism to the presence of these more Romantic traits.

Tieck's literary activity does not find its justification in his original work alone. Among the authors whose works he edited and sought to popularize were Kleist, Lenz and Novalis; he can claim, with his version of *Don Quixote* which appeared between 1799 and 1801, to be the first great German translator of Cervantes; and above all, he was an industrious pioneer of Shakespearean studies. The pages of *Alt-Englisches Theater* and *Vier Schauspiele von Shakespeare* contain his attempt to trace the gradual development of Shakespeare's art within an existing theatrical convention from some primitive *Urdrama* to the masterpieces of his maturity. This obsession, "dies grosse Genie gleichsam in der Wiege überraschen zu können," [12] coloured his attitude towards all the plays of doubtful or disputed origin, and drove him repeatedly to assert the authorship of Shakespeare without adducing more substantial proof than his own poetic intuition. If the subjectivity of this critical method has invalidated most of the conclusions which he arrived at, his study of the works of Shakespeare's contemporaries and of the technicalities of the Elizabethan stage has provided an important lead to his more systematic successors in the same fields.

Of Tieck's voluminous output very little is read today, but the full account of his influence upon his own and succeeding ages has still to be written. Only when that has been done can the effect of his fusion of artistic zeal and bold innovation be properly assessed. As it is, his reputation stands assured as the first great exponent of literary Romanticism in Germany—"der seltene Fall, dass eine entscheidende Bewegung am umfänglichsten durch einen repräsentiert wird, der gar nicht ihre höchsten Werke schuf." [13] And it is perhaps as an important figure in the history of literature rather than in the literature itself that he will continue to survive.

TRANSLATIONS

1. For the frightening, horrific, fearful our souls are also very differently disposed; when I hastily read Shakespeare for the first time everything appeared in a gloomy, terrifying light, I had overlooked all the beauty.

2. For the touchstone of true genius lies precisely in its ability to win the reader's illusion beforehand for the most daring fiction, for the most unusual form of presentation.

3. He could find no solution to the problem whether he was dreaming at this moment or whether he had previously dreamed of his wife Bertha; the marvellous blended with the commonplace . . .

4. As a child the very word mountain had been a fearful sound to my ear whenever I heard it mentioned.

> 5.   Silence of woods
>   Cheers me anew,
>   Safe from all harm,
>   Envy is far,
>   It cheers me anew
>   Silence of woods.

6. In the inmost mountains . . . , while the sound of the waters and the wood echoed through the silence.

7. The most strange and the most commonplace were so intermingled that it was impossible for him to distinguish them.

8. He cast off his melancholy as he stepped out of the shadow of the wood; for the images within us are often merely the reflections of external objects.

9. To transport you all back to the distant feelings of your childhood.

10. . . . that it places in the brightest light some great or small event which, however simply it may occur, is still marvellous, perhaps unique. This turn in the story . . . will impress itself all the more firmly upon the reader's imagination in as much as the event, despite its miraculous nature, might under different circumstances again be commonplace.

11. We are living a fairy tale, a life so wonderful as can only be found in the *Arabian Nights*.

12. . . . to be able to surprise that great genius in his cradle, as it were.

13. . . . the rare case of an important movement being most widely represented by a writer who did not produce its greatest works.

BIBLIOGRAPHY

Ludwig Tiecks Schriften, 28 vols. Berlin, 1828–54.

Ludwig Tieck, *Dramaturgische Blätter*. Breslau, 1826.

Ludwig Tieck, *Kritische Schriften*. Leipzig, 1848.

Letters of Ludwig Tieck 1792–1853, ed. Zeydel, Matenko and Fife. New York and London, 1937.

Thomas Carlyle, *German Romance*, *I*, London, 1898, contains English translations of *Der blonde Eckbert*, *Der getreue Eckart*, *Der Runenberg*, *Die Elfen* and *Der Pokal*.

KÖPKE, R. *Erinnerungen aus dem Leben des Dichters Ludwig Tieck.* Leipzig, 1855.

LUSSKY, A. E. *Tieck's Approach to Romanticism.* Leipzig, 1925.

TYMMS, R. *German Romantic Literature.* London, 1955.

WILLOUGHBY, L. A. *The Romantic Movement in Germany.* Oxford, 1930.

ZEYDEL, E. H. *Ludwig Tieck and England.* Princeton, 1931.

ZEYDEL, E. H. *Ludwig Tieck, the German Romanticist.* Princeton, 1935.

Joseph von Eichendorff

Joseph von Eichendorff

by GILLIAN RODGER

THE contrast of permanence and impermanence is one of the striking characteristics of the Romantic movement in Germany. Of its varied representatives—the Schlegels, Tieck, Novalis, Arnim and Brentano, Fouqué, Chamisso, Uhland, Eichendorff, Heine—each brought a different contribution to the period, each emphasized an individual aspect of current tendencies, each had his own particular conception of the aesthetic ideal; and, seen thus collectively, the Romantics gave rich, characteristic and enduring expression to German life and thought in the early nineteenth century. As individuals, however, they seem to have created little of lasting value. Fouqué, the idol of his contemporaries, is now widely derided for his naive and sickly sentimentality. Few now read Tieck's once popular *Märchen*. Even Brentano, Chamisso and Hoffmann have survived a century in only one or two of their many works. There is one Romantic, however, to whom this criticism does not apply. Joseph von Eichendorff, far from being remembered only for his literary historical significance, survives in twentieth-century Germany as a familiar, interesting and influential figure. His comedy *Die Freier* is the only Romantic drama, apart from *Das Käthchen von Heilbronn*, to have established itself, and indeed grown steadily in popularity, on the German stage. Not only have a great many of his lyric poems been perpetuated, for a wide public, in their musical settings by Mendelssohn, Schumann, Brahms and Hugo Wolf; some of these songs, notably *Das zerbrochene Ringlein*, have also become part of German popular tradition and suffered the rare metamorphosis of *Kunstlied* into *Volkslied*. Further, Eichendorff's relevance for the modern world can be seen in his increasing reputation as the lyrical spokesman of the lost regions of East Germany. And, of course, to all his countrymen he makes a perennial appeal by his glorification of the magical world of the German forest. One may be tempted, thus, to conclude that Eichendorff's present-day public, if large, is also predominantly emotional and that it inclines to sentimentalize his talents and value him, in a maudlin manner, for virtues which he has acquired either accidentally or by false pretences. Surely, one might think, it is more to the credit of Mendelssohn and Hugo Wolf that so many of Eichendorff's lyrics are still known; it is surely the mere coincidence of international events which has endowed him, as an East German, with contemporary significance. Unfortunately, his achievement lends itself, by its very nature, to such glib assessment. As a result, it is frequently underestimated or misunderstood and the real cause of his survival, the unique quality of his Romanticism, overlooked. On the other hand, just for this reason, serious interest in Eichendorff is the more likely to be rewarded by unexpected revelation and by insight, not only into the value of his work, but also into his position as a Romantic and into significant aspects of the general phenomenon of Romanticism itself.

At first sight Eichendorff reveals little that would allow his investigator to distinguish him usefully from his contemporaries. The very facts of his life seem to reflect Romanticism in its uneasy ambivalence. The circumstances of his youth—his birth on 10 March 1788 into an ancient, aristocratic, Catholic family, his idyllic childhood in the beloved castle of Lubowitz, near Ratibor in Upper Silesia, his carefree years as a student in Halle and Heidelberg—contrast both with the troubled state of contemporary Europe and with the pattern of his later life—his unsatisfying military service, his bitter surrender of the family estates, his prosaic years as a married man, the anxieties of his career as a civil servant and his death in retirement at Neisse on 26 November 1857. Thus the course of Eichendorff's life itself suggests the essential Romantic conflict of real and ideal, and indeed he seems, again at first sight, to have resolved this conflict in characteristic Romantic manner, by shunning the harshness of reality and fleeing to an ideal world created by his poetic talent. This, at any rate, is the inference to be drawn from the chronology of his literary life; during the happy years of his youth he produced little, but throughout his time as a civil servant he maintained a constant flow of creative writing.

Yet, if we look more closely at the superficially conventional features of Eichendorff's life and poetic activity we become aware of their distinctive character and of the individuality of his Romanticism. Can we, for example, use the familiar, if misleading, words "Romantic escapist" to describe a man who was passionately interested in contemporary events and projects, such as the rebuilding of the castle of Marienburg or the completion of Cologne Cathedral? Dare we gloss over the section of Eichendorff's work which, far from offering him an escape from reality, reflects his consciousness of the world, its troubles and preoccupations? His historical essays, his political treatises (for example, *Preußen und die*

Konstitutionen or *Über Garantien*), his works of contemporary literary criticism (the section on Romanticism in *Geschichte der Poetischen Literatur Deutschlands*, for instance) are too often ignored and, together with his autobiographical study *Erlebtes*, testify to his awareness of reality and his willingness to consider its problems.

On the evidence of such interests and works, it is thus impossible to dismiss Eichendorff as "weltfremd". On the other hand, by far the greater part of his activity was imaginative, linking him with more obviously Romantic traditions, and it is in the imaginative section of his writing that the essential nature of his achievement may be revealed. His sense of reality, illuminated at this stage, should, however, serve as a helpful clue to subsequent discovery.

One of the many fallacies attaching to the name of Eichendorff implies that he was creative only in the lyric genre. In fact he expressed himself, albeit with varying success, in all the characteristic genres of Romanticism, his diverse works together forming a significant whole. Following the lead given by A. W. Schlegel, he indulged his interest in the literature of Spain by translating a number of Calderón's *autos*, a few of the *entremeses* of Cervantes and a novel by Don Juan Manuel which attracted him, understandably, by proclaiming values which he himself cherished; "ein tüchtiger Verstand, Ehre, echte Ritterlichkeit und Andacht gehen wie ein erfrischender Waldhauch durch das ganze Buch"* [1], he wrote in the preface to his translation, *Der Graf Lucanor*. Further, Eichendorff produced some half-dozen dramas. These, if they have never been rightly assessed, are still of very mediocre value (even allowing for the success of *Die Freier*) and they range from the literary satire and undramatic extravaganza of *Krieg den Philistern!* to the serious, indeed ponderous *Der letzte Held von Marienburg*. In the last years of his life Eichendorff experimented too with the epic genre but, like the drama, it failed to offer him a completely suitable mould for his poetic talent. *Robert und Guiscard*, an improbable tale of revolutionary France, is lyrically rather than epically expressed and, although it has some moments of magic (as, for instance, the nostalgic description of Heidelberg), its oddly retrospective method of narration and its complexities of plot are not easily overlooked. *Julian* and *Lucius*, set in early Christian times, are equally lacking in the singleness of purpose, economy of style and tragic impulse which are required to transform a merely long-winded poem or a cycle of *Romanzen* into an epic.

* Joseph Freiherr von Eichendorff, *Neue Gesamtausgabe der Werke und Schriften in vier Bänden*, ed. Gerhard Baumann with Siegfried Grosse. Stuttgart, 1957–8, III, 1096. This edition of Eichendorff's works will in future be referred to in the abbreviated form *W.S.*

It is, however, when we come to examine Eichendorff's activities in the genre of the novel, or in its shorter manifestations, the *Novelle* and *Märchen*, that we first experience the fulfilment of his creative imagination and literary gifts. *Ahnung und Gegenwart*, the earliest of his full-scale novels—it was published in 1815—is a social and ethical novel, reflecting problems of the contemporary world and characteristically contrasting the triviality of court life with the life dedicated to the good and the simple, to God, music and nature. Its hero, Friedrich, as in a *Bildungsroman*, moves through various stages of experience, meeting with innumerable significant characters and ultimately finding the most valuable way of life in a monastery. This novel is compounded of episodic events, emotional relationships, glimpses of nature and over fifty songs—the literary mixture out of which Eichendorff also concocted *Dichter und ihre Gesellen*. In this work the hero Fortunat moves from Germany to Italy and back again, recapturing his student ways, making fascinating acquaintances, singing, loving and involving himself in tragic and comic happenings. The most popularly known of Eichendorff's novels, however, is *Aus dem Leben eines Taugenichts*. Its good-for-nothing hero himself tells how he left home in disgrace, played endlessly on his fiddle to express his *joie de vivre*, arrived in Italy with no money in his pocket and ultimately found the lady of his heart.

Eichendorff's short stories are, in atmosphere and theme, miniature versions of these longer novels. Closely related to the *Taugenichts*, for example, is the hero of *Die Glücksritter; Die Entführung* is a more solemn account of love and adventure; *Das Schloss Dürande* is a tale in a different mode, set against the background of the French Revolution and treating macabre themes. Most of Eichendorff's *Novellen*, by reason of their allegorical nature, approximate to the Romantic genre of the *Märchen*. Such a one, clearly, is *Viel Lärmen um Nichts* and such, too, are many of the short stories incorporated into the text of the longer novels. Strangely, in view of his delight in the supernatural, Eichendorff wrote few magical *Märchen*. One, however, appears in *Ahnung und Gegenwart* and another is included in the framework of *Dichter und ihre Gesellen*. This last is memorable for at least one happy and characteristic invention: "Es war aber gerade ein schöner Sonntagsmorgen. Ein Birnbaum ging eben übers Feld zur Kirche und rauschte Gottes Lob."*[2]

Eichendorff's prose works, rich as they are in lyrical and imaginative passages and punctuated by songs and ballads, lead naturally on to a consideration of his achievement in the genre of the lyric poem. Since he was constantly aware of "das geheimnisvolle

* *W.S.*, II, 700.

wunderbare Lied, das verborgen in allen Dingen schlummert,"* his poetry was the product of the multiplicity of his experience. His group of some twenty translations of Spanish poems, for example, shows not only his delight in the technical manipulation of verbal and metrical problems, but also his preoccupation with traditional subject-matter and style. His "Zeitlieder" were born of specific experiences and were written either in honour of friends or in commemoration of stages, events and significant locations in his life. Eichendorff's inner emotional experiences, too, the experience of nature, of love of beauty, of God, found expression in various groups of lyric poems: *Wanderlieder*, full of love for the phenomena and atmosphere of the German countryside; the poems collected under the title *Sängerleben*, which reflects aspects of poetic inspiration; *Frühling und Liebe*, a group which speaks, thematically, for itself; *Totenopfer*, in which Eichendorff contemplates death in himself and others; *Geistliche Gedichte*, revealing his griefs and inner struggles and the consolation which God's providence offered him. The subtle and irresistible charm of these lyrics lies not in profound thought or technical virtuosity, but in the freshness and sincerity of their emotional content, in their evocative quality and above all in the deceptive simplicity of their expression. "Schlicht," "gerade," wahr," "einfach"—these adjectives, the stock-in-trade of Eichendorff criticism, could equally well apply to the folk-song and of course it is to the folk-song (recalled to contemporary attention by *Des Knaben Wunderhorn*) that Eichendorff owes his unique lyrical tone of sweet and transparent earnestness.

One group of his poems, the *Romanzen*, ought by definition to be distinct from his pure lyrics, but, in fact, by reason of their recurrently subjective manner of narration, they are close relatives of the lyric. And this is the reason for their comparative inadequacy as ballads. They are, admittedly, delightful poems; they are couched in Eichendorff's easy and convincing folk-manner; their themes, in particular the supernatural themes, are handled with rare creative invention. And on the few occasions when Eichendorff's personality is withdrawn from the tale and his emotions are concealed (as in *Waldgespräch*, *Verloren*, *Die späte Hochzeit*), then a brilliantly evocative and characteristically Romantic ballad is created. The vast majority of his ballads, however, are uneasy hybrids, their dramatic and epic effect being overwhelmed and weakened by lyrical presentation and the traditional tone distorted by emotional narration.

In outline, Eichendorff's imaginative works, therefore, merely confirm his allegiance to the irrational traditions of Romantic

* *Erlebtes, W.S.*, II, 1070.

literature and fail to differentiate him significantly from his fellow Romantics. The detail of these works, however, offers clear evidence of his unique Romantic attitude and talent.

In their geographical and historical settings, for example, his imaginative works are strikingly inconsistent with Romantic fashion. For the most part, the themes of the novels and lyrics are set in the roughly contemporary world of the French Revolution, in contemporary Italy or Germany, or in the unchanging world of nature. They therefore offer Eichendorff no opportunity for escape from his immediate surroundings by flight either into a pseudo-mediaeval world or into exotically remote lands. And even when, in his ballads, he makes excursions into his own fairyland, he locates it firmly and solidly within the geographical boundaries of the real world.

The characters which he situates in these settings are also, despite their appearance, distinct from Romantic traditions of unreality. Students of all types, noble and right-thinking (Friedrich, for example), carefree and improvident (like Fortunat), excessively sentimental or sober and prosaic, jostle each other through the novels, reminiscing about their University days, singing popular songs, tramping the countryside, playing their guitars and fiddles. These are personalities of Romanticism no doubt, but they are personalities clearly founded on the fact of Eichendorff's own experience and acquaintance. The man who is mirrored in Friedrich and Fortunat, the man who describes so evocatively the pursuits, tastes and nostalgias of students, is manifestly the same man who writes in *Erlebtes* of his life in Halle and Heidelberg and who recalls his own experiences in lyrical confession. And not only the students, but also the eccentrics, actors, soldiers, aristocrats, innkeepers, hermits who people the landscapes of his novels have a basis of contemporary reality, frequently admitting of autobiographical or of allegorical interpretation. Furthermore, the situations in which these characters find themselves—meetings, reunions, journeys, celebrations, impromptu friendships, adventurous escapades, mistakes of identity, revelations of relationship—are situations natural to the flowing, involved novel of Romanticism (and indicative of the influence of *Wilhelm Meister*); they are, however, equally reflective of Eichendorff's own youthful experience of travel, social intercourse and carefree exploits and are equally linked by allegorical significance to the contemporary world of literature, society and religion.

As may be suspected, of course, Eichendorff's characterization is flat and stylized and creates recurrent types (though never caricatures) rather than individuals. His women are beautiful but featureless and repeatedly appear in a conventional attitude—standing pensive at a window, coyly teasing, blushing deeply, or in male disguise. On the rare occasions when he creates a demoniacally possessed woman, he presents her mainly as a contrast with her less colourful, ideal counterpart. His heroes are young, linked by common ideals and high-born; or, if not high-born in the social sense (as in the case of the *Taugenichts*), they belong to a moral aristocracy subscribing to the same ideals. All of Eichendorff's heroes delight in music-making, poetry, nature, travel in "the wide world" and thus contrast with his many minor stay-at-home characters of a *Biedermeier* cast. And here surely is evidence that Eichendorff's characters, situations and themes are built on a foundation not only of external autobiographical reality, not only of allegorical reality —the basis, after all, of much Romantic writing—but also of inner moral reality. His fictitious characters share his own personal delights and ideals, and the themes underlying the complex episodic structure of his novels coincide less with the wild, irrational themes of Romanticism than with the mild and practical preoccupations which he himself expresses directly in his lyrics: the search for perfect existence, friendship, ideal love, the enjoyment of nature, hunting, travelling and above all the awareness of God.

Eichendorff's choice of setting, character, situation and theme suggests, therefore, that the essence of his Romanticism must lie in his creative attitude to real experience. This impression is corroborated and clarified when we examine more closely his handling of certain significant themes. The theme of nature, for example, is particularly enlightening in this respect. Again and again his characters and situations are related to nature and to a recognizable natural location, visualized, clearly and completely, from above: the dark-green, fresh forest, in which streams glint, dark chasms yawn under rocky crags, deer graze by ruined castles and the sounds of nightingale and posthorn mingle with the subtler "Waldesrauschen." Not surprisingly Eichendorff has been accused of a lack of invention in his locations, of knowing only one season, spring, and of creating only one kind of spring. These observations are to a certain extent true; they need not necessarily be used, however, to Eichendorff's discredit. For, if his landscapes seem restricted in variety, it is not because of any lack of creative imagination on his part, but rather because one particular landscape filled his mind's eye at all times. That was the landscape of Upper Silesia, the Oder and Lubowitz, his home. The coincidence of this real location and Eichendorff's ideal landscape is proved by those lyrics in which he writes descriptively and explicitly of Lubowitz and its surroundings.

Die Heimat, for example, addressed "An meinen Bruder," opens thus:

> "Denkst du des Schlosses noch auf stiller Höh,?
> Das Horn lockt nächtlich dort, als ob's dich riefe,
> Am Abgrund grast das Reh,
> Es rauscht der Wald verwirrend aus der Tiefe.—"* [3]

On reading these and many similar lines, one realizes that the stock landscape of his novels and poems, far from being the product of a limited imagination, is in fact a vividly remembered reality, transformed into an ideal world, topographically inaccurate, but symbolic and poetic.

Since it involves thus the transmutation of precise reality into significant poetry, there is in Eichendorff's presentation of nature none of the unreal fantasy and hazy outline which characterize most Romantic scenes. And in similar terms one may account for the distinction to be drawn between the themes of love and religion as presented by Eichendorff and as presented by his fellow Romantics, by Novalis or Brentano, for example. Love, in Eichendorff's works, does not necessarily mean eroticism, nor yet does it have heavy mystical implications. As a theme it runs for the most part (except for isolated moments of sensuality) mildly, nostalgically and symbolically through his novels and lyrics. On the other hand, domestic bliss and its mirror-image, the responsibility and restriction of family ties, are conspicuously lacking in his poetic representation of love—a feature which, if it differentiates his conceptions from those of *Biedermeier*, also suggests his escapist attitude to at least one aspect of his life.

The two themes of nature and love Eichendorff constantly translates into the more profound terms of religion. The translation is frequently effected by symbolism but is always easy and natural, for his delight in nature and his intimations of love lead directly to his recognition of divine power and providence. His conception of the close relationship of God and nature is, however, neither mystical nor obscure. On the contrary, it is childlike and profoundly sincere and is of course matched and enhanced, particularly in his lyrics, by the translucent style in which he expresses it. His attitude of mind, clearly not that of a religious fanatic, distinguishes him from, for example, Brentano. Eichendorff, one must remember, was a Catholic born and bred and his religion had never needed to undergo the crisis of conversion which inflamed Brentano's mind; his faith was one of deep, broad-minded and undemonstrative conviction and was taken for granted as an essential part of his life.

* *W.S.*, I, 79.

In his own word he was no "Protestantenfresser".* As a result, Eichendorff does not dramatize his religious themes self-consciously; he does not even point an obvious moral, or, indeed, glorify moral subjects. He allows himself, rather, through his heroic characters or in his own voice in the lyrics, to express simply and modestly his profound and constant conviction of God's providence. This conviction notably affects his presentation of the theme of death, for he regularly ignores its unpleasant aspects of horror, decay and finality and suggests rather his belief in its positive significance as release or escape, symbolizing it repeatedly as a homecoming. Thus the theme of religion, which so often in Romantic literature implies affectation and pseudo-mediaevalism, springs for Eichendorff, like his other themes, from the reality of his own experience, and of all these themes it is the most profound, intimate and expressive.

It may seem frivolous to extend the examination of Eichendorff's religious theme to include also his conception and presentation of the supernatural, but indeed much that can be said of the one can be said also of the other. Just as Eichendorff's religious feelings were awakened by nature, so also was his awareness of magic heightened by it; its phenomena seemed to him to possess a mysterious live quality, explicable only in supernatural terms. Inevitably, his supernatural world, as presented mainly in his ballads, is situated, invisibly, in the heart of the forest. The recurrent fairy characters of this world, however, have their origin not in Eichendorff's imagination but in the sagas of Silesia (as told to him in childhood by his nurse), and the magical forests are the factual forests surrounding Lubowitz. In other words, although in his novels he usually explains away supernatural happenings in a rational and unromantic manner, in his ballads he presents them with simple belief. This belief had its roots, like his religion, deep in his childhood's experience and, far from conflicting with his religion, it exteriorized for him the fascination of God's realm of nature in a microcosm of magical sound, vision and scent. It is not surprising that Eichendorff's supernatural world of the forest is a world of entrancing enchantment, independent of the contemporary horror cult and contrasting in its subtlety with the extravagantly fantastic magic of Tieck and Hoffmann. Indeed, Eichendorff's use of the coined word "hoffmannisieren" betrays his dislike of the grotesque. Just as the gruesome aspects of death are in his works transmuted by his religious faith, so Eichendorff's imagination smooths over the less pleasant aspects of magic. His bewitched huntsmen do not die in

* Letter to Karl von Holtei, 13 December 1856 (*Samtliche Werke des Freiherrn Joseph von Eichendorff*. Historisch-kritische Ausgabe (ed. Wilhelm Kosch and August Sauer. Regensburg, 1908, etc., XII, 224, No. 175).

agony but simply vanish, for the ugly and the horrific have no place in his forest fairyland.

In this way Eichendorff used themes of nature, love and the supernatural to convey allegorically and symbolically his real experiences, sincere beliefs and personal ideals. The communication of these abstract conceptions must therefore depend for its success, to a large extent, on his power of description and Eichendorff is generally acknowledged to have possessed that power in a unique degree. Understandably, in view of his lyrical talent, his characteristic style of description is not analytical but rather emotional, evocative and atmospheric. He describes a landscape, for example, less by particularizing its detail than by inviting the reader to experience its atmosphere, by making in fact a direct appeal to his senses.

Eichendorff achieved this descriptive communication in various ways and most obviously by his sensitive and economical use of atmospheric words to evoke various sensations. Synaesthesia was, of course, a notion dear to the hearts of the Romantics, but in Eichendorff's works it is so far from being hackneyed as to create the more vivid effects: "Draußen aber", he writes characteristically in *Dichter und ihre Gesellen*, "war unterdes der Abend verklungen und verblüht."* (4) This method of creating atmosphere can easily be overworked and can lead to an unhappy excess in description of vague and subjective emotionalism; indeed, Eichendorff's everrecurring phrase "wie im Traum" is in this way unhelpful and uncommunicative. In the main, however, his description is saved from this danger not only by his sparing use of synaesthetic effects, but also by the flashes of imagery which lighten again and again his potentially turgid and sentimental conceptions. Eichendorff, as his ballads testify, was capable of inventing his own magic and frequently, by magical suggestions, he communicates atmospheric impressions directly and vividly to his reader's imagination. In this way, for instance, he conveys the colour, mystery and tranquillity of an old garden: "Es war, als hätte ein wunderbarer Zauberer über Nacht seine bunten Signaturen über das Grün gezogen und säße nun selber eingeschlummert in dem Labyrinth beim Rauschen der Wasserkünste und träumte von der alten Zeit, die er in seine stillen Kreise gebannt."† (5) Often, too, Eichendorff's imagery involves not the irrational terms of the supernatural but precise observation of real phenomena: the first pink streaks of dawn over the clear night sky, for example, are likened to the cloud of breath on a mirror. For this reason Friedrich Schlegel was unable to decide whether

* *W.S.*, II, 641.   † *Dichter und ihre Gesellen, W.S.*, II, 517.

Eichendorff's works were art or nature, and indeed his descriptive style has been called realistic, "realistisch-impressionistisch"* and compared to Constable's vivid communication of reality. Furthermore, from time to time, Eichendorff's predominantly imaginative description is punctuated and enhanced by a stroke of pure realism. "Das Mädchen war arg durchnäßt," we read in *Dichter und ihre Gesellen*," mit dem dünnen, vom Regen knapp anliegenden Kleide, mit den lang herabhängenden, tröpfelnden Locken sah sie wie ein Nixchen aus, das eben den Wellen entstiegen"† [6]—a sentence which demonstrates his effective combination of the two extremes of evocative description, the realistic and the imaginative.

Clearly, judged by contemporary standards, Eichendorff's manner of narration is unusually precise and vivid. He himself felt that to strip his style of its realism would be to rub and blur the fresh colours of a painting, and just for this reason he did not fall into the Romantic errors of excessive subjectivity, vagueness and emotional turgidity. And indeed there is another reason why he could never have committed these literary sins. No one could write in a maudlin manner or take his emotions and imagination overseriously who had at the same time the healthy sense of humour which Eichendorff displays over and over again in his works. It is seen not just in the conception of the happy-go-lucky *Taugenichts* figure, not only in moments of contemporary satire, nor in slapstick situations, but in the countless episodes, verbal effects and comments with which he transforms a potentially sentimental moment into a piquant vision or a sensible judgment. A description from *Aus dem Leben eines Taugenichts* demonstrates his characteristic blend of fantasy, realism and humour: "Die alte Frau mahlte indes in einem fort mit ihrem zahnlosen Munde, daß es nicht anders aussah, als wenn sie an der langen herunterhängenden Nasenspitze kaute"‡ [7]; in *Dichter und ihre Gesellen* the description of "eine seltsame, phantastisch geschmückte Weibergestalt" concludes with the delightful glimpse: "ihr schneeweißes Hemd [war] an den Nähten mit schwarzer Seide nach böhmischer Art ausgenäht, woraus sie hervorschien wie eine Heidelbeere aus der Milch"§ [8]; in the same novel, Otto, sick at heart, is frankly described by Kordelchen: "'Aber wie siehst du aus!... nüchtern und blaugrün, wie eine leere Weinflasche!'"‖ [9] The point need not be laboured. Eichendorff's fresh, stimulating and realistic sense of humour happily offsets the emotional and atmospheric qualities of his descriptive manner.

* Ernst Scheyer, "Eichendorff und die bildenden Künste," *Aurora. Eichendorff-Almanach*, XVI. Neumarkt/Opf., 1956, 26.

† *W.S.*, II, 541.   ‡ *W.S.*, II, 389.   § *W.S.*, II, 567.   ‖ *W.S.*, II, 641.

And also from a purely stylistic point of view Eichendorff was saved by the nature of his talent from exaggerated emotionalism. His prose style, distinguished of course by its lyricism, is lucid at all times and serves well his complex plots and episodes. His lyric style, based as it is on the vocabulary, constructions and rhythms of the folk-song, is a model of transparent simplicity and seeming artlessness and testifies to his profound love of music. Formally too Eichendorff keeps a firm hold on the fluid subject-matter of novel, *Novelle* or poem and steers a confident course among the obstacles which his abundantly inventive imagination provides. The conclusions of his most complex novels, *Ahnung und Gegenwart* and *Dichter und ihre Gesellen*, are reached with comparative ease and, if the multiple thematic threads are rarely all tied up, their confusion is resolved in an impression of dense unity. The action of his novels, one may feel, is impeded by the many interpolated songs, but otherwise when he uses the characteristic devices of Romantic prose-writing he does so to solve, rather than to complicate, his formal problems. Episodic confusion is frequently clarified by his recourse, for example, to the tale-within-a-tale structure favoured by Tieck; *Ahnung und Gegenwart* is presented in a significant cyclic form; audience and narrator are frequently differentiated; *Die Glücksritter* and *Das Schloss Dürande* are controlled by the sections in which they are cast. In fact, formally, Eichendorff subscribed to Romanticism, but handled the techniques characteristic of the movement in such a way as to avoid its common pitfall of rhapsodic diffusion.

In this way, as can be seen, serious examination of Eichendorff's achievement gives promise of interesting conclusions. In the first place, of course, it reveals him as an undoubted Romantic, linked by a common attitude to Tieck and the Schlegels, Brentano and Hoffmann. He was a Romantic in his love of music, in his preoccupation with spiritual values and dislike of philistines, in his fondness for supernatural invention, his delight in the folk-song, his attitude to formal problems and his predilection for certain literary genres. Yet Eichendorff's Romanticism was clearly his own and is distinguished from that of his contemporaries above all by its realistic qualities. His fictitious characters and locations founded, as they are, on fact; his most imaginative supernatural themes rooted in childhood experience and local tradition; his folk-song style and themes of student-life, the fruits of his own youth; his emotions unfeigned; his love of nature profound and personal; his religion convinced and spontaneous; his descriptive manner vividly evocative—the various features of Eichendorff's Romantic attitude and style are uniquely coloured by his constant awareness of reality.

Even his *Sehnsucht*—that most Romantic of attitudes, with its two-fold direction towards past and future—is tinged by the reflection of reality. He yearned, not for a past of Romantic pseudo-mediaeval artificiality, but for an actual place, real people, actual situations and an actual stage in his own life. His *Sehnsucht* was not a vague imagining of the unattainable, but the remembering and idealising of the already experienced:

> "Nicht Träume sind's und leere Wahngesichte,
>   Was von dem Volk den Dichter unterscheidet.
>   Was er inbrünstig bildet, liebt und leidet,
> Es ist des Lebens wahrhafte Geschichte."* (10)

Eichendorff's memory, as well as his imagination, was the vehicle of his yearning and together they created an ideal world which was neither unreal nor fantastic. In this world he perceived certain symbols of the ideal, significant symbols in that they too had played their part in his actual experience. In his poems old age, winter, autumn, fallen leaves, the symbols of decay, are more than balanced by the many symbolic presentations of ideal existence. Youth, "das gelobte Land der Jugend"†; spring, the season of youth; music, its expression; the forest, enchanted by spring; the carefree *Spielmann* who wanders, singing, through it—these symbols of the ideal coalesce in the general symbol, Eichendorff's old home, Lubowitz. And through the symbol of Lubowitz Eichendorff received deep intimations of his ideal world in its ultimate form and the future goal of his yearning, the Kingdom of God. If he yearned back, in his own recurrent word "wälderwärts," to the lost past of Lubowitz, so also he yearned forward to a future of ideal existence, a future promising not the vague illusions of a *Fata Morgana* but the recovery of happiness and the certain fulfilment of faith. At this point the popular conception of Eichendorff as a carefree and irresponsible minstrel must obviously be amended. Because of his preoccupation with the lost past of his youth and his anticipation of death, his writing is charged with a poignant and nostalgic sadness. For him *Sehnsucht* implied the anguish of *Heimweh*, in the earthly, but above all in the spiritual sense of the word.

It remains now to be seen whether any real value attaches to Eichendorff's individual kind of realistic Romanticism. Clearly, it differentiates him from his fellow Romantics in a number of significant ways. Unlike Tieck, for example, Eichendorff avoided the pitfall of artificiality; unlike Novalis, he never lost contact with the real world in flights of religious or erotic imagination; his knowledge

---

* *Sonette 5, W.S.,* I, 69.   † *Dichter und ihre Gesellen, W.S.,* II, 524.

of reality was first-hand and not, as was Arnim's, indirectly and academically acquired. Eichendorff indulged neither in the extravagances of Brentano, nor in the fantasy of Hoffmann; his subjectivity was never embarrassing (indeed his unwillingness to bare his soul is demonstrated by his unusually detached diary-writing). He avoided the worst excesses of *Schundromantik*, with its sentimental and self-conscious themes and its false and emotional style, and on the other hand he stood consciously aloof from the prosaic *Biedermeier*. His *Vaterlandsliebe* could not be confused with *Deutschtümelei*; on the contrary, he wrote in disapproval of "die ... moderne Vaterländerei; ein imaginäres Deutschland, das weder recht vernünftig, noch recht historisch war."* [11] And this was not the only aspect of Romanticism from which he deliberately dissociated himself. When he wrote of the "Verfall der Romantik"† and regretted its failure to live up to its promise, he was deploring, not, of course, the theory and intention of the movement, but its pernicious tendencies, and he repeatedly contrasted its worthless achievement with the worthy principles on which it rested. Nor did he ever weary of exhorting his aristocratic contemporaries to defend all that was great, noble and beautiful in face of the growing artificiality and vain triviality of their times.

In this way, one may perceive the negative value of Eichendorff's realistic Romanticism in his spontaneous and conscious avoidance of emotional falsity, exotic exaggeration or bizarre unreality. But what of its positive values? It has been said that Romanticism's distinctive feature was "the surrender to unbounded and uninhibited imagination"‡; Eichendorff, however, did not surrender unconditionally and his imagination was held in check, invigorated and strengthened by his awareness of the threefold reality of past, present and future. His art is romanticised reality, real-life presented in the irrational terms which memory and imagination impose. And for this reason his works are healthier, sturdier and, with their richness of allegory and above all of symbolic meaning, infinitely more significant and sincere than most Romantic writing. This is why the conception of Eichendorff as a naive and superficial nature-poet is so far from the truth. This is why he can be described not only, glibly, as Germany's greatest lyric poet or the creator of the Romantic *Lied* but also, more accurately, as "der erste Führer zur Wirklichkeit des Draußen ... , zur Natur, zur Landschaft, den wir im Reich gehabt haben,"§ as a penetrating commentator

---

* *Erlebtes*, *W.S.*, II, 1046.   † Ibid. p. 1062.
‡ Ralph Tymms, *German Romantic Literature*. London, 1955, p. 24.
§ Paul Fechter, "Eichendorff Heute," *Aurora. Eichendorff-Almanach*, XIV. Neumarkt/Opf., 1954, 13.

on contemporary social, literary and ethical problems and as a bold champion of timeless spiritual values. There were, of course, other realistic Romantics—one thinks of the tragic Kleist, of Arnim and his merciless detail, of the academic pedantry of Uhland, of Hoffmann with his bizarre observation or of the bitterly ironic Heine—but their very inability to reconcile the real and the ideal illuminates, by contrast, the rare and happy balance of Eichendorff's Romanticism, implying, as it does, not disharmony and conflict, but the close, peaceful and fruitful interaction of imagination and reality.

Is it too bold, then, to suggest that Eichendorff has outlived his contemporary Romantics by reason of his consistent awareness of reality; or that this awareness purified his poetry of the unworthy and impermanent characteristics of Romanticism; or that, therefore, his art reveals Romanticism at its best and most significant?

One must remember, however, that the Romantic formula was relevant not only to the problems of artistic creation but also to the problems of living. "Aber die Romantik," Eichendorff wrote himself, "war keine bloß literarische Erscheinung, sie unternahm vielmehr eine innere Regeneration des Gesamtlebens."* [(12)] And from this point of view too, Eichendorff may be regarded as an unusually successful exponent of Romanticism, since he resolved the striking dichotomy of his life, with its two sharply distinguished and disharmonious phases, in terms of Romantic ideals. By his art he transformed the second prosaic and troubled phase into a continuation, on an imaginative level, of his idyllic youth. In his latter years he stilled the pain of grief, loss and anxiety, so modestly revealed in his letters, by his faith in the reality of God's providence, but also by his poetic contemplation of past happiness:

> "Herbstlich alle Fluren rings verwildern,
>   Und unkenntlich wird die Welt.
> Dieses Scheidens Schmerzen sich zu mildern,
>   Wenn die Zauberei zerfällt,
> Sinnt der Dichter, treulich abzuschildern
>   Den versunknen Glanz der Welt.
> Selig Herze, das in kühnen Bildern
>   *Ewig* sich die Schönheit hält!"† [(13)]

If the symbolism of this poem is significant, so also is its title, *Sängerglück*. In this way, by his poetic activity, as well as by his religious faith, he created for himself a life of unity and inner harmony, a life which contrasts with Kleist's or Heine's and yet which is

---

* *Erlebtes, W.S.,* II, 1069.   † *W.S.,* I, 80.

in a sense more Romantic than theirs. For the dominant aim of Romanticism was the fusion of life and art, the bridging of the gulf between ideal and real, the dream-world and the world of reality. It is this Romantic task which Eichendorff was uniquely successful in performing and he thus emerges from investigation as the most significant example not only of the Romantic poet but also of the Romantic man.

It is sad that Eichendorff, who possessed such rare insight into the values of Romanticism lived to be disillusioned in the achievement of the movement: "So war die Romantik bei ihrem Aufgange ein Frühlingshauch, der alle verborgenen Keime belebte, eine schöne Zeit des Erwachens, der Erwartung und Verheißung. Allein sie hat die Verheißung nicht erfüllt, und weil sie sie nicht erfüllte, ging sie unter . . . ," he wrote.* [14] But when we, from our position in the twentieth century, look back upon the movement, its creators and its legacy of achievement, we may perhaps venture to disagree with Eichendorff. There was at least one Romantic who, in his art and in his life, fulfilled and vindicated the high promise of Romanticism, and that was Eichendorff himself.

TRANSLATIONS

1. Sound common sense, honour, genuine chivalry and the spirit of devotion waft through the whole book like a refreshing breath of forest air.

2. As it happened, however, it was a fine Sunday morning. A pear-tree was just walking through the field to church and was rustling in praise of God.

3. Do you still remember the castle on the quiet hill? There, at night, the horn sounds enticingly, as if it were calling you; the deer grazes by the ravine; the forest murmur rises disturbingly from the depths.

4. Outside, however, the evening had meanwhile died softly away and had withered.

5. It was as if a wondrous wizard had, overnight, signed his name in gay colours on the greensward and now was himself sitting fast asleep in the labyrinth by the plashing fountains and dreaming of the old days which he kept spellbound in the breathless circles of his magic.

6. The girl was soaked through; with her thin dress clinging, wet with rain, to her body and with her long hair dripping, she looked like a little water-sprite that had just risen from the waves.

7. The old woman meanwhile kept on grinding with her toothless mouth, so that it looked exactly as if she were chewing the tip of her long nose.

8. . . . a strange and fantastically ornamented female figure . . . her snow-white blouse [was] embroidered at the seams with black silk in

* *Erlebtes, W.S.,* II, 1072.

Bohemian fashion and she emerged radiantly out of it like a bilberry out of milk.

9. "But what a sight you are! . . . dreary and blue-green, like an empty wine-bottle!"

10. It is not dreams and vain chimeras that distinguish ordinary people from the poet. What he ardently creates, loves and suffers is the true story of life.

11. . . . the modern patriotic cult; an imaginary Germany which was neither properly sensible, nor properly historical.

12. But Romanticism was not an exclusively literary phenomenon, it undertook, rather, an inward regeneration of all life.

13. Now that it is autumn, the fields all around are growing tangled and the world is becoming unrecognizable. In order to alleviate his pain at this parting, when the enchantment is shattered, the poet ponders how he can faithfully depict the lost splendour of the world. Happy the heart that can, in bold images, preserve beauty *for ever*!

14. In this way, Romanticism, at its dawning, was a breath of spring, germinating all the hidden seeds, a fine time of awakening, of expectation and of promise. But it did not fulfil that promise and because it did not fulfil it, it foundered.

BIBLIOGRAPHICAL NOTE

The critical edition of Eichendorff's works:

Sämtliche Werke des Freiherrn Joseph von Eichendorff. Historisch-kritische Ausgabe, ed. Wilhelm Kosch and August Sauer. Regensburg, 1908, etc.

is still incomplete. There is available, however, an excellent unannotated edition:

Joseph Freiherr von Eichendorff, *Neue Gesamtausgabe der Werke und Schriften in vier Bänden,* ed. Gerhard Baumann with Siegfried Grosse. Stuttgart, 1957–8,

which contains *Gedichte, Epen, Dramen, Romane, Novellen, Märchen, Erlebtes, Tagebücher, Übertragungen* and *Vermischte Schriften.*

Of critical literature treating Eichendorff, the overwhelming bulk is in German and deals with general as well as with innumerable particular aspects of his life and work. Predominantly biographical information is to be found in:

Hans Brandenburg, *Joseph von Eichendorff. Sein Leben und sein Werk.* Munich, 1922; and

Willibald Köhler, *Joseph von Eichendorff. Ein Dichterleben in 11 Kapiteln.* Augsburg, 1957,

while a wide range of both dilettante and specialist studies is presented in the various numbers of:

Aurora. Ein romantischer Almanach (since 1953, *Eichendorff-Almanach*), ed. Karl Freiherr von Eichendorff, Adolf Dyroff, Karl Schodrok. Oppeln (subsequently Neumarkt/Opf. and Würzburg), 1929, etc.

Important essays on Eichendorff by, among others, Richard Alewyn, Richard Benz, Hermann Kunisch, Reinhold Schneider and Franz Uhlendorff are collected in the symposium:

Eichendorff heute. Stimmen der Forschung mit einer Bibliographie, ed. Paul Stöcklein. Munich, 1960.

The classified bibliography contained in this book is extensive and takes account of works published as late as 1959.

In the English language, while there are a great many shorter articles on specific aspects of Eichendorff's life and work, for example:

Oskar Seidlin, "Eichendorff's Symbolic Landscape", *Publications of the Modern Language Association of America*, vol. LXXII, 1957,

there is as yet no full-scale treatment of his achievement as a whole. Studies of Eichendorff may, however, be found within such general works as:

CLOSS, A. *The Genius of the German Lyric. An historic survey of its formal and metaphysical values.* London, 1938.

PRAWER, S. S. *German Lyric Poetry.* London, 1952.

TYMMS, RALPH. *German Romantic Literature.* London, 1955.

Annette von Droste-Hülshoff

Annette von Droste-Hülshoff

by BRIGITTE E. SCHATZKY

ANNA ELISABETH (ANNETTE) was born in January 1797 at the castle of Hülshoff near Münster as the second child of Freiherr Clemens August Droste zu Hülshoff and his second wife, Therese von Haxthausen. The birth was a premature one, leaving Annette with a very delicate constitution. From her first major illness at the age of seventeen, the effects of which lingered on for years, until her death in 1848, the periods during which she was free from headaches, dizziness and pain were few and brief indeed.

Annette von Droste's development from a delicate "Burgfräulein" (as she called herself with characteristic self-irony) to Germany's greatest woman poet was a slow one. Coupled with ill-health, it was her upbringing and environment which retarded and hampered her artistic growth. Born into the "caste" of Westphalia's landed aristocracy (the Drostes had lived at Hülshoff since the fifteenth century), she led the conventional sheltered life if not of a lady of leisure, then of a "Blaustrumpf von Stande." The yearning for experience and individual self-expression was counteracted by a crippling sense of loyalty to the claims of family and feminine decorum. There is a strong personal note in the lines of a youthful dramatic fragment entitled *Berta* (1813):

> "*Cordelia:* Zu männlich ist dein Geist, strebt viel zu hoch
> Hinauf, wo dir kein Weiberauge folgt;
> Das ists, was ängstlich dir den Busen regt
> Und dir die jugendliche Wange bleicht.
> Wenn Weiber über ihre Sphäre steigen,
> Entfliehn sie ihrem eignen bessern Selbst." [1]

As if to prove her submissiveness, Annette set to work in 1820 on *Das Geistliche Jahr in Liedern auf alle Sonn-und Festtage,* a kind of devotional calendar in verse intended for the use of her maternal grandmother. Based on the examination of conscience as the centre and exercise of the spiritual life, and confined to a rigid framework of prescribed Biblical texts and other Christian themes, the under-lying emotion is that of contrition ("bittere Reue") and the soul's craving for God's grace.

"Herr, ich bin ein arm und kaum noch glühend
Döchtlein am Altare deiner Gnade;
Sieh, mich löscht ein mattes Lüftchen fliehend,
Mich ein Tröpfchen von der Welt Gestade." [2]

Her microscopic gaze, which she was later to turn outwards to
the world of nature, is trained mercilessly upon the minutest motions
of the soul, cringing and writhing in ceaseless self-abasement. But
real remorse presupposes real guilt, and for all her protestations
about "sin," about "des Stolzes Klippen" and "dieser Erde
Freuden"—metaphors which rarely rise above the conventional—
the first twenty-five cantos of *Das Geistliche Jahr* fail to carry conviction, and many subtle variations on Baroque and Romantic
verse forms only serve to emphasize the basic poverty of experience.

It is significant that when Annette von Droste did undergo her
first deep emotional experience—a strangely ambivalent passion for
two young men of her acquaintance—she broke off her work on
Das Geistliche Jahr. A faint note of defiance, born of genuine suffering
now creeps into some of her poetry:

"Ihr frommen Leute wollt die Sorge kennen
Und habt doch nie die Schuld gesehn!
Doch sie, sie dürfen schon das Leben nennen
Und seine grauenvollen Höhn.

Hinauf schallts wie Gesang und Loben,
Und um die Blumen spielt der Strahl,
Die Menschen wohnen still im Tal,
Die dunklen Geier horsten droben." [3]

Outwardly her life remained quiet and uneventful. During the
first thirty years only occasional visits and excursions into the neighbourhood interrupted life at the ancestral "Wasserburg," and when,
after her father's death she moved with her mother to the nearby
"Witwensitz" of Rüschhaus—"das grüne Haus" standing in the
midst of rural calm—she wrote of it as "one of the most unchanging
places where one remains oblivious of the passage of time." Dividing
her time between attending to domestic duties, collecting coins,
medals, cameos and minerals (a life-long hobby), going for long
solitary walks over the heath or just daydreaming, she is not unlike
the heroine of her first attempt at sustained prose writing, the novel
Ledwina (1819–24). A "Freifräulein" like herself, Ledwina leads the
outwardly sheltered and ineffectual life of an invalid, oppressed by
the anxious solicitude of her nearest and dearest for her physical
well-being, while her spirit longs to break free into a world of its own.

But all this is only dimly realized, only half-acknowledged. Just as Annette's own youth was, as she put it, "verdämmert und zerfahren," so too the image of her youthful heroine is no more than a fleeting, shadowy reflection of herself in the water:

> "Ledwinas Augen ruhten aus auf ihrer eigenen Gestalt, wie die Locken von ihrem Haupt fielen und forttrieben, ihr Gewand zerriss und die weissen Finger sich ablösten und verschwammen." [4]

Languid, sick and tired almost unto death, she drifts along, her waking hours filled with daydreams, her sultry nights exposing a "grauenvolle Traumwelt" full of tombstones and peopled with macabre figures from the contemporary English "terror" tale.

The fascination of what Annette von Droste called "des Grauens Süsse" was to remain a major source of her poetic inspiration. She seems to have possessed some form of "second sight" (an early poem actually bears this description) which was only half-tempered by scepticism. Here, in the borderland between belief and doubt, between dreaming and waking was her true realm—"unser Reich, was wir mit den Engländern und Schotten teilen." The kinship with English and Scottish literature is particularly evident in three long epic poems written after a period of stagnation, which left both *Ledwina* and *Das Geistliche Jahr* in a fragmentary condition. The first, *Das Hospiz auf dem grossen Sankt Bernhard* (1828–34) tells the old story of the St. Bernard dog who saves a boy from dying of cold and helps the good monks to recover the frozen body of his grandfather. It contains, amongst others, a macabre nocturnal scene in which the bodies in the morgue, where the old man and his grandson have sought shelter, seem to come alive. The theme is man in the grip of unknown and hostile powers, but neither the conventional paraphernalia of horror nor the inclemencies of an externally conceived landscape succeed in conveying the necessary sense of inevitability, especially as the terrors of the night are offset by the idyllic peace of the monastic life and the joys of motherhood. The language already betrays a characteristic angularity and pointed rhythmical quality, but there is no attempt to adapt it to the different moods of the action, thus giving the whole a faint monotony.

If *Das Hospiz* is indebted to Walter Scott, it is Byron's influence which is discernible in the next narrative poem, *Des Arztes Vermächtnis* (1834). The plot is clearly based on Schelling's *Die Letzten Worte des Pfarrers zu Drotning auf Seeland* published in 1802: a doctor is called out in the middle of the night to attend a dying man, member of a band of criminals living in the depths of the forest. He has to make the journey blindfold on horse-back, and after a night full of horrors is made to swear an oath not to divulge what he has seen to any living soul. On the homeward journey he witnesses in a condition of semi-consciousness the brutal murder of a woman whom he had met by the bedside of the wounded man, an experience which gradually undermines his sanity. It is a work which, to quote the Doctor's own words, "schauernd sich dem kranken Haupt entwand." Identifying herself with the principal character, and as if she were herself sleep-walking, the poet follows him step by step into the regions of night and death, as, bereft of the protective power of his senses, he becomes the victim of a demonic power—"der Dunkle"—which is not entirely a figment of his fevered imagination. As in *Das Hospiz*, the horrors of the night give way to the beauteous calm of the morning, the hideous den in the forest to the peaceful dwelling in the valley. But the juxtaposition now spells a haunting sense of doubt:

> "In Tönen kehrte das Bewusstsein mir;
> So lieblich aus der Luft die Wirbel dringen,
> Gewiss, ich hörte eine Lerche singen
> Und dachte noch, sie muss den Morgen bringen;
> Ob Traum, ob Wirklichkeit, das fragt sich hier.
> War's Traum, dann trag' ich manches graue Haar
> Umsonst, und manche tiefe Furche gar." [5]

The figure of the man whose grey hairs bear witness to what he has seen appears again in *Der Graue*, one of Annette von Droste's numerous ballads. Wherever she uses traditional ghost story figures as agents of horror, it remains a matter of uncertainty whether these figures are real or illusory. Despite the poet's superior knowledge there remains the shudder of the mysterious unknown, a real sense of *Angst* lurks behind the "poetisches Gruseln" consciously aimed at.

For the setting of her third epic poem, *Die Schlacht am Loener Bruch* (1837–8) Annette von Droste returned to her native Westphalia. The result is a heightening of the realistic quality as well as a deepening of the spiritual content. It deals with one of the few important episodes in the history of the Thirty Years War, though mistrusting her own ability to render the historical material sufficiently "interesting," the poet felt obliged to incorporate a fictitious element, the Gertrud-Johannes episode. What lingers in the mind, however, are the portrait of the hero and the magnificently ponderous battle scenes—passages which surprised Schücking that they could have been written by a woman, and which are indeed without parallel in Annette von Droste's other work. The knightly valour of Christian von Braunschweig or Tilly's bold nocturnal ride through the ghostly forest to reconnoitre hard by the enemy camp seem like a wish-fulfilment of her own thwarted desires. Throughout nature plays a dominant part, not only in the many "Stimmungsbilder," but as an integral part of the action. The great battle itself is described like a natural phenomenon, unfolding like a thunderstorm from the earliest faint forebodings to the final clash of arms:

"Hell schmetterte Trompetenton;
Frischauf zu Ross, der Feind ist wach!
Entlang der Liesner hörten schon
Die Posten dumpfen Trommelschlag.
Und wimmelnd überm Heidegrunde
Das Heer sich ordnete zur Stunde;
Die Ordonnanzen flogen, laut
Signale dröhnten übers Kraut." [6]

"Not like the poetry women usually write," remarked Charlotte Brontë about the work of her sister Emily. The same might be said in the case of Annette von Droste, who bears indeed a curious affinity to the English novelist. Almost exact contemporaries, they each created out of the depths of their imagination a stark, passionate world in contrast to their own quiet, circumscribed lives. Annette's *Wuthering Heights* was *Die Judenbuche* (1837–41), a sombre and powerful work born of "ein immer tiefer dämmrigtes Nachdenken" about a subject whose very stark simplicity fascinated and disturbed her. It is the story which she had known since her youth of the "Algierer Sklave": the "Judenmörder" of Paderborn in Westphalia who, having spent many long years in Turkish slavery, returns home in his fiftieth year only to hang himself at the very scene of his old crime: the beech tree marked by the local Jewish community with a mysterious Hebrew curse.

Sitting in the ordered tranquillity of her idyllic Rüschhaus, Annette von Droste found herself drawn into a world of disorder, depravity and evil. She is as far from revelling in her morbid theme as she is from moralizing about it, proceeding rather with reticence and caution, mindful of the limitations of human reason and of the obscure, unfathomable recesses of the mind. It is this, and not any superficial desire to mystify in the sense of a detective story, which accounts for the many question-marks in the narrative, the hidden clues, the apparently unconnected happenings, the atmosphere of semi-darkness, the many ambiguities in speech and action. Brief snatches of dialogue, swift questions and answers like the thrust-and-parry of a cross-examination serve to intensify the general sense of brooding fate rather than to elucidate the particular point under discussion:

"Plötzlich fragte Simon: 'Trinkst du gern Branntwein?—
Der Knabe antwortete nicht. 'Ich frage, trinkst du gern
Branntwein? Gibt dir die Mutter zuweilen welchen?'—
'Die Mutter hat selbst keinen,' sagte Friedrich.—
'So, so desto besser!—Kennst du das Holz da vor uns?'—
'Das ist das Brederholz.'—Weisst du auch, was darin
vorgefallen ist?'—Friedrich schwieg." [7]

Such vividly illumined scenes, flashing like shafts of lightning
out of the darkness, seem to light up hidden abysses without fully
revealing them. The character of Friedrick Mergel himself is shadowy
and ambiguous. In her depiction of his strange double existence
it is as though the author herself only half guessed at a pact with
the devil. Any attempt to retreat from the path of evil is foiled, the
future seems uncertain yet inevitable. Walking behind his uncle
Simon, with whom he has a disturbing family likeness:

". . . erinnerte er unwillkürlich an jemand, der in einem Zauber-
spiegel das Bild seiner Zukunft mit verstörter Aufmerksamkeit
betrachtet. [8]

The figure of Friedrich's "Doppelgänger" is but an extension of this
mirror image—a favourite one in Annette von Droste's work. Who
is he, this Johannes Niemand? The very picture of poverty, misery
and insignificance, his presence seems to incite Friedrich to brag
and boast and assert his superiority. At the same time the latter's
life is strangely bound up with his, he feels drawn to him as to his own
reflection.

Johannes Niemand was conceived as a real person; according to
an earlier version he was the illegitimate child of Simon. Margaret's
cryptic ejaculation: "Ein falscher Eid!"still bears witness to this fact,
but it has become blurred, thus heightening the enigma, whilst not
wholly losing the link with reality. Uncle Simon, too, is a robust figure
of flesh and blood as well as the personification of evil, as, with his
red coat-tails flapping behind him like flames of fire, the world of
reality and the world of appearances merge—just as Friedrich's
father, at one moment lying in the gutter, a broken bottle-neck
between his lips, turns at the next into a ghost haunting the Brederholz like the spectre of Original Sin. Even the motif of the "Holz-
frevel" (a common enough phenomenon in the wooded regions of
Germany at the time and a real social problem) merges imperceptibly into the mysterious workings of Nature: the falling trees make a
sound like the groaning of creation, announcing the approach of an
evil fate.

What makes *Die Judenbuche* so singularly compelling is the growth
of this mysterious evil fate out of a concrete world of common sinful

humanity. This in turn springs from Annette von Droste's strong links with her native land and its people. "Ich bin ja selbst eine Bauernnatur," she asserted more than once. She not only collected folksongs and folktales for the brothers Grimm and had a perfect command of the local *Plattdeutsch*, but also had an intuitive grasp of the slow cumbrous mentality of the ordinary folk around her, of their simple, but by no means irreproachable way of life. "Die tiefe und stolze Waldeinsamkeit" in which Friedrich Mergel's story takes place acts not as a Romantic "Stimmungsbild," but is a realistically conceived milieu to explain the character of the inhabitants. The sub-title of the story—*Ein Sittengemälde aus dem gebirgichten Westfalen*—indicates that the author's original aim was to give the sociological background to a murder. The first draft did not in fact get as far as the murder, but deals solely with the "Umgebungen" of the young Friedrich. This explains the presence in the final version of the somewhat lengthy description of the village wedding, which forms a striking contrast to the terseness of the other scenes, such as the final picture of the now simple-minded Friedrich sitting by the edge of the forest chipping at a wooden spoon:

"Er schnitt ihn aber ganz entzwei!" [9]

Annette von Droste intended to incorporate *Die Judenbuche* into a larger work on Westphalia and the life and customs of its people. Though this was never realized, she continued to work along these lines, now inspired by Washington Irving's *Bracebridge Hall* to start on a kind of "Familiengemälde" in the form of a journal entitled *Bei uns zu Lande auf dem Lande* (1841-2), now collaborating with Freiligrath and Schücking on their *Malerisches und romantisches Westfalen* (her contribution being subsequently published separately under the title of *Bilder aus Westfalen*). Interesting and attractive as these are—the former shot through with a sense of humour otherwise found only in Annette's letters, the latter written in a masterly prose style—these writings are at best only side-lines of her creative work, at worst distractions from and dissipations of her true talents. The marvel is that out of this semi-journalistic activity there sprang a *Novelle* so powerful that it has become a land-mark in the history of German poetic realism.

Meanwhile, between 1837 and 1839, Annette von Droste had found it possible to complete *Das Geistliche Jahr* abandoned nineteen years earlier. The original scheme of a calendar for her grandmother has been abandoned and the result is a feeling of liberation:

"Erst seitdem ich mich von dem Gedanken, für die Grossmutter zu schreiben, völlig frei gemacht habe, habe ich rasch und mit . . .

erleichternden Gefühlen gearbeitet ... Für die Grossmutter
ist und bleibt es völlig unbrauchbar, so wie für alle sehr fromme
Menschen, denn ich habe ihm die Spuren eines vielfach gepressten
und geteilten Gemütes mitgeben müssen." (10)

The pious self-abasement of the soul has become suspect:

> "Wenn aus der Not nach Rettung Sehnen keimt,
> Ist das die Reue?" (11)

The need for divine salvation remains: if anything, it has become
more insistent, haunted as she is by the real possibility of losing her
faith. At times she tries to blame the intellect: again and again
she accuses her own "Wissen" or admonishes the "false prophets"
of her day, propagators of anti-Christian doctrines which were
gaining ground in Germany (though she herself had little more than
second-hand knowledge of their writings). The real obstacle to
salvation is her own earth-bound self:

> "Doch fühl ich dann zu anderer Zeit,
> Wie Haar dem Haupt
> Der finstren Erde mich geweiht,
> So machtberaubt." (12)

In wretched contrast to the "sweet," "pure," "mild" promise of
heaven, her soul here and now, lies dormant and heavy upon a waste
land: "matt," "verschlossen," "dumpf," "versteinert," "tränen-
schwer" and "ausgedörrt," "siech," "kalt" and "ächzend," to
quote only a few of the epithets which help to give the latter part
of *Das Geistliche Jahr* its distinctive personal note. Verses such as
those belonging to the Third Sunday after Easter, in which the
leadenness of the soul is reflected in the sultriness of a summer's
day, point forward to the best of Annette von Droste's nature poetry:

> "Die Wolke steigt
> Und langsam über den azurnen Bau
> Hat eine Schwefelhülle sich gelegt;
> Die Lüfte wehn so seufzervoll und lau
> Und Angstgefühl sich in den Zweigen regt;
> Die Herde keucht.
> Was fühlt das dumpfe Tier? Ists deine Schwüle?
> Ich steh gebeugt:
> Mein Herr, berühre mich, dass ich dich fühle!" (13)

"Mit dem letzten Federstriche im *Geistlichen Jahr*," she wrote in
1838, "wird das irdische Jahr alle seine wilden Quellen wieder
über sich strömen lassen." How true this expectation was to prove!
In the same year there had appeared Annette von Droste's first

collection of poems under the title *Gedichte von Annette Elisabeth von D. H.* and published at the instigation of Levin Schücking. A writer himself, he was the son of Katharina Schücking, a once celebrated Westphalian poetess and a close friend of Annette's. After her death the latter had begun to take a maternal interest in the young man, but the nickname of "Mütterchen" she had adopted for herself soon became an all too thin disguise for a much deeper emotional attachment. In September 1841 she went to stay with her married sister at the romantically situated castle of Meersburg on Lake Constance—in search, as she put it, of "rest, poetic surroundings and better health." Within a few days Schücking had joined her, summoned ostensibly to help her brother-in-law Lassberg with his formidable collection of old German manuscripts.

The ensuing five months, during which the two were almost daily companions, were not only the happiest in Annette's life, but brought the final, long-deferred release of her poetic genius. Devoted and enthusiastic, full of sympathetic but critical interest in her work, Levin gave her what she had so sorely lacked; confidence in her vocation. Above all, his youthful spirit gave her a new lease of life, a richer awareness of herself and the world around her. Levin himself, only half conscious of the important role he was playing in the life of a woman twenty years his senior, suddenly became the centre, the very source of her creative activity. "Was ich werde," she confessed to him in one of her innumerable letters—surely amongst the most poignant love-letters ever written—"werde ich durch Dich und um Deinetwillen; sonst wäre es mir viel lieber und bequemer, mir innerlich allein etwas vorzudichten." And again: "Schreibe mir nur oft, mein Talent steigt und fällt mit Deiner Liebe."

Outwardly the great spate of lyrical poetry which was the product of this brief Meersburg period was the result of a wager, Schücking having asserted that she could not write poems at will, but had to wait for what she herself once called "die rechte Stunde." It was the kind of challenge Annette von Droste needed. Throughout this period of animated creativity—in striking contrast to the slow gestation that went to the making of her earlier work—Levin was at her side, making suggestions, pointing out obscurities and assisting in the work of publication.

The first complete edition of Annette von Droste's poetry, which was published by Cotta in 1844 under the title of *Gedichte von Annette Freiin von Droste-Hülshoff*, contains, it is true, a quantity of mediocre poems, especially among the *Gedichte vermischten Inhalts*, the group entitled *Scherz und Satire* and the so-called *Zeitbilder*, (written in the conservative-patriotic vein of her favourites Freiligrath and Geibel).

At its best, however, it constitutes a break-through to a lyrical form of expression more spontaneous and direct than anything that had gone before. Not that it contains a great effusion of feeling, for it is characteristic of Annette von Droste that the precipitate of her deepest personal experience is found in her letters, not in her poetry. Even her few love poems—*Brennende Liebe, Die Schenke am See, An Levin Schücking*—are reticent in tone and heavy with a kind of subdued sadness.

Almost twenty of the Meersburg poems are ballads, in which the subjective element is of necessity least in evidence, especially where they are based on traditional models, as *Der Graf von Thal* and others. In atmosphere they have little of the sunny serenity of the place of their composition, being reminiscent rather of the earlier Rüschhaus ballads:

> "Im Westen schwimmt ein falber Strich,
> Der Abendstern entzündet sich,
> Grad überm Sankt Georg am Tore;
> Schwer haucht der Dunst vom nahen Moore.
> Schlaftrunkne Schwäne kreisen sacht
> Ums Eiland, wo die graue Wacht
> Sich hebt aus Wasserbins' und Rohre." [14]

This is the opening verse of *Der Fundator*, perhaps the most successful of the ballads. The gradual building up of the ghostly atmosphere by means of realistic, sensuous impressions from the world of nature —the blue haze and the vapours of the moon, the groaning of the toad, the rustling in the reeds, the "snoring" of the swans—link it with the finest part of the collection, the *Heidebilder*. As the title suggests, these once again take their inspiration from her native moorlands, and once again the intimate, "lyrical" note is absent. The language has none of the radiancy of Goethe's lyric poetry; the "spröde Rhythmik" (as Wolfgang Kayser has aptly described it) seems harsh, even jerky when compared with his harmonious verse movements. In place of a musical appeal the verse often has the quality of speech, with a strong acoustic element (it ought properly to be read aloud). She uses words not for their associative symbolism or suggestive overtones, but in their basic, elemental sense and with a bold accuracy as though she were thereby able to conjure the world of natural phenomena.

In 1838 Annette von Droste had written to a friend: "Sie wissen selbst, mein Freund, dass ich nur im Naturgetreuen, durch Poesie veredelt, etwas leisten kann." This is as near as she ever came to a definition of her own "poetic realism." Read in the light of the *Heidebilder*, "fidelity to nature" implies the attempt to capture by sensory means that portion of the natural world of which she was herself a part: the world of "Heidekolk" and "Lehm," of "Föhre," "Sand" and "Bruch." After the vague longing for infinitude of German Romanticism, it seems like a deliberate restriction of the field of observation, matched by a sharpening of the senses of perception. With an almost electric sensitivity, her ear, her very nervous system is attuned to the minutest stirrings of life around her, listening as it were to the breathing of nature:

"Man hört im Kraut des Käfers Gang." [15]

This is reflected in the choice of verbs: knistern, flüstern, rieseln, knirren, klingeln, knittern, rispeln, etc., verbs which are as accurate as they are suggestive. The characteristic movement of her verse is from a shadowy beyond to the clearly perceptible, from the incommensurate to the commensurate, as in *Das Hirtenfeuer*:

"Dunkel, Dunkel im Moor,
　Über der Heide Nacht,
　Nur das rieselnde Rohr
　Neben der Mühle wacht,
　Und an des Rades Speichen
　Schwellende Tropfen schleichen." [16]

This is partly to be explained by Annette von Droste's extreme myopia which, while blurring distant objects, enabled her to see near-by ones with microscopic clarity. But fundamentally it answers her unconscious need to oppose the formless, the chaotic by clutching at the actual, the close-at-hand, to counterbalance her own deep-seated *Angst* by the most exact notation possible of the *données* of the world around her.

Not that she ever tried to "tame" nature in the *Biedermeier* sense of turning it into a well-kept garden of flowers and vegetables. At best the haven of house and garden is but a temporary refuge from the dark and sinister forces of nature at its most elemental. Even when the boy in *Der Knabe im Moor* has safely reached home after his perilous journey across the moor, the memory of what he has seen is all too real:

"Da mählich gründet der Boden sich,
　Und drüben neben der Weide,
　Die Lampe flimmert so heimatlich,
　Der Knabe steht an der Scheide.
　Tief atmet er auf, zum Moor zurück
　Noch immer wirft er den scheuen Blick:
　Ja, im Geröhre war's fürchterlich,
　O, schaurig war's in der Heide!" [17]

The atmosphere is often strangely akin to that of *Das Geistliche Jahr*; epithets such as "grau," "blass," "bleich," "matt," "dunkel," "dämmernd" still predominate. But the twilight of the soul has become externalized in the dusk and gloom of the heath, the heaviness of the human spirit transferred to a world of nature imprisoned in its torpid creatureliness:

> "Unke keuert im Sumpf,
> Igel im Grase duckt,
> In dem modernden Stumpf
> Schlafend die Kröte zuckt,
> Und am sandigen Hange
> Rollt sich fester die Schlange." [18]

Throughout the Meersburg poems the subjective element is kept in check, if not wholly suppressed. *Die Taxuswand*, with its stoic, yet tender renunciation of happiness, or *Das Spiegelbild*, in which the haunting vision of her own reflection gives way to an acceptance of herself as she is, is as near as Annette von Droste comes to a personal confession. Both rank amongst her most moving as well as technically her most accomplished poems.

After Schücking's departure the old inertia set in, but her creative impulses lay dormant rather than dead or exhausted. In September 1842 she, too, left Meersburg to return home to Rüschhaus. It was here that she completed *Der Spiritus familiaris des Rosstäuschers* (1842), the last of her four epic poems. Based on one of the *Deutsche Sagen* of the brothers Grimm, it tells the story of a horse-dealer who, having through no fault of his own lost all he has, makes a pact with the devil; driven to the verge of madness—like Goethe's *Zauberlehrling* he cannot get rid of the spirit he has himself called up—he sacrifices his newly won wealth as well as honour and strength, and by piercing the seal of the magic bottle with a nail from the Cross, finds in the end the longed-for salvation. The scene by the lake in the fourth canto, where the *Rosstäuscher* tries to hurl away the dangerous vial and, even as he utters a prayer for forgiveness, feels it stinging and pricking his body, forms the climax of the poem. In its preoccupation with the idea of guilt as it were overtaking man unawares and leading him to remorse and punishment, the poem seems to hark back to *Die Judenbuche*. But instead of the Old Testament fatalism of the *Novelle*, the final mood of the *Spiritus familiaris* is one of Christian redemption. The boundary between the real and the illusory which hitherto had been blurred and uncertain is now drawn with a firmer hand:

> "Wo sich der Engelsflügel neigt,
> Und nicht des Drachen Kralle reicht." [19]

Though the horrors of death and putrefaction reach their highest point, they are depicted with a sensuous objectivity and sureness of touch which have their origin in a more positive, less somnambulistic *Weltanschauung*—if one can use such a word in the case of a poet so singularly antipathetic to intellectual abstractions.

In September 1843 it was necessary for Annette von Droste, now a very sick woman, once again to seek the more salubrious air of Meersburg. Sitting or, more often, lying in her turret room high up over Lake Constance, she became more and more cut off from the outside world. "Ich bin in meinem Turm wie begraben," she told Schücking, who had in the meantime been to see her—but in the company of his young wife. The meeting had been a painful one for Annette and was subsequently followed by a complete estrangement. She had become famous and much sought after (in 1845 Schumann asked her, in vain, for a libretto). But fame meant nothing to her; far better, she wrote in a letter of 1843, "die Beine auf dem Sopha zu strecken und mit halb geschlossenen Augen von Ewigkeiten zu träumen ... keiner beliebten Manier, keinen anderen Führer als der ewig wahren Natur durch die Windungen des Menschenherzens zu folgen und unsere blasierte Zeit und ihre Zustände gänzlich mit dem Rücken anzusehen."

It was during this final period that Annette von Droste produced verses of such exquisite harmony as the opening of *Im Grase*:

> "Süsse Ruh, süsser Taumel im Grase,
> Von des Krautes Arome umhaucht,
> Tiefe Flut, tief, tief trunkne Flut,
> Wenn die Wolk' am Azure verraucht,
> Wenn aufs müde, schwimmende Haupt
> Süsses Lachen gaukelt herab.
> Liebe Stimme säuselt und träuft
> Wie die Lindenblüt auf das Grab." [20]

The poem was published in a posthumous collection of 1860 entitled *Letzte Gaben*. Though again somewhat mixed in quality, it contains some of Annette von Droste's finest poetry, mostly written between 1844 and 1845. One has to bear in mind the troubled uncertainty of mood of the *Heidebilder* fully to appreciate the sense of serenity which pervades poems such as *Grüsse*, in which each "schwache Form in Dunkeln" is no longer a menacing phantom, but a "tiefvertrauteste Gestalt." *Im Grase, Durchwachte Nacht* and *Mondesaufgang* are great lyric poems by any standards, combining as they do the experience of life as a harmonious whole with a more relaxed rhythm and a loosening up of conventional metric forms. The dominant atmosphere is no longer expressed in epithets such as "heiss," "schwer" or "dunkel," but by "süss," "tief" and "leise," yet without loss to the characteristic sensory quality of the imagery. *Mondesaufgang* is at once more personal and more truly religious than the whole of *Das Geistliche Jahr*: a Wordsworthian "gentleness of heaven is on the sea," a "mildes Licht" which not only promises momentary shelter from the horrors of the night (viz. the lamp in *Der Knabe im Moor*), but banishes them altogether.

> "Da auf die Wellen sank ein Silberflor,
> Und langsam stiegst du, frommes Licht, empor;
> Der Alpen finstre Stirnen strichst du leise,
> Und aus den Richtern wurden sanfte Greise;
> Der Wellen Zucken ward ein lächelnd Winken,
> An jedem Zweige sah ich Tropfen blinken,
> Und jeder Tropfen schien ein Kämmerlein,
> Drin flimmerte der Heimatlampe Schein." [21]

Not the restless straining of the soul laden with sin and guilt, but a patient waiting upon the workings of nature, both in its threatening and in its gentle moods, produce this final sense of release from fear and doubt.

Annette von Droste had reached the end of her creative life. With the exception of a few sacred poems (among them *Die ächzende Kreatur*, a strangely tortured poem whose very title suggests a relapse into the mood of earlier days), her poetic activity, as indeed all other activity virtually ceased after about 1846. For the last two years, until her death on 24 May 1848, her lyre was silent.

It was a lyre on which many notes were never struck. The note of humour, for instance, was deliberately suppressed ("Ich meine, der Humor steht nur wenigen und am seltensten einer weiblichen Feder, der fast zu engen Beschränkung durch die gesellschaftliche Sitte wegen"). The personal struggle for inner release never issues in a cry for freedom, as in the poetry of Emile Bronte. The struggle for political freedom taking place on her very doorstep found no echo in her work—except as an occasional protest delivered with all the indignation of her "loyales Aristokratenblut." Unsustained by the discipline of the intellect, her work is occasionally obscure and contains much that is only second-rate. Yet if she did not fully exploit and develop her own capabilities, she never sacrificed her artistic integrity by attempting to go beyond them for the sake of effect or popularity:

> "Sei ein Ganzes—ob nur ein Traum, ein halbverstandenes Märchen—es ist immer mehr wert als die nüchterne Frucht vom Baum der Erkenntnis." [22]

TRANSLATIONS

1. Too like a man's is your spirit, striving too high,
   To where no woman's eye can follow you;
   This it is which fills your breast with trembling fear
   And makes your youthful cheeks grow pale.
   When women rise above their sphere,
   Then they desert their own, their better self.

2. Lord, I am a poor, small, scarcely glowing
   Candle on the altar of thy grace;
   Behold, I am extinguished by a feeble breath of air,
   By a droplet from the universal shores.

3. You think, good people, you are acquainted with Care,
   Yet you have ne'er set eyes on Guilt!
   They, they alone may speak of Life
   And of its fearful heights.

   Upward, like songs of praise, the sound ascends,
   The sun's rays dally round the flowers,
   Peacefully men dwell in the valley,
   Dark vultures make their nests above.

4. Ledwina's eyes lingered upon her own form, as the locks fell from her head and drifted away, her dress was torn up, and her white fingers became separated and merged with the water.

5. Consciousness returned to me in sound;
   So sweetly in the air the warbling trills,
   Surely I heard a lark in song,
   And thought it must the morning bring.
   A dream? Reality? That would I know.
   If dream, then many a grey hair I bear
   In vain, full many a deep furrow on my brow.

6. Clear and loud the trumpets called;
   Arise, to horse! The foe's astir!
   Along the Liesner the sentries heard
   Already the hollow beat of drum.
   And swarming o'er the barren heath,
   The troops at once fell into rank.
   The orders flew around, and loud
   The signals o'er the bracken rang.

7. Suddenly Simon asked: "Dost like whisky?"—The boy did not answer. "I'm asking thee, dost like whisky? Does thy mother give thee some now and again?"—"My mother has none herself," said Friedrich.—"Well, well, all the better!—Dost know the wood in front of us?"—"That be Breder Wood."—"And dost know what happened in there?"—Friedrich was silent.

8. ... he reminded one instinctively of someone who gazes into a magic mirror and sees in it the image of his own future with troubled intentness.

9. But he quite cut it to pieces!

10. Only after I had completely freed myself from the idea of writing for my Grandmother was I able to work quickly—and with ... feelings of relief. ... For my Grandmother, as for all very devout persons, it is, once and for all, of no use, for I have had to leave upon it traces of a much troubled and divided mind!

11. When from need for salvation yearning springs,
    Can that be true repentance?

12. And yet I feel at other times,
    As hair is joined to head,
    Consecrated to this dark earth,
    Bereft of strength.

13. The cloud ascends,
    And slowly o'er the azure vault
    A shroud of sulphur settles down;
    The warm, still air is full of sighs,
    And fearfulness stirs in the branches.
    The cattle groan.
    What moves the sullen beast? Dost thou this sultriness impart?
    Abject I stand:
    Touch me, my Lord, that I may feel thy presence!

14. A wan ray floats upon the western sky,
    The evening star is lighting up
    Above the gate where stands St. George;
    Heavy the vapours waft from nearby moor.
    Softly the drowsy swans do pass
    Around the island, where the grey watch
    From out the reeds and rushes looms.

15. You can hear the beetle walk through the grass.

16. Dark, dark the moor,
    Over the heath-land Night,
    Only the trickling reeds
    By the mill do not sleep;
    Along the spokes of the wheel
    The swelling droplets steal.

17. Then, gradually, the ground grows firm,
    And yonder hard by the willow
    The lamp sends out its homely light,
    The boy stands at the boundary.
    Backward he casts a timid glance:
    Dreadful indeed it was on the moor,
    O, ghostly it was in the heather!

18. Frog crouches in the marsh,
    Hedgehog cowers in the grass,
    In the mouldering bracken
    Toad twitches in its sleep.
    And on the sandy hill
    Snake coils itself tighter still.

19. Where angels' wings gently incline,
    And dragon's claw can gain no hold.

20. Sweet repose, sweet bemusement in the meadow,
    Wafted around by the scent of the herbs,
    Deep flowing current, deep, delirious current,
    When the cloud evaporates in the azure,
    And on to the weary, swimming brain
    Sweet laughter playfully descends.
    A dear voice murmurs and drifts
    Like lime-blossom on to a grave.

21. A silvery veil descended on the waves,
    And slowly thou didst rise, o gracious light;
    Stroking with gentle touch the dark brows of the mountains
    Which turned from judges to benign old men;
    The waves, no longer flickering, beckoned, smiling,
    From every branch I saw the drops of water sparkle,
    And every drop seemed like a cosy chamber
    Whose homely lamp sent out its glistening ray.

22. Be one thing wholly and completely—even if only a dream, a fairy-tale but half-comprehended—it is worth far more than the prosaic fruit from the tree of Knowledge.

BIBLIOGRAPHY

Annette von Droste-Hülshoff. Sämtliche Werke. Carl Hanser Verlag, München, 1952.
Annette von Droste-Hülshoff. Sämtliche Werke. Insel-Verlag, Leipzig, 1939.

Die Briefe der Annette von Droste-Hülshoff (2 vols.), ed. K. Schulte-Kemming-hausen. Jena, 1944.

Schücking, L. *Annette von Droste-Hülshoff. Ein Lebensbild.* Hannover, 1862.

Staiger, E. *Annette von Droste-Hülshoff.* Zurich, 1932.

Hesselhaus, C. *Annette von Droste-Hülshoff. Die Entdeckung des Seins in der Dichtung des 19. Jahrhunderts.* Halle, 1943.

Franz Grillparzer

Franz Grillparzer

by E. E. PAPST

THE influential authority with which Weimar, and more especially Goethe, invested the humanist and idealist tradition is gradually being revealed as a mixed blessing for the history of German literature and criticism. As the shadows disperse which surrounded the zone of Olympian brilliance and which blurred many a nineteenth-century reputation, it is perhaps not surprising that of the authors whose distinctive genius and stature begin to assume clearer outline, none should benefit more than Grillparzer, Austria's most celebrated dramatist.

Goethe and Grillparzer, Weimar and Vienna, are focal points of two distinct traditions which, despite the inextricable interplay of mutual influence, have maintained their separate identity within the German-speaking cultural complex. While the prevailing German currents received their distinctive impetus from the Protestant humanism of the Reformation and the Renaissance, Austria remained the centre of those traditionalist forces, re-energized by the Counter-Reformation, which were intent on conserving the heritage of the Catholic Middle Ages and the Holy Roman Empire. For as long as possible she resisted the secularized rationalism and anti-authoritarian individualism of Enlightenment and Pietism, which in Germany nourished a spirit of progressive liberalism and a Promethean confidence in man's ability to transcend the universe and, a second creator, fashion it in his own image. In Austria the belief in an objectively given hierarchical order died hard: an order hallowed by history and tradition, and exceeding the limits of rational comprehension and organization; a hierarchy in which man, the creature, was assigned a fixed place and to which he subordinated himself by the virtues of humility and obedience to a God-appointed pattern of creation.

It is true that Grillparzer was born into and nurtured by the belated rationalism of the Josephinist age which slowly undermined Austria's resistance to the democratic revolutions of the nineteenth century. It is also true that throughout his life (1791–1872) he could not fail to come within the powerful orbit of the liberal tradition and, in particular, that without the formative influence which Goethe and Schiller exercised upon his talent, and Kant upon his thought, his genius would have developed along essentially different lines. Nevertheless, an insistence on these and other imported influences obscures the true growing points of an imagination so deeply rooted in a living indigenous tradition. The Austrian perspective alone can throw into relief Grillparzer's true significance for German literature and reveal him as something considerably more colourful and distinctive than is suggested by the label "Epigone der Klassik" with which a Goethe-orientated school of criticism has tried to assimilate this embarrassingly "begabter Einzelgänger" into the main stream of German literature.

Grillparzer's own views on the German authors of his day often border on contempt and are themselves a measure of the extent to which he dissociated himself from a body of literature which he regarded as contrived, lacking in phantasy, enervated by philosophical and theoretical speculation. This "Empfindungsmattigkeit" he attributed not least to the stiff mannerism of an ageing Goethe. Thus even his considerable admiration for Goethe—as indeed also for Beethoven, the other Olympian of his age—is never free of a deep-rooted ambivalence. This was most keenly felt with regard to Goethe's influence on his own talent. The memorable tears which welled up in his eyes when Goethe took his arm to lead him into lunch during his brief stay in Weimar were not entirely free of a certain bitter knowledge that he was not exempt from the state of creative paralysis into which a whole generation of *Epigonen* had been hypnotized. For, as he records in the poem *Reiselust*, amidst all the disillusionment with which the German literary scene filled him:

> "Einer [Goethe] nur ist mir erschienen,
> Aber ich ertrug ihn nicht,
> Und der Abglanz seiner Mienen
> Ward statt Flügel mir Gewicht." [1]

Grillparzer's inspiration, then, was not drawn from the rarefied academic atmosphere of the Weimar court theatre, but above all from the living tradition of the Viennese *Volksbühne*. [2] Still thriving and proliferating on a legacy from which Germany had once and for all been disinherited by Gottsched's purgative reforms, the popular playwrights of the day were proud to trace back an unbroken lineage from the *Bernardoniaden* and *Zauberspiele* of a Johann Kurz or a Schikaneder, through the *Hanswurstiaden* of Prehauser and Stranitzky to the extravagant spectacles of Jesuit and Court Baroque and, still further back, to the colourful pageantry of the mediaeval mystery and morality. Playwrights rather than dramatists, with a genius for "theatre" inherited from generations of actor-authors, who improvized more performances than they ever penned plays; practitioners with a sure instinct for exploiting the resources of mime and of a highly refined stagecraft to entertain their popular, untutored audience-spectators (*Zuschauer*) who watched rather than listened to plays (*Schauspiele* in the fullest sense of the word).

In Grillparzer, the contemporary of Raimund and Nestroy, the key component of his Viennese heredity expresses itself in the innate conviction that the stage, the actors and the audience-spectators can alone validify a dramatic text, transforming it from a speculative blue-print, from a mere dramatic intention, into a living play which carries its own conviction within itself. This knowledge that the theatre was the essential medium and ultimate testing ground of his art gives the clue to those major points of emphasis in both his theory and his practice which demarcate him so sharply from the prevailing trend of German drama (and which also, incidentally, account for the wellnigh suicidal despondency with which the growing indifference of his Viennese audiences filled him). Even Schiller, for whom Grillparzer entertained a lifelong respect as a master of the dramatic art, suffered from the fundamental deficiency which condemned German drama to an academic existence as a primarily literary art—the lack of an indigenous theatre tradition, rooted in the past and validified by the test of time and popular approval.

To borrow one of the phrases with which he praises Shakespeare, Grillparzer is as much the "Gesamtschauspieler seiner Stücke" [3] as their author. This is true not only of the wide scope and firm guidance which he gives his actors, the subtle articulacy with which he fills every inflexion of the voice, every gesture and movement of the body, the attention which he pays to entrances, positioning and exits, or to the telling effect of curtain lines and situations; it is manifest in his whole ability to mould the total stage "picture" or *Bild* into an indispensable extension of the verbal medium, which itself is already worked through and through with plastic imagery. The text of a play, in his eyes, is not all that different from the libretto of an opera. It is subordinated to a total structure, of which it is only one ingredient among many. And so, far from being the sole medium of presentation, words are not even always the vehicle of the ostensible action, let alone of the "inner" psychological action of his plays.

Probably none of his works so convincingly justifies his reputation as the "Dichter des Stummen" [4] as *Des Meeres und der Liebe Wellen*. None conveys so well the texture or characteristic "feel" which, perhaps more than any other feature of his plays, is the most striking quality of his genius. The very title, indefinably Baroque in flavour, fuses abstract concept with concrete image and so establishes the full range of the medium in which the fateful love of Hero and Leander is enacted. The action—and it could scarcely be otherwise if the myth is to be dramatically exploited—is primarily focused on the insidious undermining of Hero's conscious will to fulfil her vows of celibacy by the pre-conscious stirring of her womanhood, by a passion still unborn, for which she has still found no words. Thus, if this submerged conflict is to be realized at all in the first person present of drama, it must for the most part be played out below the threshold of explicit linguistic statement.

Perhaps Grillparzer's greatest contribution not only to German, but to world drama is his conquest and mastery of a vast dimension to body forth this type of submerged conflict, which at best the conscious mind experiences only as an unarticulated state of distraction (*Zerstreuung*). And so, at all the crucial stages of the action in *Des Meeres und der Liebe Wellen* speech either fails or breaks down into absent-minded incoherence, or else is used unwittingly (and in other plays wittingly) as a rationalistic means of concealing the true movements of the heart. To the extent that their informative and explicative task is taken over by non-verbal elements, words can now be more fully utilized for performing the important task of reinforcing the psychological realism of the play.

One instance must do duty for a host of others. Bidding her ritual farewell to the gods of earthly love, Hero's eye for the first time falls on Leander. Forgetting the ritual words for taking leave of Hymen, she searches for the tongs she already holds in her hand. Absent-mindedly repeating the formula for the farewell to Eros, she is impatiently interrupted by the Priest before she has got beyond the significant apostrophe "Der du die Liebe . . ." [5] She finally crowns her confusion by pouring too rich a libation on Hymen's sacrificial flames. Thus, beneath the distraction of her mind and words, the whole nature and foredoomed course of a conflict still hidden from Hero is revealed to the audience by the symbolism of her actions and the *unintended* significance of her words. Throughout the play this "dumb language" keeps the audience informed of the true motive forces underlying the ostensible course of the action.

Thus Grillparzer has forged an instrument of unparalleled sensitivity to record in all their fully dimensioned living immediacy the finest nuances of those twilight states of the human mind, halfway between the unconscious and the conscious, between instinct and will, dream and waking, in which motives are ultimately rooted, inaccessible to the insight and control of the conscious mind and will.

In this essentially modern sense, this compatriot of Freud is one of the earliest and greatest exponents of psychological realism.

This use of drama as a totally co-ordinated symbolic sphere, in which abstract linguistic concept is both complemented and confirmed by the "tally" (σύμβολον) of verbal image, visible action, gesture and other objects of immediate sense perception, is of a piece with Grillparzer's sporadic and (on principle) unsystematic theoretical statements on art.* This mistrust of systematic thought is symptomatic of his sceptical attitude to philosophy in general, which he regarded at best as a "Brille für das geistige Auge," [6] useless to the blind and impairing the vision of the healthy. For philosophy operates with concepts (*Begriffe*) and arranges them in logically demonstrable sequences. But the precision and usefulness of concepts is dependent on their abstraction, upon the extent to which they have emptied the objects of living experience of their palpable substance. Nor can logical argument ever hope to rival the type of unprovable (*erweislos*) conviction which immediate experience (*Empfindung*) carries within itself. Thus the blue-prints of the universe excogitated by the philosopher's disembodied intellect remain for Grillparzer the arbitrary, "phantasmagorical" products of a speculative faculty run wild, unchecked by the control of sensuous verification. They achieve systematic coherence only by violating the essence of reality, which, both in its parts and its overall structure, is conceptually irreducible or— to use again a leitmotif term of Grillparzer's—*erweislos*. "Die Welt würde in diesem Augenblick zusammenbrechen, wenn ihre Verbindungen solche wären, die wir einsehen könnten." [7] To ignore this truth is in his eyes equivalent to blasphemous irreverence, a sin epitomized for him in the Hegelian system, "die monströseste Ausgeburt des menschlichen Eigendünkels." [8]

Grillparzer's theory of art is the positive complement of this negative attitude to philosophy. Although indebted, among others, to Kant, Spinoza and Bouterwek, it has a highly distinctive focus in his definition of beauty (the validifying principle of art) as the total congruence of the mental and the sense objects of perception ("die vollkommene Übereinstimmung des Sinnlichen mit dem Geistigen"). Where philosophy fragments the faculties by destroying the functional relationship of the senses and the intellect, art is "die Verkörperung des Geistes, die Vergeistigung des Körpers, die Empfindung des Verstandes und das Denken des Gefühls." [9] It integrates all the faculties into a unitive act of contemplation or *Beschauung* and thereby achieves a "Zurückführung des Gedankens

* "Art" and "artist" are used throughout in their widest sense, to correspond with the German *Kunst* and *Künstler*.

auf die Wirklichkeit." [10] Art thus aims at symbolic truth, at "ein Bild der Wahrheit, eine Inkarnation derselben," [11] at once fully experienced and understood. Any intentions which the artist fails to incarnate symbolically are invalid—and in this sense "Genialität ohne Talent ist der Teufel der neueren Kunst." [12] For "was nicht ausgeführt wird, ist leer; was nicht ausgeführt werden kann, ist verrückt." [13] The *Bildlichkeit* or *Körperlichkeit* [14] of art is its reality coefficient, endowing it with the same immediacy of *erweislos* conviction as an object of nature, which persuades us of its reality through the fact that it is. This *es ist*, [15] which it shares with nature, ensures that art embodies acts of contemplation (*Anschauungen*) which, both subjectively and objectively, are valid acts of cognition, in conformity with both the "inner and outer laws of nature."

This victory over the fragmentation of the mind and the achievement of a state of being in which all the faculties are concentrated and co-ordinated in an act of *Beschauung*, is a matter which constantly and urgently preoccupied Grillparzer throughout his life, and by no means only in relation to art. Indeed, the idea of *Sammlung* [6] (his favourite term for this integrated state) is the germ seed of all his thought and writing. For his whole conception of life and tragedy is based upon the conviction that *Sammlung* [16] alone can redeem the human condition from its state of chaotic fragmentation, which both as a state of mind and as an objective feature of the world is at the root of all tragedy. For:

> ". . . wo du [Sammlung] *nicht* bist, da zerfällt in Staub
> Das Götterbild der Menschheit und zerbröckelt,
> Wie Mauersteine, deren Bindung wich.
> Der Sohn der Erde tritt in die Natur,
> Sein Auge sieht: ein stummes totes All,
> Sein Ohr vernimmt: ohn' Inhalt, wirre Töne,
> Die Hand ergreift, läßt fahren und faßt wieder;
> Was ihn umringt, es ist ein Vieles nur,
> Und er ein Nichts im Vielen, das kaum Etwas.
> Da steigst du nieder in den engen Kreis,
> O Himmlische, und heißt und lehrst ihn gatten
> Dem Ohr das Aug', dem Aug' die sichre Hand;
> Die Zunge spricht es aus, was sie gewonnen,
> Und der Gedanke tritt, ein Neugeborner,
> In die dem Chaos abgestrittne Welt." [17]

Here too is the ultimate explanation of Grillparzer's unconditional devotion to his art as the sole source of meaning and purpose in his life, and of his chronic obsessional fear that the wells of his genius were drying up. His autobiographical writing is scarcely ever free of the anxiety that the whole "gedankenlose und gedanken-mischende Zerstreuung"[18] of his life is silting up the contemplative faculty indispensable not only to his art, but to his very hold on reality: "Mein Leben war immer ein Traum, und zwar nicht ... der eines Wachenden, sondern in der Tat Eines, der schläft." [19] Hofmannsthal has summed up the malaise which vitiated Grill-parzer's whole life in a pregnant formula: "Grillparzer's Signatur: sich selber nicht besitzen."[20] This sense of self-alienation, of lacking (to use Hero's words) "das stille Glück des Selbstbesitzes," [21] contains the seed of all Grillparzer's creative writing.

Not the least remarkable feature of his genius is the luxuriant vitality with which this seed, and the tragic dichotomy implicit in it, flowers into the rich diversity of his plays*. Although not numerous, these are varied in theme and treatment with a Protean versatility that is itself evidence of the archetypal character of the tragic conflict ultimately common to all the plays. This can perhaps best be formulated in terms of the dual loyalty which man owes to the two incompatible realms to which he belongs: the timeless spiritual realm of eternal forms, and the temporal physical realm of living experience. In neither realm is fulfilment possible, for if the eternal patterns revealed through the detachment of contempla-tion remain disembodied chimaera without the substance of living experience, the very quest for this substance plunges man into a chaotic flux of uncontrollable passion and event, in which all sense of pattern and direction is lost.

All Grillparzer's plays thus derive the course of their action from a common dynamic impetus. Driven out of a state of intact innocence, in which they are at one with the inner law of their being and the objective order of the world, his heroes and heroines enter a laby-rinth of mental and moral delusion, in which they lose their intrinsic selves. For a while they cling to the illusion of controlling their destiny, only to awaken in a prison of guilt and fateful circumstance which they themselves have erected with their desire-tainted wills and from which there is no escape. Too late they discover the truth revealed to Rustan on awaking from his timely dream in *Der*

* Although Grillparzer's reputation rests primarily upon twelve completed tragedies and one comedy, these do not constitute his total oeuvre. Apart from several dramatic fragments, mostly composed in his youth, this includes a large lyrical output, whose unemotional and reflective mode of expression contrasts surprisingly with the impassioned tone of much of his dramatic writing; the opera libretto *Melusine* (1823), commissioned but never composed by Beethoven, despite his warm reception of it; two prose tales *Das Kloster bei Sendomir* (1828) and *Der arme Spielmann* (1847); a number of undeservedly neglected epigrams; and a large body of theoretical and autobiographical writing, mainly in the form of journals, *Reisetagebücher* and a *Selbstbiographie* (1853), written at the age of sixty-three and covering the first forty-odd years of his life.

Traum ein Leben, a truth which might stand as a motto over all Grillparzer's plays:

"Eines nur ist Glück hienieden,
Eins: des Innern stiller Frieden
Und die schuldbefreite Brust!
Und die Größe ist gefährlich,
Und der Ruhm ein leeres Spiel;
Was er gibt, sind nicht'ge Schatten,
Was er nimmt, es ist so viel!" [22]

Thus the fate of Grillparzer's characters, as a recent critic (H. Gmür) has put it, is that in the purity of contemplation they cannot remain human, while in realizing their humanity through living they cannot remain pure. This dualism between *Sammlung* and *Leben*, between the *vita contemplativa* and the *vita activa*, which since Euripides has been an ever-recurrent mode of conceiving of the polarity inherent in all human existence, bears a marked affinity to the dichotomy, variously formulated by Schiller, between *Formtrieb* [23] and *Stofftrieb* [23]. But here again difference is more telling than similarity when comparing Grillparzer with the German tradition. Schiller tends to formulate the polarity in abstract concepts which make it most fruitful for discursive manipulation. Grillparzer, aware of the impoverishing effects of philosophical precision, prefers to retain all the psychological imponderables and conceives the polarity in terms of fully dimensioned *states of mind*, thus making it primarily amenable to artistic treatment. The loss to philosophy can thus be booked as a gain to drama. Moreover, this refusal to transcend the problem intellectually by abstracting it from the realm of *Empfindung* in which it is fully experienced, already precludes, or at least makes more difficult, Schiller's idealist resolution of the conflict through an act of transcendant sublimity (*Erhabenheit*).

In fact Grillparzer attempts a clearcut idealist resolution only once—in *Sappho* (1817), which in this and other respects is the least representative of his plays. Written under the first impact of Weimar influence, and in particular of *Torquato Tasso*, this work was, as Grillparzer readily admitted, to a large extent ploughed with Goethe's ox (or, in the more respectful German, ". . . so ziemlich mit seinem Kalb gepflugt"). After his spectacularly successful debut with *Die Ahnfrau* (1817), a horrific family tragedy in the tradition of the Austrian *Geisterstück* [24] and *Geisterroman*, [24] he was determined to dissociate himself sharply from the notorious vogue of Romantic fate tragedy by choosing an outspokenly classical theme and treatment for his next play.

Sappho's tragedy springs from her attempt to achieve a union between art and life, between her divine calling and her womanhood, through her love for the youth Phaon. But once the sluice-gate of her passions is open, she is incapable of stemming their rising flood. Discovering too late the self-delusion with which she has hidden from herself the true nature of Phaon's feelings, she is swept forward to the brink of an act of insensate vengeance. From this she is rescued only by Phaon's plea for mercy and his reminder that her vocation places her amongst the gods and allows her no place among mortals, from whom she can claim reverence, but never love. Transcending her passion and acknowledging her guilt, but unable to return in life to the realm of poetic *Sammlung* which she has betrayed, Sappho once more embraces her lyre and achieves freedom in the transfiguring sublimity of a willingly accepted, self-inflicted death. And so this tragic conflict, to which Grillparzer was to find no resolution in his next play a few years later, is here still resolved through a typically Schillerian act of *Erhabenheit*.

The trilogy of *Das goldene Vliess* (1820) is the first dramatic treatment of the myth of Jason and Medea to make use of the earlier parts of the legend and so lay bare the psychological process by which Medea is transformed from an untamed innocent, at one with herself and nature, into an otherwise wellnigh inconceivable figure of horror and guilt. As a motto for the trilogy Grillparzer notes in his diaries a passage from Rousseau's *Confessions* (favourite reading throughout his life): "L'on a remarqué que la plupart des hommes sont dans le cours de leur vie souvent dissemblables à eux-mêmes, et semblent se transformer en des hommes tout différents." What was still to some extent concealed under the potentially misleading motif of the family curse in *Die Ahnfrau* is now made plain in this tragedy of the will ("Trauerspiel des Willens"): Jason and Medea fall victim to the inexorable fate of self-alienation (*Selbstverlust*) inherent in the operation of the will. Man is still, as for Schiller, a creature with the distinctive characteristic of willing, but he no longer wills in accordance with genuine moral choice; he wills what he must will, what he is driven to will.

Jason and Medea together embody the twofold nature of this blind drive. Like Sappho before her, and Hero and Libussa after her, Medea embodies its more distinctively feminine variant, the irresistible enslavement of the self by the passion of love:

"Es gibt ein Etwas in des Menschen Wesen,
  Das, unabhängig von des Eigners Willen,
  Anzieht und abstößt mit blinder Gewalt;
  Wie vom Blitz zum Metall, vom Magnet zum Eisen,

Geht ein Zug, ein geheimnisvoller Zug
Vom Menschen zum Menschen, von Brust zu Brust.
Da ist nicht Reiz, nicht Anmut, nicht Tugend, nicht Recht,
Was knüpft und losknüpft die zaubrischen Fäden:
Unsichtbar geht der Neigung Zauberbrücke,
So viel sie betraten, hat keiner sie gesehn!
Gefallen *muss* dir, was dir gefällt . . . " [25]

In Jason the will assumes its characteristically masculine form as a
lust for adventure and glory, an irresistible urge to realize the self
through action (*Tatendrang*). "Nur *er* ist da," Medea says of Jason,
"*er* in der weiten Welt, Und alles andre nichts, als Stoff zu
Taten." [26] This presumptuous egoism of action ruthlessly sacrifices
the whole to the part and fixes its eyes on the moment of personal
achievement, which it wrenches out of the overall continuity of
time. Thus the Argonaut destroys the order of the universe:

"Der Masstab aller Dinge war verloren,
    Nur an sich selbst mass jeder, was er sah." [27]

Even before returning to Greece, Jason has fallen prey to the Nemesis
of circumstance and memory which his presumption has invoked:

". . . Erinnrung des Vergangenen
    Liegt mir wie Blei auf meiner bangen Seele,
    Das Aug kann ich nicht heben und das Herz." [28]

Instead of fulfilling himself he has lost himself as surely as Medea:
"Ich bin nicht, der ich war . . . Ich bin nur Jasons Schatten, nicht
er selbst." [29]

And so Jason and Medea themselves forge the fetters which are
to tie them together in a life-time of misery, each the other's peculiar
fate ("Ich dir zur Qual, du mir"). [30] The twin peak of their desires,
the wresting of the Golden Fleece from the guardian dragon and
the consummation of their union with one another (fused into a
scene of almost unfathomable symbolic depth) is in effect the
precise moment at which they set the seal on their irrevocable
joint doom—a doom which remorselessly compels them inch by
inch to estrange themselves not only from others, but from their
own intrinsic selves and grinds them down to their final acts of
despair. The trilogy ends with Jason and Medea, expelled by
Creon, wandering in a wilderness of mental and moral agony, from
which death would be a merciful release. Medea's one consolation
is that at least her children have been spared the nightmare of life.

"Nicht traur' ich, daß die Kinder nicht mehr sind,
    Ich traure, daß sie *waren*, und dass *wir* sind." [31]

Das goldene Vliess is a work of unrelieved pessimism, concluding that death is better than life, and best of all is never to have been born. Alongside *Libussa*, it is Grillparzer's most ambitious attempt to symbolize the tragedy, not of any particular type of life, but of the human condition itself. It is also the first play to achieve a synthesis of the two traditions, the Austrian and the classical Hellenic, to which he was heir.

But it is in his next play, *König Ottokars Glück und Ende* (1823) that he finds the genre which, more than any other, was able to reveal the unique nature of his genius. For Grillparzer was peculiarly sensible to the fundamental advantage of historical subjects over invented subjects. He saw this above all in their power to discipline the imagination into conformity with reality, and so to validify its speculative creativeness with a richness of real character and situation, with imponderable "life." His theoretical comments on historical drama are therefore amongst his most illuminating aesthetic statements. They are also pervaded by that religiously toned reverence for history as the repository of God's will which is a feature of all his later work and outlook. Like nature, history is "erweislos, weil . . . selber der Erweis," [32] and, as the creation of God, it must always transcend man's presumptuous attempts to understand and control it by the light of the rational intellect.

In the last analysis it is the lack of this reverence for history (of what Libussa calls "Ehrfurcht, die nicht auf Erweis sich gründet") [33] which brings about the downfall of the proud Ottokar in this chronicle of his defeat and humiliation at the hands of the founder of the Hapsburg Imperial dynasty. All the rich tapestry of Ottokar's self-centred motives and deeds is woven through with the hubris which would use his fellowmen as mere tools for the fashioning of a world in his own image. Scornful of time-hallowed traditions and loyalties, he tinkers and tampers with history, imposing upon it the pattern of his will, tyrannizing it with brute force or rationalized argument, and so calling forth the forces with which the organism of the corporate whole will restore the balance of its healthy development.

These forces find their focus in Rudolf of Hapsburg, who, in assuming the Imperial Crown, has put off his private self and become identified with his divinely appointed office—divinely appointed because its authority is not arbitrary, but rooted in history and the will of the corporate whole. In this sense Rudolf can say that it is not he who is disciplining Austria, but Austria disciplining herself through him. His actions are in the fullest sense "true" and no longer dependent on the unwitting illusion or the knowing lie on which all self-orientated action depends (—the "lie" which furnishes *Weh dem, der lügt!* with its problem theme).

Rudolf is thus the first, and indeed the only one, of Grillparzer's characters to achieve a synthesis of the *vita activa* and the *vita contemplativa*. But unfortunately he remains to a large extent unrealized as a character. In a play partially inspired by the desire to add lustre to Austria's national glory the dramatist has allowed himself to introduce something very like a saint from a mediaeval legend. Moreover, to the extent that Rudolf's redemption is not of his doing, but dependent on a transmission of divine grace, he is motivated by forces beyond the reach of secular psychology and realist art. And although at every turn Grillparzer's writing bears the stamp of a religious and specifically Catholic mould, his conception of art and life betrays the Josephinist hour of his birth; it is ultimately secular and has lost the unquestioning conviction of the operation of divine grace in history. He never again attempted a resolution of the tragic conflict in these terms.

In *Der treue Diener seines Herrn* (1828) Grillparzer again faced the tragic paradox of life squarely, this time giving it a more explicitly ethical emphasis and probing the close relationship between moral rectitude and an inability to come to grips with life, an ultimate *Lebensunfähigkeit*. Bancbanus, the one man whose loyalty and uncompromising integrity fit him best to deputize for King Andreas II during his absence abroad, is also the man whose advanced years, impartial detachment and impracticality call forth the disaster for which he and the realm have to pay so dearly. The ambiguous light which is here thrown on the nature of moral excellence is later intensified in the short prose masterpiece, *Der arme Spielmann* (1847), in which it is no longer possible to determine whether the unworldly street musician hero is a weak or a strong character, an imbecile or a saint. Intent on reproducing the music, not of Bach or of Beethoven, but of God, Jakob's playing is totally unrecognizable as music. In his life too he has lost all power to mediate between the ideal and the real. The very integrity with which he preserves his childlike innocence removes him as surely from the realm of practical humanity as the chalked "equator" with which he separates the scrupulous tidiness of his domain and the punctilious ordering of his day from the unmade beds and irregular hours of the labourers who share his room.

Discouraged by the treatment of his two patriotically inspired plays at the hands of public, censor and Emperor, Grillparzer left the field of historical drama for the three remaining plays which he allowed to be either performed or published during his lifetime.

In *Des Meeres und der Liebe Wellen* (1831), he bid farewell to the Hellenic tradition with a work which rivals the greatest of the world's love tragedies. The idyll of Hero's love for Leander is filled with such haunting sweetness that the play only just manages to justify the moral necessity for the lovers' tragic end. *Der Traum ein Leben* (1834) is conceived in the popular tradition of the Viennese *Zauberstück* to which we owe Mozart's *Zauberflöte*. Often referred to as the Austrian "Anti-Faust," this dramatic dream phantasy conceals the tragedy of a second Jason, transposing it into a lighter key and providing it with the happy ending of a fairy-tale. The play was originally planned and its first act completed between the composition of *Die Ahnfrau* and *Sappho*. It was conceived under the direct influence of Calderon's *La vida es sueño*, which Grillparzer was translating at the time and which marks the first stage of his lifelong interest in Spanish drama. This interest, in which the emphasis was later shifted from Calderon to Lope de Vega, had a profound influence on all aspects of his art, nourishing it in the field of serious drama with a Baroque tradition which the Austrian popular stage had preserved primarily in the form of comedy. *Weh dem, der lügt!* (1838), Grillparzer's one excursion into comedy, is devoted to an analysis of the relation of conscience and action, of truth and lie and is thus in a direct line with his tragedies. It, too, harks back to mediaeval and Baroque traditions—a morality play transposed into the secular convention of the popular *Lehrspiel*. [34] There is therefore a sad irony in the boorish incomprehension with which the Viennese public received this play and which finally decided Grillparzer to withhold from them his last three tragedies, regarded by many critics as his greatest: *Die Jüdin von Toledo*, *Libussa* and *Ein Bruderzwist in Hapsburg* (all finalized after 1850).

Where in his earlier works Grillparzer tended to affix a positive sign to the contemplative life and a minus to the power of love and the life of action, in his mature work there is a growing recognition of the scope which must be allowed to the principle of *Leben*. Both implicitly in the action of *Des Meeres und der Liebe Wellen* and explicitly in the Priest's warning to Hero on the eve of her taking her vows, a state of contemplation which is devoid of the fructifying power of love and untried by life is represented as unstable and as an evasion of human responsibility. *Libussa*, which together with *Ein Bruderzwist in Hapsburg* embodies the maturest fruits of Grillparzer's wisdom, goes farthest of all his plays towards a positive assessment of love, and—even if only in the form of a prophecy of a mythical future—envisages the possibility of a world in which the conflict of man's dual loyalty to an earthly and a heavenly order is resolved. When Libussa leaves her tower of clairvoyant self-possession to ascend the throne vacated by her father's death, she is yielding to an irresistible impulse of love, awoken in her by her encounter with Primislaus. But unlike Medea's and Hero's, Libussa's

love, embracing her whole people, is more akin to compassion
than to passion and throws into relief the selfishness of the aloof
detachment to which her two sisters jealously cling in their tower
of timeless contemplation.

The history of the state which Libussa now founds has all the
symbolic force of a mythologized abbreviation of the history of
human society. In a matriarchy based upon the harmonious rule of
love and childlike trust, Libussa attempts to realize the divine
order in history. But this state is of necessity unstable and short-
lived, and to satisfy her subjects' demands for a rationalized codified
administration, she marries Primislaus and hands over her power to
him. In Primislaus's state love is replaced by justice, trust by the
rule of codified law, natural growth by purposive planning. It is
an order in which Libussa has no place and to which she must be
sacrificed. But in founding Prague, Primislaus is conscious that his
is ultimately a delegated authority, and in a last prophetic vision
Libussa looks forward to an infinitely remote time when man will
have reached the limits of his power and, master of all which is
necessary for his existence, will feel the emptiness of his inner self.
Then:

> "Beschwichtigt das Getöse lauter Arbeit,
> Vernimmt er neu die Stimmen seiner Brust;
> Die Liebe, die nicht das Bedürfnis liebt,
> Die selbst Bedürfnis ist, holdsel'ge Liebe;
> Im Drang der Kraft Bewußtsein eigner Ohnmacht;
> Begeisterung, schon durch sich selbst verbürgt,
> Die wahr ist, weil es wahr ist, daß ich fühle.
> Dann kommt die Zeit, die jetzt vorübergeht,
> Die Zeit der Seher wieder und Begabten.
> Das Wissen und der Nutzen scheiden sich
> Und nehmen das Gefühl zu sich als Drittes;
> Und haben sich die Himmel dann verschlossen,
> Die Erde steigt empor an ihren Platz,
> Die Götter wohnen wieder in der Brust,
> Und Demut heißt ihr Oberer und Einer." [35]

If *Libussa* is Grillparzer's profoundest, and also his most optimistic
work, then *Ein Bruderzwist in Hapsburg* is his most personal and is
filled with the sense of anxiety and Cassandra-like impotence with
which he watched and diagnosed the political, social and moral
disintegration of his age. It is the tragedy of Rudolf II, who, a
"Hamlet on the Imperial Throne," is paralysed by the certain
knowledge of the inavertible chaos which is about to be unleashed
on Europe by the Thirty Years War, and by

> ". . . das Bewußtsein, daß im Handeln,
> Ob so nun oder so, der Zündstoff liegt,
> Der diese Mine donnernd sprengt gen Himmel." [36]

Appalled by the abyss towards which his country is being precipitated by the actions of men tainted with lust for power or with the inhumanity of religious purism, by the licentiousness of an age which has lost its moral bearings and the folly of a false liberalism which has lost its respect for the God-given hierarchical order of the world, Rudolf immures himself in his palace with his books and scientific instruments and, in impregnable solitude, seeks to silence in his breast the raging clamour of his confused times, looking to the stars and dumb nature for the order which man has destroyed. For truth can be found only:

> ". . . in Sternen . . . im Gestein,
> In Pflanze, Tier und Baum; im Menschen nicht.
> Und wer's verstünde, still zu sein wie sie,
> Gelehrig fromm, den eignen Willen meisternd,
> Ein aufgespanntes, demutvolles Ohr,
> Ihm würde leicht ein Wort der Wahrheit kund,
> Die durch die Welten geht aus Gottes Munde." [37]

But it is the inevitable tragedy of this lonely Hapsburg monarch that his vision of the eternal order of the universe is unable to rescue either his people or himself from the chaos unleashed by the destructive presumption of the will in all its multifarious guises.

With almost uncanny power Rudolf's character and fate incarnate in the living stuff of history Grillparzer's innermost convictions, and his speeches constitute the poet's testament of wisdom to his age and to posterity. The prophetic force of this wisdom is exemplified in Rudolf's vision of a world disintegrating into egalitarian anarchy, a relentless process which will not cease "bis alles gleich, ei ja, weil alles niedrig." [38] Grillparzer's alarmingly clairvoyant diagnosis of the modern age is only one instance among many of the penetrating insight and unflinching courage with which a genius, so often disparaged as pathologically "lebensscheu," [39] faced the grim reality of an unregenerate world. Far from betokening an attitude of negative resignation, so often attributed to him, the pessimism of his disillusionment only throws into relief his positive faith in an ultimate order and source of values with which he tirelessly opposed the overweening pride of the human intellect. And so, in his reply to the citizens of Prague clamouring for their democratic rights, it is with a philosophy of affirmation and hope that Rudolf sums up Grillparzer's ultimate vision of the world and his exhortation to mankind.

"Seht an die Welt, die sichtbar offenkund'ge,
Wie Berg und Tal und Fluß und Wiese stehn.
Die Höhen, selber kahl, ziehn an die Wolken
Und senden sie als Regen in das Tal,
Der Wald hält ab den zehrend wilden Sturm,
Die Quelle trägt nicht Frucht, doch nährt sie Früchte,
Und aus dem Wechselspiel von hoch und niedrig,
Von Frucht und Schutz erzeugt sich dieses Ganze,
Des Grund und Recht in dem liegt, daß es ist.
Zieht nicht vor das Gericht die heil'gen Bande,
Die unbewußt, zugleich mit der Geburt,
Erweislos, weil sie selber der Erweis,
Verknüpfen, was das Klügeln feindlich trennt.
Du ehrst den Vater,—aber er ist hart;
Du liebst die Mutter,—die beschränkt und schwach,
Der Bruder ist der nächste dir der Menschen,
Wie sehr entfernt in Worten und in Tat;
Und wenn das Herz dich zu dem Weibe zieht,
So fragst du nicht, ob sie der Frauen Beste,
Das Mal auf ihrem Hals wird dir zum Reiz,
Ein Fehler ihrer Zunge scheint Musik,
Und das: Ich weiß nicht was, das dich entzückt,
Ist ein: Ich weiß nicht was für alle andern;
Du liebst, du hoffst, du glaubst. Ist doch der Glaube
Nur das Gefühl der Eintracht mit dir selbst,
Das Zeugnis, daß du Mensch nach beiden Seiten;
Als einzeln schwach und stark als Teil des All.
Daß deine Väter glaubten, was du selbst,
Und deine Kinder künftig treten gleiche Pfade,
Das ist die Brücke, die aus Menschenherzen
Den unerforschten Abgrund überbaut,
Von dem kein Senkblei noch erforscht die Tiefe.
O, prüfe nicht die Stützen, bessre nicht!
Dein Menschenwerk zerstört den geist'gen Halt,
Und deine Enkel lachen einst der Trümmer,
In denen deine Weisheit modernd liegt.

Der Zweifel zeugt den Zweifel an sich selbst,
Und einmal Ehrfurcht in sich selbst gespalten,
Lebt sie als Ehrsucht nur noch und als Furcht.
Maßt euch nicht an, zu deuten Gottes Wahrheit." [40]

TRANSLATIONS

1. One alone appeared before me; but I was unable to support him, and the reflected splendour of his countenance added weights instead of wings to me.

2. Popular stage.

3. Actor of his plays.

4. Poet of the wordless.

5. Thou who [givest] love. . . .

6. Spectacles for the eyes of the mind.

7. The world would collapse this very instant if it were hinged together in ways which we could comprehend.

8. The biggest monstrosity hatched out by human self-conceit.

9. . . . the embodying of the mind, the spiritualizing of the body, the sensation of the understanding, and the reasoning of the emotions.

10. Reduction of thought to reality.

11. An image of the truth, an incarnation of it.

12. Genius without talent is what bedevils modern art.

13. . . . what is not executed is empty; what cannot be executed is lunatic.

14. Imagistic quality . . . corporality.

15. It is.

16. Self-collectedness. (The German term, as used by Grillparzer, fuses the ideas of concentration and composure, and cannot be adequately translated.)

17. Where you are *absent*, humanity's divine image turns to dust and crumbles like the stones of a wall which has lost its mortar. Earth's child sets foot in nature, his eye sees—a universe that's dead and dumb, his ear hears a meaningless confusion of sounds, his hand grasps, lets go and seizes again; all that surrounds him is a motley of the many, and he a nothing in the many, scarcely anything. Into this narrow circle you descend, oh heavenly one, and command and teach him to wed eye to ear, and to the eye the sure hand; the tongue pronounces what it has won, and thought, new-born, enters into the world wrested from chaos.

18. Thoughtless and thought-confusing distraction.

19. My life has always been a dream, and not . . . the dream of one who is awake but in fact of one who sleeps.

20. Grillparzer's signature: not possessing his own self.

21. The quiet happiness of self-possession.

22. One thing only is happiness on earth, one thing: the tranquillity of inner peace and the breast freed from guilt! And greatness is perilous, and renown a hollow game; all that it gives is worthless shadows, what it takes away is so much!

23. Formal drive . . . material drive.

24. ghost play . . . ghost novel.

25. There is something in human nature, which, independent of its owner's will, attracts and repels with blind force. As from lightning to metal, from magnet to iron, a mysterious pull travels from person to person, from

breast to breast. It is not charm, not gracefulness, not virtue, not justice, which ties and unties the magic threads. The magic bridge of the affections is invisible: of all who have trod it, none has seen it. What you like you *have to* like . . . .

26. He alone is there, he alone in the wide world, and all else nothing but raw material for deeds.

27. The measure of all things was lost; each man measured all he saw only against himself.

28. Remembrance of the past lies like lead on my anxious soul; I can raise neither eye nor heart.

29. I am not he I used to be . . . I am but Jason's shadow, not himself.

30. I your torment, you mine.

31. I do not grieve that the children are no more, I grieve that they *were* and that *we* are.

32. Unprovable, because itself the proof.

33. Reverence not founded on proof.

34. Didactic play.

35. The clamour of noisy labour hushed, he will hear anew the voices of his breast: love, most gracious love, which does not love insufficiency because it is itself insufficiency; the awareness of one's own impotence amidst the surge of power; inspiration, already guaranteed through itself, true because the fact that I feel is true. Then will come the time which is now passing, the time once more of seers and gifted men. Knowledge and utility will divide and take unto themselves feeling as their middle partner. And though the heavens are then locked, the earth will rise aloft to take their place, the gods will live again within the heart and humility will be the name of their supreme and unifying master.

36. . . . the awareness that in action, whether thus or thus, lies the fuel which will blast this mind thundering towards heaven.

37. . . . in stars . . . in stones, in plant, animal and tree; not in man. And he who could understand how to be quiet like them, docile and devout, mastering his own will, an ear stretched wide and filled with humility—he might perhaps learn a word of the truth which proceeds through the universe from God's lips.

38. Till everything is equal, ah yes, because everything is low.

39. Life-shy (literally)

40. Look at the world, plain for all to see, how mountain and valley, river and meadow stand. The heights, though bare themselves, attract the clouds and send them as rain into the valley; the wood wards off the predatory, savage storm; the spring does not bear fruit, and yet it nourishes fruits; and out of the interplay of high and low, of fruit and shelter, is generated this whole, grounded and legitimized by the fact that it is. Do not summon to judgment the sacred bonds which—unconscious and given at birth, unprovable because themselves the proof—fasten what the hair-splitting subtlety of reason tears asunder. You honour your father—but he is harsh; you love your mother, who is limited and weak; your brother is the closest to you of all men, however removed in words and deed; and when your heart draws you to a woman, you do not ask whether she is

best amongst her sex, you are charmed by the blemish on her neck, a flaw in her speech sounds like music, and that I-know-not-what which delights you is an I-know-not-what for everyone else. You love, you hope, have faith. And is not faith simply the feeling of unity with yourself, the proof that you are human on both sides: weak when single and strong as part of the whole. That your fathers believed what you yourself believe, and that your children will tread the same paths—that is the bridge, made of human hearts, spanning the unexplored abyss of which no lead has yet plumbed the depths. Oh do not test the props, do not improve! Your human hands destroy the invisible supports, and one day your grandchildren will laugh at the ruins in which your wisdom lies rotting. . . . Doubt breeds doubt in itself, and once reverence is split in itself, it lives on only as ambition and as fear. Do not presume to subject God's truth to the analytical niceties of reason.

BIBLIOGRAPHY

A complete historical critical edition of Grillparzer's works, diaries and diaries and letters has been supervised by A. Sauer and R. Backmann (Vienna, 1909–48). Its introductions and critical apparatus are invaluable and its text may be regarded as definitive except where superseded by R. Backmann's select edition in five volumes (Vaduz 1947 and Vienna 1952). Grillparzer's *Gespräche* have been edited by A. Sauer in six volumes of the *Schriften des literarischen Vereins in Wien* and Vol. I (new series) of the *Jahrbuch der Grillparzer-Gesellschaft* (Vienna 1941).

Translations into English have been attempted by Arthur Burkhard (The Register Press, Yarmouthport, Mass.), including: *Sappho* (1953), *The Golden Fleece* (1942), *A Faithful Servant of his Master* (1941), *The Jewess of Toledo* (1953), *Family Strife in Hapsburg* (1940).

J. Nadler, *Franz Grillparzer*, (Vaduz, 1948, and Vienna, 1951) is the fullest and most up-to-date biography. A. Ehrhard and M. Necker, *Franz Grillparzer* (Munich, 1910, 2nd ed.) is a very worthwhile older monograph. Pre-war studies of note include Ilse Münch, *Die Tragik in Drama und Persönlichkeit Grillparzers* (Berlin, 1931) and J. Müller, *Grillparzers Menschenauffassung* (Weimar, 1934). Full-length treatments in English include: D. Yates, *Franz Grillparzer, a critical biography* (Blackwell, 1946), F. E. Coenen, *Grillparzer's Portraiture of Men* (University of North Carolina, 1951), G. Stein, *The Inspiration Motif in the Work of Franz Grillparzer* (Martinus Nijhoff, The Hague, 1955).

Two important recent studies emphasize the need for a revised perspective: G. Baumann, *Franz Grillparzer. Sein Werk und das österreichische Wesen* (Freiburg/Vienna, 1954) and W. Naumann, *Grillparzer. Das dichterische Werk* (Stuttgart, 1956). H. Gmür, *Dramatische und theatralische Stilelemente in Grillparzers Dramen* (Winthertur, 1956) analyses the all-important relation of verbal and non-verbal aspects, and U. Helmensdorfer, *Grillparzers Bühnenkunst* (Berne, 1960) contains interesting essays of interpretative, aesthetic and stylistic interest.

Amongst recent bibliographies E. Hock, "Zur Grillparzer-Forschung" (*Germanisch-Romanische Monatschrift*, Vol. IV, new series, 1954) provides an invaluable survey of recent research, most of which has appeared in the form of articles devoted to single plays. Alongside R. Stiefel's full-length study, *Grillparzers Goldenes Vliess* (Berne, 1959), important shorter interpretations include E. Staiger on *Ottokar* (*Trivium*, Vol. IV, 1946, and reprinted in *Meisterwerke deutscher Sprache aus dem 19. Jahrhundert*, Zürich, 1948), M. E. Atkinson on *Des Meeres und der Liebe Wellen* (*German Life and Letters*, Vol. IV, 1951) and the three contributions to B. von Wiese's *Das deutsche Drama* (Vol. I, Düsseldorf, 1958) on *Ottokar* (W. Neumann), *Bruderzwist* (G. Baumann) and *Libussa* (E. Hock). B. von Wiese himself gives a masterly analysis of *Der arme Spielmann* in *Die Deutsche Novelle* (Düsseldorf, 1956).

Many articles of interest appear in the *Jahrbuch der Grillparzer-Gesellschaft*, now resumed in a "Dritte Folge."

Friedrich Hebbel

Friedrich Hebbel

by MARY GARLAND

HEBBEL started his diary on 23 March 1835 with these words:
"Reflexionen über Welt, Leben und Bücher, hauptsächlich aber über mich selbst, nach Art eines Tagebuchs . . .

Ich fange dieses Heft nicht allein meinem künftigen Biographen zu Gefallen an, obwohl ich bei meinen Aussichten auf die Unsterblichkeit gewiss sein kann, dass ich einen erhalten werde. Es soll ein Notenbuch meines Herzens sein . . ."[1]

This high-spirited statement of the young man of twenty-two—Hebbel was born on 18 March 1813—with its touch of arrogance and hint of intimacy has not lost its strangely moving appeal some hundred years after his death on 13 December 1863. Yet self-confidence and belief in latent powers was the only source of strength from which Hebbel could draw in a life devoted to independent literary pursuits and poetic creation, in years of deprivation and hours of tortuous doubts. For Hebbel knew neither the security of a stable family background, a formal education, nor even, in years of manhood, a settled occupation.

A mason's son, Hebbel was born in the little town of Wesselburen in Dithmarschen. His brief autobiographical sketch *Aus meiner Kindheit* (begun in 1842) gives us—though with poetic illumination —his own impressions of his early childhood. It is hard in an age of social reform to realize the material want which the family endured. More bitter still were the humiliations that accompanied poverty. Hebbel's wounded pride and his suffering soul is echoed throughout his work in varied form and became the driving force in the formation of his character and ideas.

In the circumstances his education began favourably in a dame school, though he was never allowed to forget that he was a poor man's son. The stories of the Old Testament were readily absorbed by his imagination and took their place beside the many fairy-tales in which his mind moved already as in a second world. Yet this world of the child's vivid imagination was not so much populated with good fairies as with phantoms that tortured his soul by night. With the unusually rapid development of his senses the mysterious aspects of life that were, in embryo, the problems to which he was to dedicate his life, began to oppress his mind.

His education was continued by the new village schoolmaster Dethlefsen, through whose kindness he made his first acquaintance with poetry. Dethlefsen's library was small and Hebbel had soon absorbed it, but the foundation was laid, his mind had taken its bent. Despite the teacher's opposition Hebbel's father decided in 1825 that it was time his son helped to support the family. For a time Hebbel went to work with his father, desperately unhappy and unsuited to the job, until in an hour of passionate revolt he broke with both, his father and manual labour. When the father died in 1827 his mother sent him as an odd job boy to the parish bailiff to be trained as "Kirchspielschreiber." His status was merely menial and he longed in vain for outward recognition. But the library of the Kirchspielvogt Mohr exercised a decisive influence upon him. His creative powers began to find expression, the poet in him matured. If his talent were not to be permanently crippled he had to get away from Wesselburen. A letter to Uhland and the Danish playwright Oehlenschläger brought no practical help, but at last, in 1835, the editor of the *Pariser Modeblätter* in Hamburg, Amalie Schoppe, made arrangements for him to come to Hamburg, where he was to resume his education and qualify for university entrance.

It is hard to imagine the man, who is reflected in the aphorisms of his diary of this year as a grammar school boy, which he, to all intents and purposes, now was. He had been his own teacher during adolescence and he soon realized that he had come to Hamburg too late to make up for wasted school years in Wesselburen. He dropped his plan to matriculate, but not the plan to study at a university. His sense of dedication, which is implied in the opening of his diary and expresses itself repeatedly there as well as in some of his letters and poems, must have been all the stronger for the want of a regular education. It helps to explain why his childhood and early development foreshadows so clearly his development as man and artist. He had grown to tackle alone the queries of his searching and often perturbed spirit. Even his contact with the "wider world" did not remove this sense of isolation and self-reliance. In the years, when the influence of a teacher might have been strongest, he had to do without one. Yet his sense of independence had fostered his pride. He intuitively felt that he had to mould himself.

There followed ten years of rapid progress, which were simultaneously the hardest years of material want and deprivation, as well as inner conflict. Largely owing to the help of Elise Lensing, who, through the warmth of her personality and devotion, brought light into his uneasy stay in Hamburg, Hebbel was able to go to Heidelberg University in 1836, from where he moved six months later to Munich. He later referred to this period as the time during which his personality was made. Some of his finest lyrical poems stem from his time in Heidelberg and Munich. In Heidelberg, too, Hebbel had struck up a deep friendship with a fellow student, Rousseau. When he died in October 1838 Hebbel lost the only man who had ever been really close to his heart. A few weeks before, he had received news of the death of his mother. His diary, recording his gratitude and recalling her hard life, includes the following words, which give us a moving glimpse of his childhood and at the same time disclose some features in his character, which could torment a friend, no less than himself.

"Sie war eine gute Frau, deren Gutes und minder Gutes mir in meine eigne Natur versponnen scheint: mit ihr habe ich meinen Jähzorn, mein Aufbrausen gemein, und nicht weniger die Fähigkeit, schnell und ohne weiteres alles, es sei gross oder klein, wieder zu vergeben und zu vergessen. Obwohl sie mich niemals verstanden hat und bei ihrer Geistes und Erfahrungsstufe verstehen konnte, so muss sie doch immer eine Ahnung meines innersten Wesens gehabt haben, denn sie war es, die mich fort und fort gegen die Anfeindungen meines Vaters ... mit Eifer in Schutz nahm und lieber über sich selbst etwas Hartes, woran es im eigentlichsten Sinne des Worts nicht fehlte ergehen liess, als dass sie mich preisgegeben hätte. Ihr allein verdanke ich's, dass ich nicht, wovon mein Vater jeden Winter, wie von einem Lieblingsplan sprach, den Bauernjungen spielen musste, was mich vielleicht bei meiner Reizbarkeit schon in den zartesten Jahren bis auf den Grund zerstört haben würde; ihr allein, dass ich regelmässig die Schule besuchen und mich in reinlichen, wenn auch geflickten Kleidern öffentlich sehen lassen konnte." [2]

These two tragic losses threw Hebbel into a fit of depression and hypochondria. The mental strain told on him all the more, because lack of food had begun to undermine his health. In March 1839 he left the scene of his sorrows and set out on foot for the long journey back to Hamburg, where Elise was awaiting him. During his recovery from an illness, that brought him to the brink of death, he wrote his first tragedy: *Judith*, which he completed in January 1840. By 1841 he had finished *Genoveva* and his first comedy *Der*

Diamant. In 1842 he went to Copenhagen and was granted by the Danish King six hundred thalers a year for two years which he used for travels in France and Italy. In 1842 the first collection of his poems appeared. 1843 found him in Paris, where he wrote his domestic tragedy *Maria Magdalene.* From here he passed to Rome and Naples.

As his funds were running out and his grant was not renewed except for a final sum of two hundred thalers, he reluctantly left Italy in 1844. His natural goal would have been in Hamburg, where Elise Lensing still lived. Yet he set out amid grave inner conflicts. Elise had been his friend and benefactor for the past ten years. She had sacrificed her savings to him and she was the mother of his children, the first born son having died while Hebbel was in Paris. However, by now his attachment towards her had relaxed, and, rent with poverty as they both were, he felt he could not sacrifice his independence in gratitude towards her and legalize the union. He interrupted his return journey in Vienna, where he was introduced to an actress, Christine Enghausen. A profound mutual understanding and affection arose, which led to their marriage in 1846. However uneven the path towards a settled life had been, the period of productivity that soon commenced, was undoubtedly only made possible by the fact that he had at last found his peace of mind and an existence of comparative security. In 1847 he finished *Ein Trauerspiel in Sizilien* and *Julia,* which had been conceived in Italy. But his three tragedies *Herodes und Mariamne, Agnes Bernauer* and *Gyges und sein Ring,* completed in the years of 1848, 1851 and 1854 respectively, are marked by an increasingly balanced picture of his art and outlook. In 1849 he dramatized an early narration, *Der Rubin,* "Ein Märchenlustspiel," his second and final attempt at comedy. 1860 saw the completion of his most grandiose project: the *Nibelungen* trilogy. Intermittently he worked on a new subject, a tragedy on *Demetrius.* He completed four acts before he died in his fifty-first year.

He had enjoyed a circle of friends and followers. He had gained recognition, of which that of the Weimar Court and Theatre must have been the most gratifying. In Vienna, however, Heinrich Laube had closed the Burgtheater to his plays. Hebbel's remark in his diary after the completion of *Gyges und sein Ring* in 1854: "das erste Stück, das ich in den Kasten lege" [3] reflects upon this unhappy relationship, under which he and his actress wife suffered alike.

Although Hebbel considered drama to be "die Spitze der Kunst" [4] he achieved a mastery in the lyric, which he cultivated successfully throughout his life. He could capture the fleeting

moment and imbue it with a universal significance without depart-
ing from its essential fragility. Much of the poetry is frankly reflective. In it he expresses the attitudes which animate his plays,
but with a serene harmony, which the plays by their nature could
not achieve. The note of suffering, when it occurs, is all the more
poignant and even heart-rending. His range of form is wide,
but he is at his best in compact poems and in the taut intricacy
of the sonnet. Their delicacy and richness can form a striking
contrast to the robust vigour and gaunt sparseness of his dramatic
verse.

Hebbel's plays, as he repeatedly emphasizes, are expressions of
a philosophical attitude, attempts to interpret the particular and
individual in terms of the universal and eternal; but they are at the
same time alert and penetrating studies of character, which plumb
depths which few other playwrights have attempted. This matching
of philosophical and psychological elements is the unique feature of
Hebbel's drama.

On the 8th of October 1839 Hebbel made in his diary the entry:
"Gestern fing ich meine Tragödie 'Judith' an und schrieb ein paar
Scenen, die mir gefielen. Heute schrieb ich fort, und es glückte
wieder." [5] Fear, lest his creative vein might cease to flow, caused
him to add: "Von meiner Poesie hängt mein Ich ab; ist jene ein
Irrtum, so bin ich selbst einer!" [6] The biblical story of Judith
had for some time been in his mind as a suitable subject for his first
tragedy. It reveals at once a striking assimilation of ideas. The story
itself interested Hebbel largely because of the action of a woman
killing a man. He disbelieved the statement, that Judith was supposed to have danced and feasted for three months after the murder,
and allowed herself to be celebrated as a national hero. He was
convinced that so serious a violation of the laws of nature could
only have tragic repercussions upon the supposed heroine.
It is characteristic that Hebbel should have endowed this incident
of the story with universal significance. The relationship of the
sexes pre-occupied him as one of the fundamental problems of life.
An instinctive grasp of the limits of human nature was particularly
strongly developed in him, and in this way he presented in his first
tragedy what he considered to be the central problem of human
existence in the more complex form of the mental physiognomy
of the sexes, as well as that of the individual. Hebbel's tragic
characters are always made to grapple with the order of the universe,
God, fate. His Judith is not allowed to enjoy her triumph as a
national hero. He even went so far as to dispute the possibility that
a woman can kill for the sake of an idea. Judith sets out believing
that, after three days of fasting and praying, she has become the tool

chosen by her God to liberate Jerusalem. Yet to enable her to strike
the fatal blow she needs an access of strength that no pious delibera-
tion or dedication to the cause of her people can give her. The root
of her own individuality, which lies in her unconscious sensual
being, needs to be stirred to make her capable of the murder. Her
deed was a miscalculation. Nevertheless—and this is the tragic
irony of her situation—it was not a misinterpretation of the divine
will. The heathens were doomed and she was destined to seal their
doom. Yet God abandoned her soul and gave free play to the frustrated elemental sensual forces within her. Her conflicting emotions
turn into furious hatred when Holofernes mocks at her most sacred
feelings—but only because she expects respect from the man who
had first awakened her individuality. Had he not done so she might
have failed in her mission to kill him. But now no reasoning or
religious contemplation can blot out in her heart the instinctive
knowledge that she had violated her own fundamental nature.
Hebbel links the question whether she has conceived, with the
judgment of God, since her feeling of guilt lies outside human
jurisdiction. Despite the final question mark, however, Judith's
fate is truly tragic, the shattering of a personality.

The combination of Judith's spiritual and sensual nature is in
its basic conception as revealing a testimony of Hebbel's effort to
penetrate the mysteries of a woman's nature as Penthesilea is of
Kleist's. But unlike Hebbel, Kleist had resolved the tensions in his
character through her belief in the immortality of the soul. With
Hebbel there is no such catharsis. He had a strong conviction of the
cruel indifference of the divine towards the individual. His conception of tragic necessity was, especially in his first plays, incompatible with that of the German classicists. In contrast to them the
life of the individual, he felt, was subordinated to the balance of the
universe. Despite his consciousness of his own powerful individuality
a profound sense of humility pervaded his awareness of the universe.
This had been deepened through his contact with current philosophical thought (notably Schelling). But as a man of the north German coast, alert to the threat of elemental forces beyond the shelter-
ing dyke, Hebbel was attuned to the thought of unseen metaphysical powers. This underlies the tragic character of Judith,
showing how a human being can, even under divine auspices,
be led to self-destruction. The individual here counts for nothing in
the working of the universe. Equally illuminating is the ignominious
death of the superman Holofernes at the hand of a woman. The
myth of Napoleon is reflected in varied form throughout nineteenth-
century historical drama. Behind the remote historical background
of Holofernes, threatening Bethulia, and beyond Hebbel's own

conception of the excessively masculine hero, his reflections on
Napoleon become apparent, when he sees Holofernes' tragic guilt
in the general's adulation of his own individuality. He despises men
of inferior power and yet cannot bear to share this world with one
whom he can respect. "Schade, dass ich alles, was ich achte,
vernichten muss." [7] In displaying, as an individual, an excess of
power over mankind, he upsets the balance of the universe. With
this subordination of the individual to the idea of the universe
Hebbel links his idea on progress. Neither a philosopher, nor a
historian, he nevertheless felt strongly drawn towards metaphysical
speculation and the study of the evolution of mankind. His conception of historical drama reached far beyond the national sphere.
He expressed impatient disapproval of romantic attempts to recon-
struct a glorified mediaeval past, against "dieses Inspiritussetzen" [8]
of bygone ages. In an age of nationalism he kept apart from day-to-
day problems, until the revolution of 1848 awakened in him a deep
sense of solidarity with the idea of a German unity which must
include Austria. Schiller's *Wallenstein*, too, he refused to see as the
answer to historical drama. Instead he renewed the link with
Lessing's conception (*Hamburgische Dramaturgie*, 24. Stück), adding
"dass das Drama dessenungeachtet den höchsten Gehalt der
Geschichte in sich aufnehmen kann und soll." [9]

From his childhood Hebbel had felt at home in the religious
past, long before the political past had been added to his knowledge.
This explains in part his predilection for religious subjects. This
background had been the first stimulus to try to bring order into the
working of the universe. However pessimistic his conception of the
fate of the individual was, he believed in a balanced universe.
Through his conviction, that the evolution of mankind was balanced
by a divine power he sought to overcome inherent nihilistic tendencies. His conception of *Geschichtsphilosophie*, which Hegel had
already expressed in his system of triads, although Hebbel arrived
at it independently, appears already in *Judith*, where it serves as a
kind of catharsis. The power of Heathendom is broken at a critical
hour, when the progressive force of Christianity was threatened
with obliteration. Through Holofernes' death the progressive forces
of regenerated humanity are liberated and the jubilation of the
people of Bethulia justified. Holofernes' mockery against the
invisible God had found its powerful answer from above.

These two fundamental ideas, which Hebbel took as the basis of his
tragedy, the personal tragedy of Judith and his metaphysical
conception, were already formulated in his mind some months
before he began to write the work, stimulated by his reflections on
Schiller's "romantic tragedy":

"Die Gottheit selbst, wenn sie zur Erreichung grosser Zwecke auf ein Individuum unmittelbar einwirkt und sich dadurch einen willkürlichen Eingriff . . . ins Weltgetriebe erlaubt, kann ihr Werkzeug vor der Zermalmung durch dasselbe Rad, das es einen Augenblick aufhielt oder anders lenkte, nicht schützen. Dies ist wohl das vornehmste tragische Motiv, das in der Geschichte der Jungfrau von Orleans liegt. Eine Tragödie, welche diese Idee abspiegelte, würde einen grossen Eindruck hervorbringen durch den Blick in die ewige Ordnung der Natur, die die Gottheit selbst nicht stören darf, ohne es büssen zu müssen." [10]

This same conception of deity underlies also *Genoveva* and is summarized in the voice of the spirit of Drago. However, in this play Hebbel adds to his metaphysical pattern a novel conception of tragic guilt as something which need not arise from ethical guilt: beauty in its purest form as virtue, may bring tragic guilt upon an individual. This Hebbel was to portray, however, more convincingly in Agnes Bernauer, with whom it is coupled with beauty of outward form. Despite her suffering Genoveva never becomes a tragic heroine, for her martyrdom leads towards salvation.

Hebbel's real fascination with the subject lay in the tragedy of Golo. With him he did not portray an ideal, but human nature as it revealed itself out of the depth of his own inner experience. Genoveva and Margaretha are symbols of Good and Evil wrestling for his soul. None of Hebbel's characters reaches such heights and depths of passion as Golo. The stages, by which, in his attempted destruction of Genoveva, he is led towards self-destruction, form a striking study in mental pathology, which Hebbel saw as an essential aspect of tragedy. His Golo, in contrast to the earlier conceptions of Maler Müller and Tieck, is basically noble and his tragedy is "so erschütternd und tragisch im höchsten Sinne, weil sein edelstes Gefühl durch böse Fügung missgeboren in die Welt tritt." Amid vain attempts to escape his destructive passions his humanity degenerates as he commits ever greater crimes. It is only when he has sent Genoveva to meet her death, that the fury of his frustrated passions recedes and permits him a final awareness of his guilt, though no prayer for salvation:

> "Das Mass des Grausens, statt der Seligkeit
> Hab' ich geleert . . .
>   . . .
> Jetzt steh' ich da, wo das Erbarmen mich
> Nicht mehr erreicht, . . .' [11]

Despite the final catharsis there remains a note of depair in Hebbel's portrayal of Golo. It is a reflection of his own dualistic nature, which finds symbolical expression when Golo deprives himself of sight.

The background to Hebbel's only domestic tragedy is also inspired by personal experience. His *Vorwort zu Maria Magdalene* was designed as a review of his ideas on drama in general, but also to justify his revival of this predominantly eighteenth-century tradition to his own contemporaries. It was written after the completion of the tragedy. However, already in 1839 a brief comment on the social drama of Lenz implies his attitude:

"Dem Lenzschen Schauspiel: *Die Soldaten* fehlt zur Vollendung nichts weiter, als die höhere Bedeutung der verführten Marie. Eine grosse erschütternde Idee liegt dem Stück zum Grunde, aber sie wird durch dies gemeine sinnliche Mädchen zu schlecht repräsentiert. Dies Geschöpf taugt nur zur Hure, was zwar nicht den Offizier rechtfertigt, der sie dazu macht, aber doch das Schicksal, welches es geschehen lässt . . ." [12]

Our sympathy with Marie is no "tragische Rührung." Hebbel misses, "dass, worauf alles ankommt, ihr Geschick in keinem Missverhältnis zu ihrer Natur steht." [13] In Klinger's *Das leidende Weib* on the other hand, both characters appear to him "reiner und göttlicher nach dem Fall . . . wie vor demselben." [14]

Hebbel's choice of title immediately draws attention to the higher significance which he attached to his "fallen woman." Klara sacrifices her life out of the conviction that her death will save the life and honour of her father. Even so the poignancy of her tragic fate is deepened by the torment of her soul on the threshold of death, when she breaks through the barriers of her middle class environment and perceives the sacredness of life in the light of the divine. Not fear of death, but a higher sense of responsibility towards herself and her unborn child permeates her whole being. She becomes aware of her father's profound error in coupling his life with a conception of honour that has no spiritual sanction, and she sees that her duty towards her father conflicts directly with her duty towards God. Yet Anton's force of character convinces her, that her final step is inevitable.

Although filial devotion had inspired her sacrifice Klara leaves this world therefore with no sense of exalted satisfaction as we see it, for instance, in Egmont's Klärchen, but with a helpless feeling of despair at her fate. The conciliatory gesture of Klara's tragedy is only apparent in the title of the play.

Hebbel follows the tradition of realism for this type of drama with a number of vividly portrayed characters. But Meister Anton, as important for the balance of the play as Klara, represents more

than the rigid father. Psychologically he reflects Hebbel's own father
and also Hebbel himself. Only Klara's problem found its stimulus
in Munich. Meister Anton has next to no Bavarian blood in his
veins. He recalls Hebbel's northern origin and among the features
of his character Anton's innate pride and willpower were conspicuous in Hebbel himself. The more tender aspects of his character find little scope in the play. Yet Hebbel illustrates in him one
who has had to put up a fight for existence, against hunger, and
more still against the humiliations that accompany poverty. His
sensitive pride as an ethical being has developed in him a strong
sense of honour which is the backbone of his existence. He econom-
izes with the display of his emotions, but has come to be quick to
suspicion and on the defensive against a potentially aggressive
world.

The social aspect of the play is traditionally an important feature
of the realistic prose drama. As its chief representative Meister
Anton becomes, however, the symbol of an age. In contrast to
his forerunners, Hebbel finds the social conflict, not in the clash
between two social classes, but within the narrow world he portrays,
an attitude which he asserted unambiguously in the preface. Yet
through its lack of political background this world appears to be
static and is an expression rather of the plight of Hebbel's personal
existence than of his preoccupation with historic development, to
which he was to return in *Herodes und Mariamne*. All the same he
brings into the final stage of the play a sense of motion. Meister
Anton's final words of dazed bewilderment are carefully calculated
to indicate the representative character of his individuality. His
bitter experience does not end with his disappointment over his
daughter, which obliterates his humanity at the news of her death,
but with a deep sense of frustration over the world that has shaped
him and yet has to account for his human failure. The final stress
on "die Welt" begins to shift the static background, the pretence
of stability collapses in face of this admission of decline. Yet in the
light of Klara's spiritual emancipation some hope is set up on the
ruins of this world, pointing beyond its decline. The personal
experience of Hebbel's characters remains a tragedy of despair, but
even though this was a reflection of his heart, he has sought to find
a balance on a higher level in conformity with his requirement for
the whole genre of "domestic tragedy."

Hebbel's development as a dramatist found a great climax in
Herodes und Mariamne. The precision of its unique structure finely
balances a combination of the historical and the psychological
drama. The historical background offered everything essential for
his idea: a world fermenting with friction on the eve of the birth of

Christ. Like Holofernes, whose direct literary successor he is, Herodes has to hold his own as the tide is about to turn against him. His precarious position far above the people of Judea and yet below Antonius and Octavianus respectively, brings out the neurotic nature of Hebbel's dictator and is not only a great advance on the cruder conception of Holofernes, but one of the most striking studies of the political usurper in German drama. Herodes has sought power not for an ideal, but to satisfy the propelling urge of his nature. Yet in the height of his power he lives in fear and loneliness, which the world feels in the ruthless assertion of his authority. This forms the framework of the tragedy.

The murder of Aristobolus darkens Herodes from the outset of the drama. It is symbolical for his disregard of human life, the decline of his humanity under the stress of his feeling of insecurity and threatened loss of power. The end of the drama sees this deterioration in its final stage. As Aristobolus was murdered before the play opens, so the impending mass slaughter of the innocents closes the tragedy.

Aristobolus introduces into the play its most classical feature, for he silently assumes the role of fate and becomes the symbol of an ancient idea, without impairing the psychological tragedy of character. The fact that we know little of him only heightens his significance as a symbol. It is of equal importance both historically and psychologically. In fact it holds the two aspects together. Aristobolus is a constant reminder of Herodes' ethical guilt, he has become the driving force behind Alexandra's passionate antagonism and he is a symbol of love for Mariamne, He stands between Herodes and Mariamne and is the initial cause of the tragedy of mistrust. Different emotions become attached to his name, both hatred and love, and both combine to render the action inevitable. Mariamne's last words to Herodes in the hour of her death are followed by "Du, Aristobolus, sei mir gegrüsst!" [15] a serene gesture confessing to the bonds of her love with a simplicity and purity which she could only experience in the face of death. The triumphant exclamation of Alexandra:

"... Ha, Aristobolus!
Du bist gerächt, mein Sohn, und ich in dir!" [16]

on the other hand, sneers at the fallen king and tyrant as the ideological victory is proclaimed by the approach of the three kings. The quick succession of personal tragedy and political doom makes Herodes almost a tragic character, an impression which is heightened by Hebbel's skilful use of tragic irony following Alexandra's words. The humiliating scorn of his greatest antagonist provokes a fierce determination to fight for his survival as king. Here, as indeed in other aspects, he stands close to King Philip in Schiller's *Don Carlos*, who at the moment of tragedy strikes the same note with his obstinate:

> " . . . Die Welt
> Ist noch auf einen Abend mein." [17]

In spite of the prominent choice of the last King of Judea as the main character and the importance of the play as a historical drama, the problem of love is of far greater significance to the characters than the political element, all the more so, since Mariamne is seen— primarily—as the representative of her sex. She is the focal point of the tragedy.

Male possessiveness characterizes Hebbel's most passionate characters from Golo to Kandaules. It is the root of Mariamne's personal tragedy as the wife of Herodes. The harsh assertion of her outraged personality cools the temper of compassion. It is, however, an essential part in the design of the dual tragedy, that Mariamne should not kill herself at the moment of realization: "War denn je ein Mensch so arm!" [18] To have done so would have been a mere act of individual despair. It would have destroyed the universal symbolical character of this conflict between the sexes. Herodes is not to be spared the bitter lesson, that only by taking her life could she restore her true image in his heart.

The repetitive construction has been much criticized; Hebbel himself defended it resolutely. It undoubtedly underlines his austerity of purpose in portraying this marriage that encounters a tragic conflict in spite of the basic constancy of mutual love. The dialogue between Herodes and Mariamne, in which their hearts search for one another and yet every word spoken fails to build a bridge, indeed only deepens distrust and misunderstanding, is in its tragic irony a masterpiece of dramatic art.

Hebbel's step from a remote historical past to the immediate problems of his own day was hastened by the 1848 revolutions. His "Deutsches Trauerspiel," *Agnes Bernauer*, is a political confession. *Maria Magdalene* mirrors a society in decay. In *Agnes Bernauer* it is the state which is threatened with decline. Both plays reflect, in different ways, the age in which Hebbel lived. The experience of revolution had taught him the value of tradition and stability. Liberal reforms, however hopeful they appeared at first, Hebbel came to regard suspiciously as playing with fire. His various comments on the political unrest reveal how strongly he began to appreciate the traditional institutions of government, that it had taken countless generations to build. To lend his views the force of conviction he rightly chose a historical background that was still firmly anchored in this tradition and inspired confidence in the future. However, some time prior to his political incitement his preoccupation with Agnes Bernauer's fate at the hands of the Bavarians had resulted in a dramatic plan that was to illustrate his theory, that tragic guilt is not identified with ethical guilt, but with tragic necessity. His new tragedy was to suffer under the dual purpose it served. Agnes fails, in Hebbel's view, not despite of, but because of extreme beauty and virtue, victim of a cruel fate, the meaning of which is to her still more obscure than it is to Klara. Agnes's death for the idea of the state remains a disquieting feature of the play, despite the great pains Hebbel took to make her doom appear inevitable. It is difficult to accept Herzog Ernst as the executor of the divine will. His dynastic interests lead to an act of political realism and are as such diagonally opposed to the idea of evolution, of which Hebbel in his portrayal of Ernst and Preising is not entirely unaware. In spirit much of the relationship between Kleist's Great Elector and Homburg, for whom Hebbel had profound appreciation (critical essay, 1850) is reflected in the Duke and his son. Yet Hebbel's play with its ethical values set on tradition stands worthily beside the Prussian's acknowledgement of the sacredness of "das Gesetz." Both writers pay homage to a historic reality that faced its greatest challenge in nineteenth-century Germany.

Agnes Bernauer is Hebbel's only contribution to national historical drama. With its masterly dialogue it is at the same time his final contribution to the realistic prose drama. His increasingly balanced personality found, without losing any of its individuality, its most congenial expression in the classical form. His previous plays have already given a strong hint in this direction. In *Gyges und sein Ring* he achieved his aim. None of the basic problems that tortured the youth are dismissed, but the urge to overcome doubt and despair by serene acceptance characterizes the maturity of the artist. Fourteen years earlier the author of *Judith* has wrestled with the difference of his type of drama compared with others, thus touching upon the difference between Greek tragedy and modern tragedy:

"Ihr Unterscheidendes liegt wohl darin, dass ich die Lösung, die andere Dramatiker nur nicht zustande bringen, gar nicht versuche, sondern, die Individuen als nichtig überspringend, die Fragen immer unmittelbar an die Gottheit anknüpfe." [19]

And adding: "Was besser ist, das eine, oder das andere, weiss ich nicht." *Gyges und sein Ring* is the first of his tragedies, in which

none of the characters suffers the frustration over an inexplicable
fate, an inscrutable divinity. Kandaules' violation of Rhodope's
humanity, symbolized by the Ring, corresponds to the violation of a
universal law, in the same way, as Rhodope's insistence upon
Kandaules' atonement expresses the divine will. Unlike Herodes,
Kandaules is given strength and maturity to see in Rhodope's
verdict not an act of personal vengeance, but a revelation of the
divine, which he fully recognizes in meeting his death. This co-
ordination between a disinterested universal power and the recognition and submission of the individual is further emphasized by
Rhodope's suicide, which removes any trace of personal inclination,
that might have made her appear happy at the side of Gyges, and
reunites her with the sublime spirit of Kandaules, sealing her
immutable dedication to the idea.

The passage from Holofernes to Kandaules, from Judith to
Rhodope, is a long one. Yet through the restless endeavour of his
complex individuality to shape and realize an art aspiring to
permanence in form, as well as to an interpretation of man's
universal problems, Hebbel's spirit of dedication never falters.
He impresses as a man, who clearly creates out of conviction. The
noble trio in *Gyges und sein Ring* show a swing towards the "sentimental" poet in Schiller's sense, and yet are truly a product of
Hebbel's individuality.

In Rhodope, too, reappears his theory, that beauty can be the
cause of tragic guilt. That he should have succeeded in his portrayal
of Rhodope in blending this idea with the idea of acceptance of fate,
is but one example of how his theories continued, basically unaltered,
to be a challenge to his creative genius in each phase of his development. Similarly, the pathological study, which is more revealing
in the character of Kandaules, than his role as reformer, simplifies
the pattern. The only character before him, that had made a
voluntary renunciation, is Golo. Herodes, though not insensible of a
feeling of guilt, had been too proud to admit it. Kandaules neither
intends evil like Golo, nor does he deliberately violate his wife's
humanity, like Herodes. He is the first of Hebbel's characters,
whose atonement rather than guilt dominates the tragedy, the
first not to be defiant.

In both these plays of his Viennese years it is the woman that
sets the pace in the ethical development of character. Hebbel's
portrayal of the mature women, embodying the standard of ethical
values, the spirit of humanity and the divine—first introduced into
German drama by Goethe's *Iphigenie*—is a marked feature of his last
plays, although his *Nibelungen* trilogy must be excepted because of
the nature of his material and his treatment.

In his dedication to his wife Hebbel recalls the day on which the characters of the mediaeval epic first sprang to life for him:

"Und Hagen Tronje sprach das erste Wort."[20]

Hagen Tronje, the man of action, who bears with stoic tenacity and deterministic resolve his guilt and doom, is a hero eminently suitable for Hebbel's dramatic design and sombre interpretation of tragic necessity. It is he, who compels us to appreciate the ethics of a remote age, its weakness and strength. Without him the pathological study of perverted passion would have been dead matter and Dietrich's message empty words.

An epic is more closely akin to music than to drama, as Wagner, in his own and different way, demonstrates. No one saw more clearly than Hebbel himself at the performance of Raupach's "Nibelungen-Hort," in which his wife played Chriemhild, that, for the dramatist, the epic story needed a new and psychological approach. Yet he retained characteristics of the epic as a support, especially the hint of mysticism, so conspicuous in the figure of Frigga. The panoramic expanse of the trilogy in its Shakespearean, kaleidoscopic breadth was also suggested by the epic, and has *Genoveva* as its only forerunner, moving between the sunless North south to Etzel's court *against* the flow of the Rhine, river of fate and guardian of the fertile land of Burgundy, where deer and wolf, song birds and raven enrich the setting or promote a sense of destiny.

Yet this adornment is strictly subordinated to a careful dramatic framework. The "Vorspiel," *Der gehörnte Siegfried*, forms an exposition of the three distinct worlds as well as the main characters. It brings the action into motion when Gunther resolves to conquer Brunhild. The stage is set for future action and for tragedy. For within the brief compass of the "Vorspiel" manifold guilt is discernible.

Hagen mocks at the Cross. Neither Holofernes nor Herodes had scorned religion with impunity. The same pattern is followed in "Siegfrieds Tod": Kriemhild turns her back on the Cross and remains unmoved by the priest's entreaties. His final admonition

"Gedenke dessen, der am Kreuz vergab" [21]

cannot halt the action, but its symbolic significance points to the final episode of "Kriemhilds Rache," in which Dietrich accepts the crown from Etzel with the words

"Im Namen dessen, der am Kreuz erblich!" [22]

The motive of the Cross runs through all parts of the play, a constant reminder of a historic and spiritual revaluation. Similarly Frigga's defiance of the Cross, which forms the opening words of *Siegfrieds Tod*, is rendered vain by the defeat of Brunhild.

Gunther's guilt emerges clearly from the "Vorspiel"; his bargain with Siegfried over Brunhild and Kriemhild reveals a disregard of the women's individuality, which is so important an aspect of Hebbel's drama, and Gunther, though of lesser stature, pays for it more dearly than any other of Hebbel's tragic heroes.

Siegfried, tempted by the prize of Kriemhild, shares this guilt. If any of Hebbel's male characters was fated to be a tragic hero in every fibre of his being, it is he, who uses Brunhild as the coin (*"der Pfennig"*) with which he seeks to secure Kriemhild's hand. Siegfried misuses the cap of darkness as Gyges does the ring. His account of how he has made his skin invulnerable points, however, in Hebbel's sense, to a deeper tragic significance. In killing the dragon he has shown an excess of strength, and in reaping a supernatural reward he has disturbed the order of the universe. It justifies Hagen's murder:

"Darf denn noch fechten, wer nicht fallen kann?" [23]

It justifies Brunhild's claim on his love; Siegfried himself never realizes the tragic irony of his words in the "Vorspiel":

"Denn Brunhild rührte, wie sie droben stand,
    In aller ihrer Schönheit nicht mein Herz." [24]

He does not conceive that the magic of the dragon's blood and the voice of the birds, who link his name with that of Brunhild, have a significant implication, the full extent of which Brunhild reveals:

"In dir und mir
    Hat Mann und Weib für alle Ewigkeit
    Den letzten Kampf ums Vorrecht ausgekämpft." [25]

However, Siegfried unwittingly uses his strength to prepare the way for the Cross, beside which there is no room for the immortal Goddess of fate—"schicksallos, doch schicksalkundig," [26] which the virgin Brunhild feels herself destined to become.

Thus no character shows more completely than Siegfried Hebbel's conception of tragic guilt, which, though not disregarding ethical guilt, sees necessity ($'A\nu\alpha\gamma\kappa\eta$) as its essence.

As in the epic, Brunhild is lost sight of after the death of Siegfried; her symbolic significance, however, persists. Already in *Siegfrieds Tod* Brunhild's love for Siegfried is emphasized, and nowhere more clearly than in the scene with Frigga. The realization that she was

". . . Ihm selbst zum Weib zu schlecht," [27]

illuminates with striking simplicity her injured love. And while she avenges herself with no less justification than Rhodope, Siegfried's death is the real beginning of her suffering. When she is last mentioned, in the final part, she is described as having taken Kriemhild's place in Siegfried's shrine. It is the symbol of a delusion: the end of the predestined harmony of man and woman.

In Kriemhild lay for Hebbel the real justification of the drama. The chaste maiden, the loving bride, the jealous wife and injured widow is completely divorced from Brunhild's mystic fatalism. However, even apart from the subsequent development of her character, her destiny, too, is basically tragic, since heaven itself speaks with two voices. While Brunhild feels justified in believing that the knight with the sword Balmung is the only man who may have a claim upon her, Kriemhild's inmost feelings recognize in Siegfried the falcon of her dream. This suggests beyond the duality of man and woman a dualism of fate, which is also implied by Siegfried's own position between the two worlds.

Kriemhild's betrayal of Siegfried's trust confirms that his heart has erred and that he had indeed been tragically deaf to the voice of the birds. In this light Kriemhild's betrayal fits into the vast pattern of an inexplicably disharmonious world that dominates the atmosphere of this play.

The breach of trust surprises in one who loves so deeply, though it may hint at hidden passions. Kriemhild's subsequent development shows her between the world of her ancestors and the beginning of Christianity. Only when she has experienced humble remorse without the comfort of forgiveness, when she has claimed justice without receiving it, does she turn away from the faith of her cradle. Ute's assertion that Kriemhild will not desecrate the "Holy Sign" is confounded by Kriemhild's ferocious and barbaric words spoken to Hagen:

> "Ich will zurück in meines Siegfrieds Gruft,
> Doch muss ich mir das Totenhemd erst färben.
> Und das kann nur in deinem Blut geschehn." [28]

The will for vengeance remains the only outlet for her tormented soul. Yet the basic helplessness and dazed wonder, with which she conceives at moments her own merciless destiny in a world of cruelty and suffering—and here there is a parallel to Golo—subtly redeem her character as obsession dispels her humanity. It shows like a glimmer in the ashes as Giselher entreats her to put an end to her work of destruction, since the Burgundians cannot alter their course, to which she replies:

> "Kann denn ich?" [29]

And to Hagen's striking counter-accusation:

"Und büss 'ich nicht?" [30]

words addressed, significantly, to the only two men that still exist in her world.

Hagen's growing stature in the last part, when his sense of inevitable doom replaces the somewhat incongruous cynicism he exhibits in the second part, gives the final tragedy its unique balance. Shrewd enough to have sensed Brunhild's love for Siegfried and the implications of Kriemhild's marriage to Etzel, he is the only character in the play to comprehend the extent of the conflict and to recognize the inevitability of the fate of the Burgundians, as well as Kriemhild's implacable vindictiveness:

"Was heucheln wir, Kriemhild?
Wir kennen uns." [31]

To Giselher he goes so far as to acknowledge:

"Sie hat ja recht, ich tat ihr grimmig weh!" [32]

Only the living world of reality exists for him; with cynical, obstinate pride he calmly takes the sword Balmung from the side of Siegfried's body in the chapel, honouring neither the dead nor the Cross. It is a final expression of his jealousy of Siegfried, but more important still, it is a grave warning to Kriemhild, the opening chord of a relentless resistance, which is subsequently reinforced, when he consigns the treasure, with unconscious allegorical significance, to the depth of the Rhine, for the Gold and the Cross are conflicting forces. So he makes sure, well in advance of the clash of arms, of his final triumph over Kriemhild. As the thought of death dominates his mind it expresses itself in word and action. His murder of Otnit is, for him, no more an isolated act of vengeance, but deliberate defiance, which drives Kriemhild into the situation in which she must bring about the total destruction of all her kin.

Hagen Tronje spoke the first word—"Und Hagen lebt!" [33] . . . to steer the course of the "ship of death," until victor and vanquished lie mingled in one common death and the Cross is erected by Dietrich.

Hagen had been very close to one side of Hebbel. The other Hebbel now resumes the lead, the patient seeker after yet another tragic dénouement. For while the Nibelungen trilogy was giving him, notwithstanding his modest remark that he had only restored an old clock, a profound sense of achievement and brought him more recognition—and fees—than any other of his plays, the seeds of *Demetrius* germinated but slowly. Yet the fragment turns out to be the most revealing personal document of his final development. None of his historical tragedies shows such a complexity of opposing forces. The careful balance of historic development in co-ordination with the cosmic idea, also planned, but not completed in his projected *Moloch*, finds no room in his panoramic picture of political chaos in Eastern Europe. The study of tragic discord among the Slavonic peoples, which had been stimulated by Schiller's fragment, which Hebbel at one time intended to complete, was as extensive as any historical research he ever undertook. Yet despite the realism of the political intrigues around him, Demetrius himself is an entirely idealistic character, who surrenders to his own sense of justice. He is the first ruler in the German historical drama of the nineteenth century to be offered power and to refuse it for the sake of truth. Demetrius is, in tragedy, the answer to an old plan "zu einem höchsten Lustspiel": [34]

> "... einer, der sich für einen Prinzen hält und nun nicht weiss, ob er, der selbst über seine Geburt nicht gewiss ist, Versuche machen soll, den Thron zu erobern, oder nicht. Was er auch tue oder unterlasse: beides ist vielleicht Frevel und Schande, also ein Mensch, der nicht einmal weiss, was für ihn gut oder bös ist. Eine sehr fruchtbare Idee." [35]

This suggests that Hebbel was particularly attracted by the psychological problem rather than by the historical significance of his character. But while the ethical balance of the play rests on his isolated individuality, the world around him is denied the benefit of his ideals and is left disrupted. One is led to suspect that Hebbel's experience of the political development of Germany must in some measure be responsible for the sudden obstruction of his idea of balance. The events in the Paulskirche and the Prussian King's refusal to accept the imperial crown offered to him in the bid for a united Germany, suggests a parallel to the conception of Demetrius. The refusal of a crown out of seemingly unlawful hands must have touched Hebbel's heart, for it resulted in yet another age of particularistic strife. As he elaborated this idea in *Demetrius* he could not attempt a harmony in which he had lost faith. *Agnes Bernauer* had been an appeal; *Demetrius* takes, as an historical drama, the form of resignation, a resignation, however, which has its own historic significance if it is seen as the expression of an age. Instead, the individual becomes the bearer of the highest ethical ideal. Hebbel had already in *Der Rubin* created the idealist, who would be the just ruler the world needed—and received. But this was, significantly, a fairy-tale.

Demetrius is basically Assad's tragic counterpart. The idealistic conception of Hebbel's tragic character is emphasized by the initial guilt, the murder (Assad commits a mock murder), in the "Vorspiel," for which Demetrius readily accepts the verdict of death. The crime, committed as a violent reaction against insult to his humble station and designed as a pointer to his tragic fate, is the first clue to the strong autobiographical element in Demetrius. But although the first acquaintance with his character is a reminder of a young, vulnerable Hebbel, the subsequent revelation of his individuality amounts to a revaluation of man's self-assertion. Both disciple and master, Demetrius responds to the strange call to go in quest of truth and terminates it, when he is certain of his error. No argument other than that of his truthfulness is recognized by him, notwithstanding all the temptations of power. Demetrius's idealism had superseded obstinate pride, resisting a—still—potentially aggressive world.

The portrayal of Marfa is a notable addition to Hebbel's mature woman characters. Her importance for the plot is as decisive as that of Alkmene in Kleist's *Amphitryon*. Hebbel's subtle psychology and dignified restraint shows his mastery in the figure of the mother, who had to decide upon the sole evidence of her instinctive feeling the identity of her long lost son. Like Demetrius, she is a solitary figure, vainly seeking divine revelation. She emerges from the structure of the fragment a symbol of fate, her indecision promoting the tragic irony that underlies Demetrius's bid for the Russian throne.

Of the principles governing the original conception of Hebbel's works, as well as his own criticism of them, there is an abundance of evidence. Yet although Hebbel himself was the keenest observer of his own individuality, he left, through the complexity of his tragic characters, the possibility of widely differing interpretation; there is no one way traffic possible through his work. Like Kleist, Hebbel felt drawn to the unusual and sought truths that lay hidden far beneath the surface of human existence. Unlike the Jungfrau von Orleans Hebbel's Judith is neither virgin nor woman; her fateful walk into Holofernes' camp has a dual purpose, a conscious one and a semi-conscious one. Golo's voluntary death is both atonement and protest against a destructive world. While Genoveva remains the figure of the legend, she is also representative of her sex, foreshadowing, as Siegfried's wife, Mariamne's problem. Herodes is both king and lover. However, whereas the despotic nature of the king is not irrelevant for his attitude towards Mariamne, he does not rule over her as over one of his subjects, but is—as a man—dependent on her. Mariamne's passionate cry

> "Dies Amt
> Ersah er für sich selbst!" [36]

brings her in line with the stoic self-destruction of her Maccabaean ancestors and still remains an assertion of her love, both vengeance and caress. Duke Ernst no less than Agnes is crushed by the God which accepted his sacrifice. Kandaules' injury to Rhodope is explained by the pride of the king and yet has its roots in repressed emotions. Even Rhodope, however serene in her conviction that she acts as a substitute of the divine, remains a woman, reasserting her love, when the harmony of her existence has been broken. Kriemhild's vengeance is more than the insistence on justice; it is an aberration of grief and of remorse. With Marfa the tragic irony is deepened through her spontaneous feelings of affection for the wrong son. Even Demetrius, after his resignation—and acceptance— is denied a glorified death, and, like Mariamne, is forced to escape reality under a mask. The very complexity of Hebbel's portrayal of character serves, however, to illuminate, from different angles, his unflinching belief in the tragic necessity of man's fate. And despite the balanced formal perfection he attained, despite the serene spirit of acceptance evident in his last plays, his early sense of insecurity, far from fading, underlies a dissonance persisting through his work. In his last, unfinished, tragedy it can be heard with undiminished force:

"Der Himmel selbst ruht auf gespaltnen Kräften" [37]

is as true for Hebbel as it is for "Demetrius."

TRANSLATIONS

1. Reflections on the world, life and books, but especially on myself, after the fashion of a diary . . . I begin this notebook not simply for the benefit of my future biographer, though, in view of my prospects of immortality, I can be certain that I shall have one. It is to be a notebook of my heart . . .

2. She was a woman of good heart, whose good and less good qualities seem to be woven into my own nature. With her I have in common my outbursts of sudden anger and rage, as also the capacity quickly and completely to forgive and forget in all things, great and small. She never understood me, indeed the limitations of her intellect and experience made it impossible for her to do so; yet she must have had some inkling of my innermost nature for she it was who over and over again . . . energetically defended me against my father and rather suffered hard treatment (which is meant literally) than left me unprotected. To her alone I owe that I did not have to be a farm boy, a favourite idea of my father's to which he recurred every winter; if this had happened, given my sensitiveness, I should have infallibly have come utterly to grief in my boyhood. To her

I owe alone, too, that I was able to go regularly to school and could show myself in tidy though patched clothing.

3. The first play that I put back into the drawer.

4. The summit of art.

5. Yesterday I began my tragedy *Judith* and wrote a few scenes which satisfied me. Today I went on with it and was again successful.

6. My poetry is my whole self; if it is a failure, then I am one, too.

7. A pity that I must destroy everything I respect.

8. Preserving in spirit.

9. That, nevertheless, the drama can and must embody the highest essence of history.

10. God himself, when He acts directly on an individual in order to achieve some great end and so intervenes arbitrarily in the mechanism of the universe, cannot save His tool from being crushed by the very wheel which it has checked or diverted. This is probably the most noble tragic idea in the story of "Die Jungfrau von Orleans." A tragedy reflecting this idea would be most impressive because of the insight it would afford into the eternal order of nature which God himself cannot disturb without impunity.

11. I have drained the cup of horror, not of happiness,
   . . . .
   Where I now stand no mercy can reach me any more.

12. Lenz's play "Die Soldaten" would be perfect if only Marie, the girl who is seduced, could be given a more exalted significance. It possesses a great and deeply moving idea, which this commonplace sensual girl but ill represents. The creature is only fit to be a whore and though this does not justify the officer who makes her one, it justifies *fate* in letting it happen . . .

13. What really matters, that her fate is commensurate with her nature.

14. Purer and more divine after their fall than they were before it.

15. Aristobolus, I greet you.

16. Aristobolus, my son, you are avenged, and I with you.

17. For one evening yet the world is mine.

18. Was ever man or woman so poor?

19. The essential difference is this: I make no attempt at the solution which has eluded other dramatists; passing over the individuals in their insignificance I link the problems immediately with God.

20. Which of the two is better I cannot say.

21. Hagen Tronje spoke the first word.

22. Remember Him, who forgave upon the Cross.

23. Remember Him, who dies upon the Cross!

24. May he fight who cannot fall?

25. For Brunhild, for all her beauty as she stood up there, could not touch my heart.

26. Man and woman have fought out, in you and me,
   for all eternity the final struggle for supremacy.

27. Immune from fate yet with knowledge of fate.

28. Not good enough for a wife for him.

29. I must return to Siegfried's vault, but first I must dye my shroud and that I can only do in your blood.

30. And can I, then?

31. And do I not suffer in penitence?

32. Why should we make pretence, Kriemhild? we know each other.

33. She is right, I did her terrible injury.

34. And Hagen lives!

35. For a sublime comedy!

36. ... one who believes himself a prince and hesitates, being without certainty of his birth, whether he should take steps to gain the throne or not. Should he act or should he refrain from action in either case he may commit a crime and suffer disgrace. He is a man who, in his own affairs, cannot distinguish good and evil. A very fruitful idea.

37. This office he reserved unto himself.

38. Heaven itself rests on divided forces.

BIBLIOGRAPHY

HEBBEL. F. *Sämtliche Werke. Historisch-kritische Ausgabe.* Ed. R. M. Werner. Berlin, 1901 ff, 24 vols.

HEBBEL. F., *Werke.* Ed. B. v. Wiese. 9 vols. 1941.

HEBBEL, F., *Werke.* Ed. G. Fricke. 2 vols. 1956.

KUH, E. *Biographie Friedrich Hebbels.* 2 vols. 1877.

WALZEL, O. *Hebbel und seine Dramen.* 1913.

PURDIE, E. *Friedrich Hebbel, A study of his life and work.* 1932.

Wiese, B. v. (in) *Die deutsche Tragödie von Lessing bis Hebbel,* vol. 2, 1948. (4th ed. in one volume, 1958.)

Theodor Storm

Theodor Storm

by WILLIAM F. MAINLAND

"DA hörte Gabriel einen Ton, dumpf, als käme er aus der Erde; und der Boden unter ihm schütterte kaum merklich. Da war es wieder und bald noch einmal. Was geschah drüben, daß jetzt zur Nachtzeit die Kanonen gingen?—Regine schien nichts davon gehört zu haben; denn sie hob den Kopf ein wenig und sagte: 'Es schlägt zehn Uhr im Dorf.' "[1]

This text occurs near the end of a little prose idyll which Storm called *Ein grünes Blatt* and published in 1850. From the eight decades which extend round that year the political and social historian records events and movements of such resonance that it seems hardly possible for any man living at that time to have remained unmoved by them. Liberal reform in England, the July Revolution, the continued ravages of industrial development, the Marxist manifesto, the Crimean War, the American Civil War, the war of 1870: in the midst of these things, of which we recognize the vast effects, little lives went on and people were happy or troubled in the ordinary business of living. "Kein Klang der aufgeregten Zeit drang! noch in diese Einsamkeit."[2] So the cottager of Storm's poem *Abseits* spent his days in humble contentment "behaglich blinzelnd nach den Bienen."[3] The odd thing is that Storm himself, who held a post of responsibility in the government of his native town and in the administration of justice, a man who enjoyed lasting fame as one of the the greatest story-tellers and lyric poets of his time in Germany, who even suffered exile as a result of the Danish incursion of 1852 and coined the phrase "kein Klang der aufgeregten Zeit!" seems to have been only distantly, indirectly aware of the events and thoughts which were disturbing and re-shaping the life of Europe. Even when we read his patriotic verses, we perceive the truth of the phrase in which his friend, the literary historian and critic Erich Schmidt characterized Storm as an observer of events in his time: "Ganz und gar kein Politiker."[4] Storm's patriotism was intense, but it was strictly local, and apart from Holstein did not embrace any other parts of Germany. In a solemn leave-taking he wrote: "kein Mensch gedeihet ohne Vaterland" [5]: he was leaving Holstein for Prussia.

An experience which Storm relates from his own childhood helps us to understand this strange sequestration of his mind. One of his favourite and most enterprising playmates was a cobbler's son, who went by the nickname of Hans Räuber. In the autumn evenings, when it got too dark to play, the two boys would take a lantern with candle-ends and creep into a cask which stood in the yard of Theodor's home. There, by the light of their lantern, completely hidden by the staves and the boards which enclosed their little world, they would while away the hours till supper-time telling stories— "Geschichten vertellen." [6] "Diese Tonne war das Allerheiligste, das nur von mir und Hans bezogen wurde . . . ging es doch sachte aufwärts, so ging es doch endlich hübsch über die Alltagswelt hinweg, dass der Schul- und sonstige Erdenstaub lustig aus den flatternden Gewändern flog . . . im Nebel der Tiefe lag es unter uns, während wir die reine Luft der Höhe atmeten . . . noch lange nachher mußte es uns jeder vom Gesichte ablesen können, daß wir in uns einen Glanz trugen, der nicht von dieser Welt war." [7]

When, in 1873, Storm re-published three stories (*Die Regentrude, Der Spiegel des Cyprianus, Bulemanns Haus*) which had first appeared some ten years before, he collected them under the title *Geschichten aus der Tonne*. This motif of the cask recurs in the story *Von Jenseit des Meeres* (1863–4) where a little girl, the daughter of a coloured woman by a rich planter, takes the place of Hans; and she, also huddled in a cask, tells stories to the boy to whose parents she has been for a time entrusted. Years later, when she goes to find her mother, her childhood friend follows her and brings her back as his bride. This involves a long voyage and an encounter with outlandish people and customs. But there is no vivid account of these things from the pen of Storm, who on other occasions describes in detail the setting of his stories. It could be argued that to dwell upon the scenes "jenseit des Meeres" would have disturbed the unity of the narrative. This explanation, though technically adequate, can only be productive if we try to see beyond it. But when we do, we begin to perceive that the unity of Storm's art, and of his life, is the outcome of his own experience of his own region, a very tiny region of "Watten" (the mud-flats and shallows), of "Halligen" (the low-lying miniature islands) and of the little strip of hinterland bordering Husum, the "graue Stadt am Meer." [8] In that town there lives to-day a retired sea-captain, landlord of an hotel, who tells stories of his life in the days of the sailing ships. In Storm's boyhood there must have been many such whose tales might have kindled his imagination; but if they did, there is little evidence of response in his writings.

The model of the full-rigged barque hanging in the choir of the old church in *Hans und Heinz Kirch* (1881–2), symbol of the seafaring life of the community, does not evoke any stories of the sea, any mental pictures of far-away places, as it would have done with Robert Louis Stevenson. Only for a brief moment, when Heinz, as a six-year-old boy, lies out on the bowsprit singing, we catch the tang of the sea air; for the rest Storm is as silent about his hero's wanderings as Heinz himself, who rarely wrote home from his distant voyages. The story is of ambition and thwarted love and bitter hostility between father and son in a little sea-port. True, it is a port on the Baltic, because it was there that Storm picked up the theme of the story. But there is nothing essential which could not have belonged to Storm's own North Sea region. No other setting is allowed to intrude, because no other setting could excite Storm's interest. Not even from the *Nordseebilder* (1825–6) of the inland poet Heine, whom he greatly admired, did Storm catch the sea-fever. He seems to have remained all his life a longshoreman at heart. Even when the adventures of certain of his characters take them to parts of Germany which Storm had visited, there is little specific attempt to describe town or landscape setting. A good example of Storm's venture into unfamiliar landscape is to be found in *Ein Bekenntnis* (1887), written shortly before his death. A visit which he had paid to the Tyrol provided him with material for description of the mountainous region. But the brief passage in which the narrator tells of his walk and of the discovery of his friend in the sanatorium leaves the impression that the strange surroundings, though carefully noted, have not stirred any deep feelings. Occasionally, in order to suggest regional character, Storm introduces a flavouring of local dialect, for which he seems to have had a retentive ear. Lisei, the dainty little dark-haired girl in *Pole Poppenspäler* (1873–4), speaks in a Bavarian dialect; and when Storm had occasion to quote something or other which the poet Mörike had said to him, he adopted a few peculiarities of Mörike's native Swabian speech.

To the English reader at least Storm appears as the provincial, with a constant and absorbing affection for his own region, its natural features, its people, its traditions and its folklore. It was a central fact in his life, accepted without question, that he, as the son of a respected patrician family, belonged to Husum in the province of Schleswig-Holstein. The sense of stability and continuity which the consciousness of family and home gave to him was strengthened in a variety of ways. There was for example a traditional association with certain families of more humble standing which had worked for the Storms for some generations; there was also the almost

habitual longevity of his family; he was able to remember his
maternal great-grandmother.

But such a narrow, fixed and comfortable pattern, however
deeply we may at times regret its absence today, had its disad-
vantages which became apparent in Storm's behaviour and in the
complexity of his emotional life; these we cannot ignore if we hope to
interpret his writings. The frank conceit of the provincial was sometimes disconcerting to his friends elsewhere. In Berlin he boasted
of the cooking in Holstein and claimed that nobody could brew tea
except the people of Husum. Another, more profound, yet equally
typical response of the provincial to cosmopolitan life is to be seen
in Storm's criticism of the cultured society of Berlin, with which he
became familiar partly through his membership of the literary
côterie "Tunnel über der Spree"—which he was invited to join in
1853—and partly through his professional duties as a lawyer during
the early period of his exile from Schleswig-Holstein. In Berlin
it was the sincerity of his own people that he missed. The Berliner,
in his opinion, thinks not in the first place of personality, but of
rank and title, "und dergleichen Nipps, für deren auch nur mittel-
mäßige Würdigung mir, wie wohl den meisten meiner Landsleute
jedes Organ abgeht" [9] (letter to Fontane, Easter Day, 1853).
Forgetting perhaps that in Husum his birth gave him an unearned
title to respect among the "lower orders," he had a deeply rooted
antagonism to hereditary aristocracy. Despite lasting friendships
with Count Reventlow and Landrat v. Wustrow, Storm was
apt to look on the nobility as "Gift in den Adern der Nation" [10]
(Köster, 1, 37) and an embodiment of insolent arrogance. Redemption, to Storm's way of thinking, was open to the rare individual
who, like Anna (Im Schloss, 1861), encounters and grows to appreciate a nobility greater than that of birth: nobility of mind. Yet at
this very time Storm was himself irretrievably caught up in prejudice
and pride: "Es scheint mir im ganzen die goldene Rücksichtslosigkeit zu fehlen, die allein den Menschen innerlich frei macht und die
nach meiner Ansicht das letzte und höchste Resultat jeder Bildung
sein muß" [11] (to Fontane, loc. cit.).

Storm was so obviously proud of the idea, and of the phrase
"goldene Rücksichtslosigkeit," that he used it in his poem Für meine
Söhne (1853); and he was no doubt pleased when his friend the
novelist Heyse quoted it in a sonnet addressed to him: "Wach
schilderst du des Lebens bunte Szenen/Im Panzer goldner Rück-
sichtslosigkeiten." [12] Fontane, urbane, cosmopolitan, found this
provincial cult of tactlessness a little offensive. In Von Zwanzig bis
Dreissig (Berlin, 1898, pp. 367–71) he tells of a morning walk with
Storm in the Tiergarten in Berlin. They had been discussing con-

temporary lyric poetry, and breakfast was suggested. Storm proposed Kranzler's—one of the most fashionable restaurants. Eyeing his companion's unconventional garb, and especially the old and shapeless knitted shawl—a present from his grandmother—which he had draped round his shoulders, Fontane tried to dissuade him. But it was no use: it had to be Kranzler's. Arriving there, Storm engaged in one of those little foibles which many English people regard as typical of most Germans. Two chairs were vacant in a window embrasure, but instead of sitting down, Storm took up his position in the narrow space between window and buffet and continued his monologue on contemporary poetry, the ends of his shawl swaying violently this way and that the more deeply engrossed he became in his theme.

This sort of deafness, which is not of the ear, but of the whole constitution, a lack of perception of the varying effect of one's words and actions on others, is not of course peculiarly provincial, though it is doubtless aggravated by a secluded and restricted upbringing. Storm remained the boy in the cask—that little world, "das Allerheiligste," in which he had felt himself elevated above "die alltägliche Welt."

Storm had little encouragement or incentive at home or at the grammar school in Husum to observe even from books the interaction of varying temperaments and minds. Bürger, Hölty, some Goethe and some Schiller are usually mentioned as his chief reading at that stage. He appears to have known nothing at all about the Romantic poets of Germany: for a time he thought Uhland (1787–1862) was a mediaeval troubadour. At Lübeck, where he was sent to school at the age of seventeen, he was suddenly introduced to literature as an urgent and absorbing experience. There, and at the universities of Kiel and Berlin, where, following his father's example he studied law, he became the *enthusiast*. It is to the starving of his perceptions and then to this sudden enthusiasm that we must look if we are to understand the particular way in which Storm reveals a paradox common among many men of great creative gifts. The poet is sensitive, he must be, as an observer of things and people; but though we have scores of examples, we continue to be disturbed because poets do not always translate this sensitivity into action; they are often blatantly inconsiderate of those very feelings which they interpret with such precision in their poetry.

The "Rücksichtslosigkeit" of Storm was not the prime cause, but it was an intermediary cause of much unhappiness for himself and those near and very dear to him. He came back to Husum, took up practice of the law, and married his cousin Constanze Esmarch. She was a woman of practical understanding and considerable charm; like her husband she enjoyed music, and her contralto voice was much admired on convivial evenings in the Storm household. There can be no doubt that Storm loved her greatly. But it seems that Biese takes an unnecessary risk in his charitable, sentimental biography (*Sämtliche Werke* I, 31) when he says: "Constanze ist die erste und einzige, die ihn eine glückliche Liebe bekennen lehrte." [13] For we know that Storm professed a deep affection for Bertha von Buchan (Wooley, pp. 11–47) and proposed marriage to her after four years' acquaintance in 1841 when she was sixteen. We know also from the confession to Brinkmann (21 April 1866) after Constanze's death that there had been a coolness and restraint in his relation with his wife. "In meiner jungen Ehe fehlte eins: die Leidenschaft. Meine und Constanzes Hände waren mehr im stillen Gefühl der Sympathie in einander liegen geblieben." [14] That Constanze may have recognized this in her own way, that she knew of Storm's affection for the much younger Dorothea Jensen, that on her death-bed she pleaded that Dorothea should take her place and look after the seven children—these things do not make a very convincing picture of "glückliche Liebe." "Die erste und einzige"— it is better to leave a man to say that himself, and even then not to quote his words as the final truth of the matter: "Liebe ist nichts als Angst des sterblichen Menschen vor dem Alleinsein" [15] (*Im Schloss*, 1861).

Storm was unreasoning in his demands. He accepted the convention that a wife should be practical in the running of a household: in view of his own inept economy this was highly desirable. The women he portrays conform to the pattern of the non-intellectual; obviously a favourite character is the girl who makes Vetter Christian's life so easy for him (*Beim Vetter Christian*, 1872). Yet he expected Constanze to listen intelligently to his stories in the process of composition and professed that she helped him by doing this. Before they were married, he somewhat arrogantly pointed to the effects of her mediocre education on the style of her letters and recommended certain reading to her, including *Abélard and Héloïse*, Heinse's *Ardinghello* and the Song of Songs! From his wife—despite his own capacity for infidelity—he demanded absolute fidelity: "Auch wenn ich tot bin, mußt du mein bleiben, ganz, ewig!" He found expression for the mingled jealousy and longing of the lover who tortured himself by the suspicion that his kisses are not the first:

> "Gesteh's, es lebt schon einer,
> Der dich heimlich geküsst einmal,
> Der deinem Kindermunde
> Der Lippen Zauber stahl.

Und gäbst du mir alle Liebe,
Und liebt ich dich noch so sehr,
Ich könnte dich nimmer umfangen
Und herzen dich nimmermehr.

Es zieht mich zu dir hinüber
So gewaltig und liebewarm—
Was bist du so unwiderstehlich schön,
Und doch so bettelarm!"[16]

(Pre 1843)

If this, or something like it, had been written by Heine, we could accept it with less discomfort, because we should think that he was dramatizing a situation; to do this consistently is to maintain control, to avoid a primitive and ugly hysteria of passion. Storm, by his nature, had no such certain control; and the system of his early moral training at home was apparently not devised to give him any armament against the obsession which later beset him. It has been said that there was no lack of genuine affection in his parents. But it was of the undemonstrative kind in which the northern temperament tends to take a somewhat excessive pride. A laconic father was probably more than a little responsible for the untidiness of Storm's emotions. In a parade of vigour, of manliness, of moral fortitude and principle, and protesting a belief in the purity of his own nature, Storm was able to delude himself intermittently and to shield himself from the humiliation of utter dependence upon others. He clamoured for his children's affection and was grief-stricken when his favourite son Hans became an incurable dypsomaniac. When he did look at his shortcomings, his weaknesses, he had an almost crippling sense of guilt. The guilt of the father—"culpa patris"—the dominant motif which he introduced into the stories *Aquis submersus* (1875-6), *Carsten Curator* (1877), *Eekenhof* (1879), *Der Herr Etatsrat* (1880-1) and *Hans und Heinz Kirch* (1882) testifies in harrowing fashion to Storm's self-torturing indulgence in the notion of sin. Such release of feeling was salutary, but it could not touch the core of evil in his life—the *hybris*, the pride which refuses to admit the bankruptcy of the individual human heart in any reckoning with outer circumstance and with mortality.

Storm professed no orthodox religious belief. He was an atheist, at the very least an agnostic:

"Und nun begann er mit schonender Hand die Trümmer des Kinderwunders hinwegzuräumen, das über mir zusammenge-brochen war . . . Ich sah den Baum des Menschengeschlechts heraufsteigen, Trieb um Trieb, in naturwüchsiger ruhiger

Entfaltung, ohne ein anderes Wunder als das der ungeheuren
Weltschöpfung, in welchem seine Wurzeln lagen." [17]

(*Im Schloss*, 1861)

He had a great capacity for happiness—even in the alien surroundings of Heiligenstadt, where he lived throughout most of his exile,
But behind the happiness of friendship, of music, of the family
circle—the bright busy little world which he had constructed for
himself, there was a constant shadow—the irrational dread of
retribution. (Like many professed atheists he was superstitious.)
The love-song of the nightingale is answered by the boding cry
of the owl:

"Zur Rechten hell ein Liebeslied,
  Zur Linken grell ein Sterbelied!" [18]

(*Käuzlein*, pre 1843)

The death of Constanze, shortly after the return to Husum, may have
seemed inevitable confirmation of his occult conviction. The other
food on which such a mind can live, and live more happily, religious
faith, had been withheld from him in his childhood. "Ich habe
durchaus keinen Glauben von der Kindheit her" [19]: his father, a
Protestant, paid little heed to religious practice, and what Storm
acquired before he could think for himself was something fiercely
negative—a traditional mistrust of Roman Catholicism. The poem
Kruzifixus (1865) gives the measure of Storm's sharp antagonism,
but a more subtle and more revealing attack is made on Roman faith
and practice in the story *Veronika* (1861). A young woman, whose
husband tolerates her observance of Catholic ritual, discovers a growing affection for an architect. With acute and discreet perception
Storm observes the stages of her sensuous awakening. A moment of
outer danger corresponds with an emotional climax: as her husband
is discussing business on a country estate, she and the architect
stroll over to a mill, and there, amidst the confusing noise, when
she can see his lips moving but cannot hear what he is saying, the
mechanism of the mill threatens to entangle her hair. He puts his
arm round her to save her, and in that moment as their lips meet,
she recognizes how near she is to losing all self-control. As they drive
back and she says goodbye to her companion, she gives him her
gloved hand. The previous touch of the bare hand, in this story as
elsewhere in Storm, indicates a precise intensity of feeling, and the
dominant motif of renunciation is made apparent by the mention
of the glove. The handling of the episode is somewhat sultry, and
cloying to our present mood, but Storm goes further in the next
episode. The young wife goes to confession and finds that she can-

not confess. The reason is that she is alarmingly aware of the priest as a man, "a virile figure of middle age, redolent of rude health and animal strength." She goes home to her husband to confide in him, and tells him, and him alone, of her transgression. The implication here is unpleasant and can be understood only in part when we recall that Storm regarded sexual attraction as "Begründerin" and not "Inhalt der Ehe." [20] In the husband of the narrative Storm saw the ideal role which he himself would have liked to play: the husband who does not ruthlessly condemn infidelity as Storm did, but who understands and forgives, and so gains complete control over the spiritual welfare of his wife. As a husband he was greedy to play many parts—lover, spouse, uncle, father, father confessor.

Storm himself demanded confidences, and himself felt the need to confess. But to whom should he address his confession? Not even friends whom he had known for years could be recipients of all the confidences he might have wished to share, though he maintained with some of these friends—Heyse (edited by G. J. Plotke, 1917–18), a then very prominent author of fiction, Mörike (edited by H. W. Rath, 1921), Gottfried Keller (edited by A. Köster, 1904, 1909[3] and P. Goldammer, 1960)—a voluminous, at times sentimental, occasionally, we must suspect, wearisome correspondence. Sometimes he touched even there on the great and harrowing preoccupations of his mind: "das Problem der Einsamkeit und das Rätsel des Todes." [21] For the expression of the frenzy of this man who was unable to entertain a religious faith either in a personal God or in survival, we have to look elsewhere. One glimpse we catch of him —at once grand and pitiable; in the stifling silence when Constanze had died he found his way to his piano, and sitting down, played ceaselessly. Of this we know from hearsay. The tangible things we have are his writings—fragments of a confession; and perhaps we may use the phrase in a more acute sense than when we repeat it in its original reference to Goethe's works. On the dykes by Husum Storm placed no figure of Faustian stature, with eyes blinded to things present yet conjuring up the vista of untold years. But in Hauke Haien there is something of the Promethean, defiant and suffering; and if this was in Hauke Haien, it was also part of Storm who created him. The difference is this: Storm lacked the essential, destructive zeal of the innovator. He declared himself for tradition, and from this came strength and weakness. Memories of childhood kept alive through the long years spent in the same familiar surroundings gave Storm—like Jean Paul's contented little schoolmaster Wutz—the comforting sense of continuity. But when that continuity was broken, as it was in the years of exile, he was deeply disturbed. "Er hatte den altgermanischen Zug, das Leben in der

Heimat als Glück, das Leben in der Fremde als 'Elend' anzusehen" [22] (Fontane, *Von 20 bis 30*, pp. 344, quoting Paul Schütz).
In Heiligenstadt the literary output was curtailed by lack of time
(he had only one free morning a fortnight), but the incentive of
familiar things was also lacking. Storm could not summon to his
aid any substantial and sustaining view of history; of the way in
which things had come about or of how they were moving he had
little perception. He did not see the past with that amplitude and
clarity which characterizes the works of three great contemporaries
of widely varying disposition—Gustav Freytag, Wilhelm Raabe and
Conrad Ferdinand Meyer. Storm was rather the amateur antiquarian, and, like most such, he had a preference for one period;
his favourite was the mid-eighteenth century, and some of the most
treasured books in his library were works illustrated by that master
engraver Daniel Chodowiecki, typical products of that time.

Storm's affection for undisturbed continuity was accompanied
by a poignant awareness of decay. The aspect of change which he
saw most vividly was the crumbling of old established things. *Auf
dem Staatshof* (1858) presents the last years in the life of a family
of landed gentry. Anne Lene, the sole heir, is engaged to the squire,
a cruel and arrogant man, who breaks the engagement. As she says:
"Er hat so Unrecht nicht gehabt; wer holt sich die Tochter aus
einem solchen Hause!" [23] Marx, the lawyer's son, who tells the
story, was her childhood friend, and coming back discovers his
love for her: " 'O Anne Lene ' rief ich und trat auf die Stufen . . .
'ich—ich hole sie! Gib mir die Hand, ich weiß den Weg zur Welt
zurück.' . . . 'Nein' rief sie, und es war eine Todesangst in ihrer
Stimme, 'du nicht, Marx; bleib! es trägt uns beide nicht.' " [24]
The floor of the pavilion above the water, where they have played
in childhood, gives way, and she is drowned. The symbol and the
catastrophe are as clearly contrived as the collapse of Mrs.
Clennam's house in *Little Dorrit* (completed the year before Storm's
narrative). Some of the ingredients are familiar to us: the ruthless
squire, the beggar-woman who accuses Anne Lene's family of
robbing her, Claus Peters, boorish but capable, the new man of
property who buys up the old estate. And this is not the only one
of Storm's stories which turn on the decay of the family with its last,
sensitive heir as central figure. There is a straight line of descent
from the Storm of *Auf der Universität* (1862) and *Ein Bekenntnis*
(1887), and the Gustav Freytag of *Soll und Haben* (1855) to the
Thomas Mann of *Buddenbrooks* (1901) and *Zauberberg* (1924).

Storm knew the need for regeneration. In lighter mood, as in
Beim Vetter Christian (1872), he could see the good sense of the older
generation (the uncle) in league with the optimism of the young

(Julie) overcoming old habit and the diffidence of the apparently confirmed bachelor—Christian. But more often he saw struggle and sorrow before the final revival of hope. *Viola tricolor* (1873) is a retrospect upon his own life. "O bleibe treu den Toten" [25] (1848) the title of one of Storm's most poignant lyrics, contains the theme which threatens disaster to the second marriage of the antiquarian who is the principal character of this story. Ines, the second wife, finds no true acceptance by her husband or her stepdaughter until, on the brink of death after the birth of her daughter, fear and longing and hope are awakened in her husband's heart. Storm knew that for regeneration courage was needed. In *Immensee* (1849) the verdict ran: "you have not the courage," in *Pole Poppenspäler* (1873–4) Lisei puts the question and emphasizes Paul's affirmation triumphantly: "if you have the courage—so have I."— In both cases, be it noted, the challenge is uttered by the woman. But courage is a hard thing to sustain when the heart is a prey to fear, and full of the memories of its own past.

Where did Storm himself find the courage, or, to put it more precisely, where did he find the cohesion of purpose which is the core of courage and withstands the disruption of fear? He found it partly as *paterfamilias*, partly in his civic work, but much more clearly and more constantly in the pursuit of his art. His stories are, it is true, the repository for many of his own troubles. These are, in varying degree, the troubles of the ordinary man; it seems to be a misrepresentation of the general appeal of Storm to call them, as Thomas Mann does, "Dichterängste." [26] The "Dichter," the artist, comes into his own in finding articulate expression for them. In Storm's life the struggle of the artist with the sufferings of the man presents a chequered pattern of success and defeat. He was not able completely to grasp an experience, to shape it and set it at arm's length all the time. He knew that this was needed, that the artist must not let the self obtrude in the work of art. The injunction is explicit in *Eine Malerarbeit* (1867): "Du siehst . . . es geht um die Kleinigkeit, das liebe Ich aus dem Vordergrund in den Hintergrund zu praktizieren." [27] The painter, malformed and grotesque, nurses his grievance against nature and society, and gives way to jealousy. He paints a picture of a young couple (known to him) in a forest glade; their happiness is contrasted with the cruel sardonic expression of the face of the artist himself who appears in the foreground. When he has fled, and found in other surroundings that he can help young people—bringing out the talent of a farmer's son and acting as guardian for his own niece—the rancour of his nature is overcome. He paints another picture in the same setting, but the young couple is now recognizable as his niece and his protégé, the artist himself being discreetly placed as a benevolent figure who no longer dominates the composition. But the artist must still be in the picture, life is still something which involves him, and that involvement is explicit in the painting. More satisfying is the story *Ein stiller Musikant* (1874–5). Here the man of good will who has shown great talent as a musician comes to realize the weakness of his own character, to know that he cannot dominate, cannot advertise himself, cannot even play the piano when others are listening. Storm himself is in this story: his taste in poetry is identical with that of the musician. But the identity is successfully concealed because there is here a sustained interest in the artist's own specific problems. The contrast between this and *Malerarbeit* is easily explained: Storm was much less at home in talking about pictures than he was in talking about and making music. In this connection the comment seems rarely to have been made that although Storm is regarded as a great descriptive writer, the graphic and painterly qualities are singularly meagre in his descriptions. To the painter a "Halligfahrt" outside Husum is a challenge of colour even on a dull day. It could provide inspiration for a whole series of water-colour drawings. All is fluid, sky merging into water, the dark line of a dyke giving illusion of a horizon, till the eye picks up beyond, against the faint yellows and russets and browns of the sky—hardly realized as substance—the blue-grey of a "Warf"; or on the other side, again suspended in the universal wateriness of sky and land and shallows the faintest emerald gleam to show where, leagues away, the "Geest" lies. The strength of Storm's description rests rather in shape and light, in movement and in stillness. It seems almost at times that his colour sense was deficient, that he may even have been, in some moderate degree, colour-blind. It certainly suggests lack of observation when he says in *Von Jenseit des Meeres* (1863–4): "Jenni's schönes, blasses Antlitz . . . war so hell vom Mond beleuchtet, daß ich den bläulichen Schmelz der Zähne zwischen den roten Lippen schimmern sah." [28] This is conceptual description, for nobody can see that lips are red in the moonlight. But apart from the outcome of sensory observation, aural or visual, the personal involvement of Storm is implicit in his stories in varying degrees. He was concerned, at times naively, with the relationship of his stories to his own experience. Like the lonely old landlady in *Marthe und ihre Uhr* (1847) who looks on the characters in Mörike's novel *Maler Nolten* (first version: 1832) as real, and imagines further episodes in their lives, Storm associated himself with the figures he drew from the life around him. Partly of course this belongs to the fashion of his time, and not only in Germany. Dickens also liked to keep in touch, to ensure that his readers kept in touch with his characters. And the amiable little trick of bringing up-to-date news about them at the end of the narrative, which we find in Dickens as in Storm, is part of the more or less romanticized realism of the time. But Dickens's characters have a much wider range of temperament, a much more varied expression than Storm's. Kinship with the writer and kindred experience are more apparent in Storm. The pre-occupation of the writer with his own feelings, with his past as his own past, leaves its mark also on the work of Storm's great Swiss contemporary, C. F. Meyer. But Meyer had a greater talent in *projecting* his stories, in creating a setting remote in time, and making it and his characters appear as separate from himself and his own environment. It is significant that the style of Meyer was alien to Storm, who once expressed the wish that he might come upon some story of Meyer which he could admire without reservation; his opinion of Meyer's art, as he saw it, is summarized in the word "gemacht" (see letters to Heyse: 7. & 28. vii, 1882 and to Keller 13 March 1883). The difference is a difference of temperament, of habit, of environment. There is a poem of C. F. Meyer in which he gives us a sudden glimpse and an enduring statement of the inspiration of his art. At home in a landscape where he could see the glow of sunset on the far-off snow of alpine peaks he knew that this belonged to his life, and that it was for ever in his poetry:

> "In meinem Wesen und Gedicht
> Allüberall ist Firnelicht,
> Das große stille Leuchten." [29]

Captured and reflected in the intricate facets of his prose and verse, the "Firnelicht" becomes and remains, as he calls it "ein kleines stilles Leuchten." [30] We are always aware of the distances and of Meyer's response; with Storm we feel rather the nearness of things in the poet's own life. Meyer had the greater intellectual discipline. For the "großes stilles Leuchten" there is in Storm's writing the flickering of sheltered candle-light from within the "Tonne."

It is not fundamentally paradoxical that Storm was at pains, by technical devices, to thrust his stories into the past. Some of his works are now classical examples of the so-called "Rahmenerzählung." This is a commonly used term (see *inter alia* E. K. Bennett, *A History of the German Novelle*, 1934; J. Klein, *Geschichte der deutschen Novelle*, 1956[1]) but not the most appropriate. Walther Brecht's "répoussoir" is in some ways more attractive because it suggests more clearly recession and perspective. Again Dickens provides an English parallel—*Master Humphrey's Clock*, a very clumsy framework for such stories as *The Old Curiosity Shop* and the afterthoughts on *Mr. Pickwick*, or *Mugby Junction*.

What is the purpose of such enfolding of the story? It gives the author the pleasure of wrapping up a parcel; the reader is then invited to enjoy the unwrapping. It is a fictitious device made to overcome the idea of fiction. If the author has taken all the trouble to wrap something up, the reader will think that that something must be genuine. On looking at some of the wrappings, however, we find that what we have been handling is very similar to a set of chinese boxes of which the innermost is not strikingly different from the others, admirable for its ingenuity rather than as a sign of fresh creative talent. If we admire the workmanship, we expect, at the core of the whole structure, a superlative achievement of skill. Instead, the author tries, without much success, to persuade us that what we have found is an objective truth. When, in *Renate* (1877–8) for example, Storm pretends to be the editor of letters which have come by a roundabout route into his hands, the subtlety of the device is suspect. This may be because it is one of many forms of circumventing the old prejudice against phantasy, against fiction as such, which by familiarity and by loss of that prejudice we can no longer appreciate. The illusion that a true story was being told may have been firmly created for Hartmann von Aue's audience of the early thirteenth century when he stated:

> "Ein ritter sô gelêret was
> daz er an den buochen las . . .
> nû beginnet er iu diuten
> ein rede die er geschriben vant." [31]

The eighteenth-century reader may have been titillated by Wieland's assurance that he was writing the *history* of Agathon (first version 1766–7) and so could do nothing to alter the behaviour of the hero by inventing any episodes. But to the present-day reader such subtleties become a little thin when he observes by the underlying uniformity of style that one man, the author himself, is responsible for the whole narrative and is not even attempting to vary the speech from character to character, that he introduces dialogue (sometimes, as in *Von Jenseit des Meeres*, purporting to be overheard) so complex and so unnaturally coherent that its independent existence baffles belief. Here the new mastery of differentiated dialogue in Fontane contrasts very strikingly with the thinly disguised monologue of Storm's narrative.

Yet it is clear that Storm as a story-teller was an immensely conscious and conscientious craftsman, who thought much about the construction of his stories. This is apparent when we watch the intensification of episode in the more substantial ones such as *Immensee* (1849), *Aquis submersus* (1875–6) and *Schimmelreiter* (1886–8), and the careful selection of significant detail in stories of more slender proportions (*Grünes Blatt*, 1850; *Angelika*, 1855; *Pole Poppenspäler*, 1873–4; *Carsten Curator*, 1877). There is further evidence of Storm's care for construction and of his thoughts on the narrator's function and method in his prolonged correspondence with Keller, Heyse, Mörike to which reference has already been made. Among the most human are those letters addressed to Ada Christen, known in Vienna as a sensational poet and an indifferent actress (edited by O. Katann, *Storm als Erzieher*, 1948). Here in two very simple but incisive statements Storm reveals something of his method and his principle. " . . . , daß ich, wenn es mir nicht von selbst kommen will, die Sache weglege, b i s es kommt"[32] shows the practised artist's reliance on the creative processes of his own mind. "Die Konzeption anlangend, so ist mein Streben darauf gerichtet, daß das Einzelne immer für sich etwas ist, und doch dem Ganzen dient"[33] (letter 2 March 1873) shows a legitimate interest in the form rather than in the idea, and might be compared with one of Otto Ludwig's definitions of Poetic Realism: "ein erhöhtes Spiegelbild des Gegenstandes, aber nach dem Gesetze der Malerei zu klarer Anordnung gediehen."[34] Elsewhere, concerning his own most favoured form of prose fiction, the "Novelle" he wrote: "die heutige Novelle ist die Schwester des Dramas und die strengste Form der Prosadichtung. Gleich dem Drama behandelt sie die tiefsten Probleme des Menschenlebens, gleich diesen verlangt sie . . . Ausscheidung des Unwesentlichen"[35] (*Eine zurückgezogene Vorrede aus dem Jahre 1881*, Köster, vol. viii, p. 122). The dramatic quality of the "Novelle" appealed to Storm, who by his art tried to control the conflict which was an essential part of life as he experienced it. The strict economy of this form of story was also congenial because his own experience was concentrated rather than expansive. The novel ("Roman") of his day permitted the leisurely self-indulgence of the writer whose mind was a storehouse of many things. The museum and art gallery of Storm's mind was not so richly endowed. It contained a sizeable collection of landscapes and figures of his own region executed in varying light, sparsely coloured and often lacking detail to a surprising degree (here and there the detail, for example the often quoted gesture of a "bleiche Hand,"[36] is as purposeful as in the chiaroscuro of a Rembrandt composition). A smaller section is given to pictures of the historical past, and a still smaller to the phantastic in which the motifs of the fairy-tale (*Häwelmann*, 1849; *Hinzelmeier*, 1850; *Regentrude*, 1864), of folklore (*Schimmelreiter*, 1886–8), of second sight (*Hans und Heinz Kirch*, 1881–2) played a modest part. But in that mostly sombre light, if the metaphor of the Storm museum may be stretched so far, the glass of the pictures and of the show-cases reflects again and again not the other objects (like the mirror in the Arnolfini composition by Jan van Eyck) but the carelined features of the story-teller himself—a story-teller who could never quite separate the shape of things stored in his memory from the shadowy configuration of his own day-dreams, his own sufferings. There is dramatic structure and dramatic suspense in his narrative, and the succession of episodes is the devising of a skilled narrator. But the form which lay nearest to the heart of Storm was neither epic nor dramatic. It took some time for the literary historians to see in him, as in C. F. Meyer, the lyric genius—the poet appreciated and esteemed by outstanding writers of prose such as Fontane and T. Mann. It is significant that Storm perceived the work ("Arbeit") in Meyer's lyric poetry, and that he demanded that this be subordinated to feeling ("Empfindung"). In the verses which emerge (in Romantic fashion) in the midst of narrative (see *Immensee*), in occasional poems, in all the intensely personal response to episodes in his own life, this characteristic of nineteenth-century lyric is dominant. For Storm the lyric was the mode of composition to which he entrusted his deepest feeling: "sobald ich recht bewegt werde, bedarf ich der gebundenen Form" [37] he wrote in a letter to Mörike (2 December 1855).

With remarkable perception he listed those of his poems which he felt were most charged with the meaning of his own experiences. These include: *Das aber kann ich nicht ertragen*, 1847; *Oktoberlied*, 1848; *Abseits*, 1848; *Heute, nur heute*, 1849; *Für meine Söhne*, 1853; *Kein Wort, auch nicht das kleinste*, 1853; *Nachtigall*, pre 1857. From this range of poems bearing, as Storm himself says, the imprint of his personality in its quest for beauty, we may derive much help towards an understanding of his character and his genius. For the present writer who sees in Storm above all the man who clung to life in a haunting confusion of love and fear, the most poignant is the lament *Einer Toten* (1847) which commemorates his sister:

> "Das aber kann ich nicht ertragen,
> Daß so wie sonst die Sonne lacht;
> Daß wie in deinen Lebenstagen
> Die Uhren gehn, die Glocken schlagen,
> Einförmig wechseln Tag und Nacht;

Daß, wenn des Tages Lichter schwanden,
Wie sonst der Abend uns vereint;
Und daß, wo sonst dein Stuhl gestanden,
Schon andre ihre Plätze fanden,
Und nichts dich zu vermissen scheint;

Indessen von den Gitterstäben
Die Mondesstreifen schmal und karg
In deine Gruft hinunterweben,
Und mit gespenstig trübem Leben
Hinwandeln über deinen Sarg." [38]

To move from the oppressive seventeenth-century graveyard sonnets
of Gryphius (1663) through the mysterious visionary laments of
Novalis (*Hymnen an die Nacht*, 1800) to the strangely consoling lyric of
Rilke ("Er wußte nur vom Tod, was alle wissen," [39] 1908), and then
back to the hopeless sorrow of Storm's bereavement brings a revelation of the dominant role which the "Todesgedanke" has played in
German poetry. Storm's poem, in its great and sombre beauty, in the
inevitable limitation which his unbelief imposed upon it, can guide
us and reconcile us in our efforts to understand the self-torture, the
ideals, the continued struggle and the rare victories of this man
who, descending into the "Alltag" which he never really understood,
bore sometimes in his face the "Glanz, der nicht von dieser Welt war."

As we leave the market-place of Husum and, walking along the
Norderstrasse, come to the Gasthaus St. Jürgen, we may pause in
front of the monument to Theodor Storm. That vast block, weath-
ered, insensate, opposing its grey and black to the yellow and russet
of frail leaves that drift down from the autumn trees, will seem to us
perhaps unbearably oppressive; and yet we realize that it is the most
appropriate memorial to a man who steadfastly refused the spiritual
assurance of a life beyond. That dense, immobile mass is a symbol
of negation. All hope seems dead; light, as an alien thing, has no
place here. At such a moment we need to recall, actively, the little
assembly of figures in his stories and the key to their sufferings in the
personal lyric of their creator.

Recognizing in these the articulate expression of general human
conflict and suffering in which every generation shares, we may find
that the dead weight of that stone no longer stifles our sympathy for
Storm, and that in recognizing his genius we can revive the modest
hope which he expressed near the end of his life in *Eine zurückgezogene Vorrede aus dem Jahre 1881*. He left it to posterity to pronounce
the verdict on his work, "denn so viel ist gewiß, der einzige
Probierstein des poetischen Werkes ist die Dauer." [40]

TRANSLATIONS

1. At that moment Gabriel heard a sound, hollow as if it came from underground; a hardly perceptible tremor shook the earth at his feet. It came again, and then a third time. What could be happening over there that the guns should be firing in the night? . . . Regine seemed to remain unaware; she raised her head a little and said: "It's striking ten by the village clock."

2. No sound of strife did yet intrude upon this blessed solitude.

3. Watching with drowsy eyes the bees.

4. No politician, whichever way you looked at him.

5. No man can thrive bereft of home.

6. Making up stories.

7. This cask was the Holy of Holies occupied by Hans and myself alone . . . Although the ascent [into the world of imagination] was gentle, it took us happily above the ordinary world, till the dust of the school room and of workaday life was whisked merrily away as the breeze took hold of our clothes . . . Below us, hidden in the mist it lay, whilst we breathed the pure air of the heights . . . Long afterwards nobody could fail to see from our faces that we still had within us a light that was not of this earth.

8. Husum.

9. And such like baubles which I, like most people from my part of the world lacked the organ of perception to appreciate with even a low degree of accuracy.

10. Poison in the veins of the nation.

11. They seemed to me to lack entirely that glorious bluntness which alone makes a man free in himself and in my opinion must be the ultimate, the supreme outcome of civilized life.

12. In the armour of glorious bluntness.

13. Constanze was the first and only woman who taught him to confess to happy love.

14. In my early married life one thing was lacking: passion. It was rather with a tranquil sense of sympathy that her hand would rest in mine.

15. Love is nothing but fear of mortal man at the thought of being left alone.

16. Confess it! There is another who kissed you a long while ago, and secretly stole from your childish lips the magic of love. And though you may say you love no one but me, and though I may love you tenderly I could not ever again hold you in my arms and whisper endearments to you. To you I am drawn with all the warmth and fervour of love. In your beauty no one could resist you, and yet you are so unutterably poor.

17. And then he began with considerate hands to clear away the ruins of childhood's miracle which had collapsed about me . . . I could see the tree of the human race growing, shoot after shoot, unfolding in the tranquil strength of natural evolution; a miracle—yes, but none other than the miracle of creation. Therein lay its roots and its strength.

18. The lay of love came sweetly from the right, and from the left the piercing knell of death.

19. From the days of my childhood I have had no faith whatsoever.

20. Foundation . . . substance of wedlock.

21. The problem of solitude and the enigma of death.

22. He shared the ancient Germanic characteristic of regarding life on his native soil as happiness, and life away from home as misery.

23. He wasn't so far wrong after all.—Who would go and fetch a daughter from such a house!

24. "Anne Lene," I cried, as I set foot on the steps "I-I will fetch her. Do you give me your hand. I can find the way back."—"No," she exclaimed, and in her voice there was fear as of death. "Not you, Marx! stay! it will not carry the two of us."

25. Keep faith with the dead.

26. A poet's fears.

27. You see . . . there's just this little detail: you have got to push your precious ego from the foreground into the background.

28. Jenni's pale and beautiful face was so clear in the moonlight that I could see the bluish glint of her teeth between her red lips.

29. Transfusing all my life and work the tranquil glow of the everlasting snows.

30. The little tranquil glow.

31. A knight there was, full learned he, could read in books right cunningly, that now beginneth to recount a tale which he found writ.

32. That if the matter will not come of its own accord, I put it aside until it does.

33. As regards the conception of a work, my effort is always to make the individual part such that it is complete within itself and yet subservient to the whole.

34. An intensified mirror-image of the object but taking a clear and orderly shape according to the law of the painter's art.

35. The "novella" of to day is the sister of drama: the most disciplined form of prose-fiction. Like drama it deals with the most profound problems of human life, and like drama it demands the exclusion of all that is inessential.

36. Pale fingers.

37. When I am really moved I have to turn to metrical form.

38. But these things I cannot bear—that the sun still looks down joyously upon the world and that, as when you were living, the clocks still tick and the bells peal and day follows night in never-ending monotony; that when the lights of day have faded, the evening still brings our thoughts together as it used to do, and that, where your chair once stood, others have sat, and nothing seems to miss you. Then through the railings the thin scant rays of the moonlight grope their way and fall upon your tomb and, like sad phantoms, stray above your coffin.

39. Of death he only knew what all men know.

40. For this much is certain: the only touchstone of a poet's work is its permanence.

BIBLIOGRAPHY

(A selection of titles in addition to those mentioned in the text. It is realized that not all of the following may be easy of access. For the assembling of this material, and for constant help throughout the writing of the chapter I am indebted to Dr. Eva Engel of the Modern Language Department, University College of North Staffordshire.)

EDITIONS

Köster, A. 1921, 8 vols.

Storm, Theodor. *Sämtliche Werke*, 1951 (2 vols. India paper), Winkler-Verlag, München.

POEMS

Parnass: a readily available edition.

For the dating of individual poems see:

Wooley, E. O. *Studies in Storm*. Indiana University Publications, 1943.

LETTERS

Storm, Gertrud (ed.) 1915–17, 4 vols.

WORKS OF REFERENCE

Biese, C. J. A. *Storms Leben und Werke*, 1921 (3rd ed.).

Bonwit, M. *Der leidende Dritte*, 1952 (The problem of the renunciation of love).

Bracher, H. *Rahmenerzählung und Verwandtes bei G. Keller, C. F. Meyer, Th. Storm. Ein Beitrag zur Technik der Novelle*, 1924.

Brecht, Walther. *Storm und die Geschichte*, Deut. Vierteljahresschrift 3 (a searching and perceptive article).

Fontane, Th. *Von Zwanzig bis Dreissig*, 1898 (a humane, shrewd and critical study).

Klein, J. *Geschichte der deutschen Novelle*, 1956 (3rd. ed.).

Leuhertz, R. *Die lyrische Einlage bei Th. Storm*, 1933.

Mann, Th. *Leiden und Grösse der Meister*, 1935, pp. 183–207 (an enthusiastic study, valuable for its comment on poetry).

Schmidt, E. *Charakteristiken*, 1902 (2nd ed.), pp. 437–79 (excellent for its constructive criticism and earliest reference to symbolism in Storm's writing).

Stuckert, F. *Th. Storm, sein Leben und seine Welt*, 1955.

Von Wiese, B. *Die deutsche Novelle von Goethe bis Kafka*, 1959 (4th ed.), 2 vols.

There are single translations of some short stories available in English, e.g. *The Senator's Sons* (Harrap's Bilingual Series, 1947).

Gottfried Keller

Gottfried Keller

by F. M. LINDSAY

I

GOTTFRIED KELLER is the representative author of the German Swiss. In a way that is true of no other Swiss man of letters his fellow-countrymen have taken him to their hearts. Other great Swiss authors, like Jeremias Gotthelf and Conrad Ferdinand Meyer, may excel Keller in particular qualities, and either of those men can be regarded more fully than Keller as the literary embodiment of a particular social group, in Gotthelf's case the rich farmers of Canton Berne, in Meyer's the old Zürich patriciate. But Keller, with his roots in the village of Glattfelden and his life spent in Zürich, with his excursions to Munich, Heidelberg and Berlin and his constant awareness of his cultural dependence on Germany—this contrasting with his political independence —is a more complete and more universal poet and author than those others.

Switzerland has made a distinguished and distinctive contribution to German literature. When Luther with German "Dämonie" was shaking the foundations of Christian spiritual life in Europe, Zwingli, his Swiss counterpart, was making a cool, rational Swiss appraisal of the needs of the reformed church and arriving at equally radical but less stormily expressed convictions. Niklaus Manuel is remembered among early German dramatists for his vigorous and expressive Reformation plays. In days when German literary life was almost at a standstill the great Albrecht von Haller composed notable poetry, but only as a hobby, for Haller was more famous in his profession as anatomist and physiologist. The names of Professors Bodmer and Breitinger of Zürich are familiar to the student of literary history, even if he has never read their works, as the men who discerned which direction German literature needed to take in the 1740s. Salomon Gessner was another talented Züricher of the generation which immediately precedes the great awakening of German literature in the 1770s. Goethe was bound by ties of affection to Switzerland, and one of Schiller's best-known plays has become the Swiss national drama. In the nineteenth century Switzerland contributed quite disproportionately to her size to German literature with the authors already mentioned, to say nothing of the poet Leuthold and the historian of the Renaissance, Jakob Burckhardt. In more recent times the names of Carl Spitteler, Max Frisch and Friedrich Dürrenmatt show that Switzerland's venerable literary tradition is still very much alive.

The individuality of Swiss literature is difficult to convey in a few sentences. While it could clearly enjoy no separate existence apart from German literature it has a strongly characteristic flavour and often reflects attitudes which would be unthinkable in Germany. Swiss political institutions are reflected both directly and indirectly in German Swiss literature, as the reader of Keller's works soon realizes. Certain fundamental human rights have enjoyed continuous recognition in Switzerland for longer than in Germany, and there may be a connection between this and the fact that Swiss literature shows less sign of storm and stress, of Faustian striving for unattainable absolutes, of the Kafkan calling in question of the justice and value of life than that of Germany. Kleist would have been unthinkable in Switzerland; Nietzsche was there only as a foreign professor, he had no organic link with the place.

The most eminent men of letters in Switzerland have firmly and sensibly opposed the idea of a dialect literature; this can only have a limited appeal, and it is preferable to speak in German with Swiss overtones to the whole German-speaking world rather than enjoy the cosy, parochial self-indulgence of talking in accents understood but by a few about things which in any case would not interest the many. Keller always wrote in the standard German language even though this cannot have been easy or natural for him.

II

Gottfried Keller was born in Zürich in 1819. His father, a woodturner, was a person of great energy and very considerable artistic ability. The poet certainly inherited most of his artistic gifts from his father. His mother, the daughter of a country doctor, was a good but very down-to-earth person. Rudolf Keller died when his son was only five, and the widow, being left in fairly straitened circumstances, had to take in lodgers and let off most of her roomy old house in the Zürich *Rindermarkt*. Gottfried was a solitary child, given to brooding and daydreams. His teachers were for the most part rather insensitive and unimaginative, and he did not much enjoy school. But he learned quickly those subjects which interested him, and it must have come as a great shock to his mother when he was expelled from the *Industrieschule* at the age of fifteen; he had taken part in an unpleasant persecution of an unsatisfactory master who had been dismissed, yet it seems improbable that he was the ringleader or merited so severe a punishment.

When the question arose what to do with the boy, Gottfried declared emphatically that he wished to become a landscape painter. His mother tried to talk him out of this, but he was all the more determined to have his own way. After several years of trying to learn at home under unsatisfactory teachers, Keller set off for Munich in 1840, resolved to learn something there about landscape painting. Two and a half years later he returned to Zürich, having spent all his patrimony and made little if any progress as a painter. His sense of failure deepened in the following few years, till suddenly, in the mid-1840s he turned to literature and quickly produced some poems, mainly inspired by the political poets, Grün, Herwegh and Freiligrath. Now Keller was hard put to it to make himself sufficiently master of the technical side of versifying to reduce his abundant poetic material to some kind of order. In 1846 he was able to bring out his first book of poems.

Gradually Keller became known in Zürich as a poet, and in 1848 his native canton gave him the money to enable him to study in Heidelberg. He hoped one day to become a dramatist. In this period falls his acquaintance with Ludwig Feuerbach, the atheistic philosopher, who swept away the last remnants of Keller's inherited religious faith, and for years remained the principal intellectual influence in Keller's life. Keller moved from Heidelberg to Berlin in 1850 and spent several years there. By now he was engaged in writing *Der grüne Heinrich*, the great burden of his Berlin sojourn. The work was not completed till 1855.

Between 1842 and 1855 Keller was in love over and over again with a succession of young women, for the most part tall, handsome Amazons who would certainly never have considered uniting themselves for life with his four foot ten inches. Henriette Keller, Luise Rieter, Marie Melos, Johanna Kapp, Betty Tendering, all, and especially the last two, made a deep impression on him. *Der Landvogt von Greifensee* reflects Keller's constant attempts to achieve a satisfactory relationship with the other sex.

From 1861 till 1876 Keller served as First Secretary of Canton Zürich. This period of official activity made heavy demands on his time and energy, and he took pride in carrying out his duties efficiently. In 1856 he had published the first volume of *Die Leute von Seldwyla*, but no further literary work appeared for many years. By the early 1870s he was beginning to long for his freedom, and the publication of his *Sieben Legenden* in 1872 marks the first re-emergence of the poet and prose-writer from the burdens of office. He continued to serve as *Staatsschreiber* for several more years, but he was by now seriously concerned about the works which he still hoped to write. In 1874, just before his retirement Keller completed Part II of *Die Leute von Seldwyla*.

In the years after 1876 Keller was extremely productive. In 1877 appeared the *Züricher Novellen*, in 1880 he revised and greatly improved *Der grüne Heinrich*, 1883 brought *Das Sinngedicht* and the new and augmented edition of his poems, 1886 the novel of his old age, *Martin Salander*.

By 1885 Keller's health had begun to fail, and his sister Regula, who had kept house for him since his mother's death, was now a dying woman. Although he still had faith in the younger generation Keller withdrew more and more from outside contacts. It was widely but falsely believed that he had become sour and misanthropic in his old age; though the years had brought him his fair share of disillusionment and disappointment he remained to the end fundamentally a man of good will. Regula died in 1888, and after this his health deteriorated rapidly. Keller was a sick man, quite uninterested in the public celebrations of his seventieth birthday in July 1889. But although he was clearly incurably ill, death did not claim him till nearly a year later, on 15 July 1890.

III

In later life Keller was proud that it had been "der Ruf der lebendigen Zeit" which had stirred him into poetic activity in 1844. He was roused by the example of the German political poets into writing his first verses. For the most part these tendentious political poems impress us as rather naive, even ridiculous nowadays. The *Jesuitenzug*, for instance, which is intended to be menacing, even frightening, now seems merely funny. It had been reasonable enough in his father's day for a democrat to have a healthy dislike for aristocrats and priests, but within one generation the situation had become quite different. The nature poetry from Keller's first collection has worn better, and often in only slightly modified form his early nature poems were preserved by the aged poet in his *Gesammelte Gedichte* of 1883. The cycle entitled *Lebendig begraben* was adversely criticized by Varnhagen von Ense, that connoisseur of poetry, who on the whole reacted very favourably to Keller's verse, and the modern reader generally finds these poems in poor taste. However, Keller's genuine feeling for nature, his keen painter's eye, his evident liking for his fellow-men and the plants and animals of the field, and an occasional moment of high poetic inspiration combine to make his verse memorable and important as a personal document of the poet's life.

In the *Gesammelte Gedichte* the *Spielmannslied*, which is the first poem in the collection, characterizes Keller's poetry most effectively; he makes no excessive claims for himself, but he does through the parable of the sower make it clear that he regards himself as a true poet; he would not claim that he has always made the most of himself, that he has never been slack or heedless or missed an opportunity; yet now and again "a hungry little bird" has gathered nourishment from him, he has provided the sustenance that sent the bird soaring heavenwards again, and he has therefore not entirely betrayed his mission.

Unter Sternen, a short poem originally written in 1846, communicates Keller's love of night; this was, of course, a characteristic of much Romantic poetry, in Germany and elsewhere. But Keller's poem appears to be the record of a particular and precious experience; in the evening starlight, he claims:

> "Hier fühl ich Zusammenhang
> Mit dem All' und Einen." [1]

This poem, with its joy in the beauties of creation, places Keller among the true nature poets of Europe, side by side with Goethe or Wordsworth. His famous *Abendlied an die Natur* is a hymn of homage to the benign and refreshing influence of Nature to which he turns for comfort in every difficult situation in life; Nature has given him the only pure pleasures he has ever known with no bad after-taste, no regrets or repentance. When Keller fails to appreciate Nature's benefits, his heart will be sick or corrupted. When his end comes, he is happy to think of reposing under Nature's green grass. He loves and accepts the natural order, which he regards as fundamentally beneficent.

Abend auf Golgatha is the most direct evidence we possess that Keller may have turned away from Feuerbach towards the end of his life. This is a beautiful and subtle short poem about Christ on the cross. It is evening, getting dark, and the dew is falling. A large moth comes and settles for a moment on Jesus' gleaming white shoulder and then flies off into the darkness. But Christ is not quite deserted, for His mother, Mary, who is also His creature, embraces the pillar of the cross. Within these eight lines Keller uses the words "der Erlöser" (Redeemer), "des Herrn" (the Lord), "das Kreuz" (the cross), "der Schöpfer" (Creator), "das Weib, das er zur Mutter sich schuf" (the woman whom He created for His mother). It is possible that he wrote the poem only or mainly because of its admirable pictorial quality, but it seems to me more likely that he wanted to say those weighty words, of whose truth he was by now (1881) more than half convinced, in as non-committal a way as possible.

Keller handles the hexameter here with great skill, and this is undoubtedly one of his best lyrics.

We do not remember Keller primarily as a lyric poet, but in the poems mentioned and a handful of others he has produced work which ranks with the best written in the German tongue. His best known and best loved poem, *Abendlied (Augen, meine lieben Fensterlein)* is the work above all others in which the quintessential Keller, the man of the seeing eye, who treasures the precious gift of life, reveals himself. Here Keller achieves that rare synthesis of thought, emotion and form which constitutes a true work of art. *Winternacht*, a delightful poem in which the imprisonment of natural forces in the winter is symbolized by the nixie's struggle to emerge from below the ice of a frozen pond, is another poem that haunts the memory.

IV

Der grüne Heinrich, even in the very imperfect form in which it first appeared in 1854 and 1855, was recognized as a work of genius by those most competent to judge. It is the story of Heinrich Lee, the clever son of a poor widow in Zürich. In the later version (1880) Heinrich tells his life's story in the first person, from his dim memories of his father who died when he was quite small to his withdrawal as a still comparatively young man to a minor administrative post in a Swiss mountain village. His childhood and adolescence are recalled in considerable detail, and we soon know intimately the imaginative child's life in his mother's big, rambling old house in the centre of a then very much smaller Zürich. With disarming frankness we are told of the child's first religious doubts, his difficulty in behaving honestly, the few occasions when he knew he had done something really shameful to other people without being found out. We learn that Heinrich early makes the discovery that even children can be completely and radically depraved; this is shown by his experiences with a horrible juvenile usurer, Meierlein, who tries to enforce payment of debts by methods which, as Keller points out, would be perfectly legitimate in the adult world, but which no right-thinking person would dream of allowing one child to use against another. Then we hear of Heinrich's expulsion from school and of his fateful decision to become a landscape painter. He is sent to his uncle's house in the country for a time. His adolescence is dominated by the conflict of his two loves, that for the country schoolmaster's delicate daughter, Anna, and that for the handsome young widow, Judith, a living embodiment of the power and abundance of Nature. After various unsuccessful attempts to find a reliable teacher in Zürich Heinrich persuades his guardians to let him have the money left for him by his father, and goes off to Munich to study art. There he is not very successful; he wastes some of his time, he does not have the means to pay a good teacher, and in any case landscape painting has gone out of fashion. So by the time he has been two years there he has spent his all and gained nothing. We hear of his friendships with the other painters Erickson and Lys, who are contrasted as a talented and likeable Philistine and a man of more genuine and problematical genius who has the most sublime disregard for other people's feelings. Keller himself as a young painter in Munich did not have friends like these; the loyal Johann Salomon Hegi was nothing like as accomplished a painter. Heinrich resolutely refuses to do what he would consider inferior work to help to pay for his studies, but in the end he finds himself reduced to painting flagpoles for a royal wedding in order to pay his rent and have something to eat. However, he takes pleasure in his honest labour and its reward. The later part of the book is much inferior. We cannot easily believe in Heinrich's introduction to Count Dietrich's castle and the events that happen to him there— the Count turns out to have bought all Heinrich's paintings and studies from the junk-shop dealer in Munich who had given Heinrich next to nothing for them. The Count's adopted daughter, Dortchen Schönfund, falls in love with Heinrich, does what she reasonably can to encourage him, but he is too slow and cold. In the end Heinrich leaves the castle with the Count's good will, a large sum of money and the uneasy feeling that he could have had Dortchen if he had but tried. The whole castle episode harks rather of a fairy-tale ending. At home Heinrich is just in time to say farewell to his mother on her deathbed. After a little time he takes a position in a country valley as a minor official; his life is brightened by the return of Judith from America whither she had emigrated. The two do not marry, but take great pleasure in one another's company. Judith dies during a great epidemic while she is nursing sick children; she has become a much more charitable if less passionate person meantime.

Der grüne Heinrich is a great novel in the tradition of the German *Bildungsroman*, which gives the story of a single individual's development from innocence and ignorance to maturity and wisdom. Heinrich Lee is in many ways the most engaging hero of all the German *Bildungsromane*. A clever child with an inquiring mind, he has the modesty and diffidence that prevent him from seeming disagreeably precocious. From a very early age he makes his generally accurate observations about other people; we find his frankness about his early faults of character disarming. The death of Heinrich's father results in a particularly close and affectionate relationship between the boy and his mother. When Heinrich tells lies and steals, what rescues him from his wayward and irresponsible behaviour is more than anything the fear of losing his mother's confidence and causing her serious offence. The story of Heinrich's two loves in his native village is one of the great delights of the book; instead of loving one girl in different ways Heinrich divides his capacity for loving into the spiritual, respectful worship from afar which he bestows on Anna—she cultivates a kind of ideal remoteness, and on the one occasion when Heinrich so far forgets himself as to kiss her, her emotional equilibrium is seriously upset by the incident—and the passionate, sensuous love for the strong, healthy, beautiful Judith. With Judith Heinrich is often tempted almost beyond endurance, but she is considerably older than he and refrains from seducing him. Later in the book after his two brief excursions with Hulda and Dortchen Schönfund, Heinrich sees Judith again, but by now their relationship is quite different, serene, mature, based on the memory of those stormy passions of long ago. They do not marry, and from what we know of Keller's views on marriage and relations between the sexes in general we can be sure that he does not mean us to understand that Heinrich and Judith are ever "lovers."

Der grüne Heinrich has its *longueurs*, of course; most readers find the account of the Munich Carnival tedious in the extreme, and the story of Albert Zwiehans' amours (really introduced to show the dangers of not being able to make up one's mind between two women) tries the reader's patience sorely. The *Meretlein* story, another digression, comes earlier in the book, seems more closely related to the hero's difficulties with his teachers, and is altogether more tolerable. Later on, the whole episode in the Count's castle suggests that Keller was becoming impatient of the book and was prepared to use almost any means to bring it to an end quickly. While the last book of *Der grüne Heinrich* has some good pages one loses that feeling of being in close touch with reality which makes Books I and II so memorable.

The work gained enormously from being re-written in chronological sequence and in the first person throughout in 1880. The original version was much too disjointed, being partly written in the first, partly in the third person. The style of the book was carefully scrutinized, and many improvements of detail were made. But Keller discarded *Judiths Bad*, a most artistically affecting passage in the original book, in the interest of avoiding cheap erotic effects. To Emil Kuh he wrote as early as 1871 that it was "die roheste und trivialste Kunst von der Welt . . . in einem Poem den weiblichen Figuren das Hemd übern Kopf wegzuziehen," [2] and made it plain that he was no longer prepared to seek popularity by such methods. Most of his readers would be inclined to think that Keller's judgment betrayed him over *Judiths Bad*, even if in principle they sympathized with the attitude that made Keller drop it in 1880.

The first book of *Der grüne Heinrich* rings true on every page. Not only does Heinrich enlist our sympathy, we relive his life with him, step by step, and reflect how much of his experience is universal human experience. There are no boring passages, because every reader is reminded of his own early days and thinks how remarkable it is that Keller should remember his childhood and adolescence so much more distinctly than we ourselves.

The novelty and wonder of the world in childhood are recaptured in all their freshness by this author who retains so much of childlike naïveté in his grown-up character. Then we are delighted by Heinrich's love for Anna; we fear a little for him when he begins to see too much of Judith; it is almost with relief that we learn of her departure for America. But as the book progresses we begin to make reservations about it. The story of Meretlein is still more or less relevant; Heinrich's teachers show little understanding of him, and this cautionary tale of what can happen when a very sensitive child is treated with an exemplary lack of understanding by parents and teachers has a direct bearing on the theme of the book. The long account of Albertus Zwiehans and his amatory vacillations is too much for our patience, even if it may not be completely unrelated to the theme of the book. When we read of Heinrich's first impressions of Munich we are thrilled as the author was evidently thrilled by his first contact with the wealthy Catholic culture of South Germany, but later on we realize that Keller has not been as selective as he might have been; his account of the Munich artists' Carnival celebrations is allowed to run to seed, and even the most indulgent reader finds himself tempted to skip some pages. The fourth book is not as dull as the third, but is full of improbabilities. It is plain that in his anxiety to use to literary advantage as many elements as possible of his real life experience Keller has scarcely maintained a due sense of artistic proportion; the romantic fantasy of Heinrich's chance meeting with Dortchen, his introduction to Count Dietrich and his sojourn at the castle, Dortchen's love for him, his failure to respond, all strike us as far fetched and quite out of keeping with the earlier part of the book. Then at the very end we once more become reconciled to the work; the hero's reunion with Judith and his withdrawal to his modest civil service position seem to us a good and seemly ending.

Der grüne Heinrich is an untidy, sprawling work, measured by the neat, competent standards of today's novelists, but it is the honest record of a well-lived, full life, and has many beautiful pages. If not Keller's most accomplished work it is certainly his richest.

V

The Seldwyla stories (*Die Leute von Seldwyla*), begun while Keller
was working on *Der grüne Heinrich*, were published in two parts, in
1856 and 1874 respectively. They demonstrate convincingly that,
while Keller might still have a good deal to learn about the novelist's craft, he was capable of a high degree of *expertise* in the handling
of the *Novelle* form. The earlier set of five stories shows a somewhat
more indulgent attitude towards the shortcomings of his fellow
Swiss than the second series, which was the product of his late
maturity. Keller may be allowed to speak for himself in the famous
words of his introduction to Part I of the book:

> "Seldwyla bedeutet nach der älteren Sprache einen wonnigen
> und sonnigen Ort, und so ist auch in der Tat die kleine Stadt
> dieses Namens gelegen irgendwo in der Schweiz. Sie steht noch
> in den gleichen alten Ringmauern und Türmen wie vor drei-
> hundert Jahren und ist also immer das gleiche Nest; die ursprüng-
> liche tiefe Absicht dieser Anlage wird durch den Umstand
> verhärtet, dass die Gründer der Stadt dieselbe eine gute halbe
> Stunde von einem schiffbaren Flusse angepflanzt, zum deutli-
> chen Zeichen, dass nichts daraus werden solle." [3]

Although the town of Seldwyla serves as the background of
all the stories, most of them are concerned with exceptional people
who happen to have lived there. Thus the first story, *Pankraz der
Schmoller*, deals with a boy, Pankraz, who has close affinities with
Heinrich Lee. Pankraz conquers his serious fault of character and
manages to succeed brilliantly in his chosen military career; a
great disappointment in love and a painful encounter with a hungry
lion in the Arabian desert prove to be the means of grace that
enable him to master the negative elements in his own make-up.
Pankraz is really a *Bildungsroman* in miniature, and the reader is
left with the feeling that the theme called for more ample and
leisurely treatment. *Romeo und Julia auf dem Dorfe*, the most powerful
and affecting story in the collection, tells of the quarrel of two
originally good and moderately successful peasants, Manz and
Marti, and of its disastrous consequences for their children Sali
and Vrenchen. Finding it impossible to achieve the natural fulfilment of their love in marriage because of the dispute between their
families, Sali and Vrenchen spend a single gloriously happy day
together, make their nuptial bed on a hay barge and in the grey
light of dawn drop into the water and drown. The newspapers talk
prudishly of the degeneration of morals, but Sali and Vrenchen,
whose love is absolute and all-demanding, find it equally impossible

to separate for ever or to marry; their tragedy has an awful inevitability. Keller's wonderful descriptive powers and his mastery of colour and symbol are revealed in this story. *Frau Regel Amrain*, another offshoot of *Der grüne Heinrich*, is concerned with the education of Fritz Amrain, a young Seldwyler, by his mother, Frau Regula. Deserted while still a young woman by her improvident husband, Frau Regel makes it her main task in life to educate her youngest son to ideal citizenship. She steers him carefully past all the pitfalls of childhood and adolescence and last of all sends him to cast his vote when, as a grown man and husband, he is prepared to neglect his civic duty. No doubt this book is very improving, but the didactic intention is too obvious, and the British reader rebels at the idea of a young man remaining quite so closely tied to his mother's apron strings. *Die drei gerechten Kammacher*, one of the most entertaining stories of the collection, illustrates Keller's thesis that three just men could not live together under the same roof. The three combmakers are all men with a rather wooden idea of justice; essentially mean and grasping, they all hope to buy the same business and to marry the same woman. Keller's gift for caricature and his tendency towards the grotesque find free rein in the *Kammacher*. It was a story which was particularly dear to the author's heart, and he always tended to have a good opinion of people who thought well of this work. Like all the best comedy *Die drei gerechten Kammacher* has tragic overtones. The figure of Züs Bünzlin, that terrible woman whom all the combmakers wish to marry for her money, is a monument to the cautious bachelor's fear of the designing human female. *Spiegel das Kätzchen* is oddly out of place among the other mainly realistic stories, being a fairy-tale with talking animals, a magician, and a witch on a broomstick. It purports to explain the proverb: "Er hat der Katze den Schmer abgekauft," by telling the story of a little cat, Spiegel, who, hungry and neglected, sells himself to Pineiss the magician. The latter wishes to use his fat for nefarious purposes connected with his art. Spiegel contrives to thwart Pineiss and remain alive; the moral of the story is that we should not try to take advantage of the distress of our fellow-creatures. Spiegel, an entertaining fantasy, would certainly make an excellent children's story. The stories of Part II have a single theme in common, the need for a man to be himself, to forget sham and concentrate on living a full and good life within his natural and proper limits. In *Kleider machen Leute* the tailor Strapinsky causes confusion and trouble for himself and others because he has always romanticized himself and assumed clothes which do not befit his station; he does not mean to deceive the world, but when the world shows itself ready to take him for what he is not he makes no effort

to put things to rights. *Der Schmied seines Glückes* was a young man
who had so little self-respect that he was prepared to pretend to be
the illegitimate son of an eccentric, rich relative in return for being
made the old man's heir. All might have been well if John Kabys
had not been foolish enough to seduce the old man's wife. She
became pregnant, and John found that the husband did not take
kindly to the suggestion that someone else must have fathered his
wife's child. And so very soon John found himself disinherited; the
rest of the story tells how he had to resign himself to a modest career
as a maker of nails. *Die missbrauchten Liebesbriefe*, *Dietegen* and *Das
verlorene Lachen* all deal with the same theme of being true to oneself
and not poisoning life and confusing human relations by pretence.
The first of these contains some entertaining literary satire, the
second has a historical background and the last is a short novel of
contemporary life about a husband and wife who forsake their true
natures for trade and religion respectively, and are restored to one
another by natural affection; here again Keller allows Nature to
rectify the wrongs brought about by a perverted and unhealthy
culture. Compared with the first stories of the collection the later
five seem a little contrived and doctrinaire; Keller's powers of poetic
invention have become relatively restricted, but *Kleider machen Leute*
is a true work of art. *Dietegen* bears close affinities to *Ursula*, which
was based on the same source book, Melchior Schuler's *Taten und
Sitten der alten Eidgenossen* (1839), and *Das verlorene Lachen* anticipates
Martin Salander.

VI

In his *Sieben Legenden* (1871) Keller uses as his source some legends
of the saints as retold by Ludwig Theobul Kosegarten (1758–1818),
a Protestant Prussian minister, in a somewhat sentimental and
cloying manner. Kosegarten takes the point of view that the desires
of the flesh are bound to be sinful, and he sets great store by asceticism and self-denial, in this respect even outdoing his sources.
Keller's approach is very different. Although in most instances he
adheres fairly closely to the narrative frameworks of his originals he
alters the spirit of the Legends completely, and in fact, Keller's
legends are tributes to the good, natural life, which must be regu-
lated only by reason and common sense, not impoverished by a
damaging asceticism. This asceticism need not be religious in
origin; the heroine of the first story, a clever Alexandrian girl,
Eugenia, forces herself into an impossible situation through the
conceit of the bluestocking. By trying to make her admirer, the
Proconsul Aquilinus, meet her on her own terms she alienates his
affection; in her unhappiness she assumes men's clothes and takes
refuge in a monastery, becomes a monk and then even abbot; only

through pure chance is she rescued by Aquilinus from her false
situation and restored to her proper sex and surroundings as his
wife. Eugenia causes herself and Aquilinus great distress by her
attempt to deny her femininity in favour of an unnatural intellectualism, and she is fortunate in being falsely accused of pursuing
a lecherous widow who had taken a liking to the personable young
abbot. When Proconsul Aquilinus investigates the case and discovers who the abbot is, all is well. Aquilinus and Eugenia marry,
and he, too, becomes a Christian. *Die Jungfrau und der Teufel* shows
the Virgin Mary in the guise of protectress of her children. Count
Gebizo loved to make a parade of his generosity, so that he was
prepared to hand over his wife to the devil in return for money. The
Virgin changes places with the good and beautiful Bertrade, goes
with the devil, and when he is about to make love to her, assumes
her true form and puts him to flight. On the way home from handing
over Bertrade Gebizo falls down a cliff and perishes. The Virgin
now has to find Bertrade a new husband, and *Die Jungfrau als Ritter*
tells how she assumed the form of the diffident knight Zendelwald,
defeated all comers in the tournament, the winner of which was to
marry Bertrade and gracefully withdrew when the young man
arrived in time to claim the lovely prize the Virgin had won for
him. Zendelwald is one of Keller's delightfully modest self-portraits.
Die Jungfrau und die Nonne portrays the Virgin in her role of match-
maker and upholder of family life. Beatrix, a young nun, runs away
from her cloister, marries a handsome knight and has a family
of eight sons. In her absence the Virgin does her duty as sacristan
of the nunnery; when her children are grown up Beatrix returns and
finds that her absence has not been noticed. At a great festival
in the cloister each nun brings a gift to the Virgin. Beatrix, old
and worn out by child-bearing and rearing, cannot think what to
bring. Then, as the service begins, her husband appears with the
eight sons, who kneel before the altar. In symbol of their accept-
ability as offerings a garland of oak leaves appears on each young
head. Beatrix's natural desire to fulfil herself as a woman has
not been regarded in heaven as a fault; indeed she is honoured
above the other nuns by the Virgin. *Der schlimm-heilige Vitalis* tells
of St. Vitalis, who dedicates his life to the reclaiming of prostitutes.
An enterprising young woman manages to turn him from his career
of self-denial and unnatural well-doing and makes of him a model
husband. In *Dorotheas Blumenkörbchen* Keller describes the efforts
of a well-favoured girl to elicit a declaration of love from an amorous
but diffident and reluctant swain. Dorothea is a Christian, but
Theophilus, her lover, is not. They quarrel, and Fabricius, the
Roman governor, pursues her. When she will not yield to him,

Fabricius has her tried and put to death. From Dorothea an angel comes to Theophilus bearing a heavenly gift of fruit and flowers. He accepts the Christian faith, is put to death by Fabricius, and his soul is united with Dorothea's in heaven. The last paragraphs of this beautiful little legend describing the reunion of these two blessed souls have a Dante-like flavour. *Das Tanzlegendchen* tells of a maiden named Musa who loves dancing. One day King David appears to her in a vision and promises her heavenly joys if she will refrain from dancing on earth. This she agrees to do; she dies the death of a mediaeval saint on a bed of moss in her cell, and is received up into heaven where she immediately joins a dancing throng. In heaven the Nine Muses have been invited up from the underworld for a visit that day. Out of gratitude the Muses rehearse a chorale which they sing in heaven, but its tone is so nostalgic, it reawakens such tender memories of happy days on earth for many inhabitants of heaven that the Muses have to be brought to silence by a heavy peal of celestial thunder and sent back to hell. There is a division of interest in the *Tanzlegendchen* between the story of Musa and the fate of the Muses in heaven. The story is too slight to contain two main themes, and, despite one or two extremely well written paragraphs, it is the weakest of Keller's legends. Keller shows in his legends that for men and women on earth there is no more holy duty than that of living a good, wholesome and natural life. Any intellectual or religious exercise which is at variance with this first duty of mankind should be abandoned. Sometimes life is tragic, as in *Dorotheas Blumenkörbchen*; then it will be a comfort to have lived according to the best insights of our human nature.

VII

The *Züricher Novellen* (1878) are very different from *Die Leute von Seldwyla*. The earlier collection of stories was about imaginary people in an imaginary Swiss town. In the *Züricher Novellen* Keller is mainly concerned with historical figures in his native city. This makes these *Novellen* more credible than the earlier collection, but it also cramps the author's style occasionally. One is sometimes very aware of the trouble Keller took over his historical backgrounds. At least one of the stories, *Der Narr auf Manegg* concerns a person in a state of mind quite remote from ordinary experience; it is the weakest in the collection. *Ursula*, the last *Novelle*, though interesting as the document of a collective religious aberration, is not in Keller's best vein. Keller is again much preoccupied with the question of a good and wholesome development of the human personality. His characters fail or succceed in life according to whether they are true to themselves or not. A rather flimsy framework story lends

unity to the collection. A young Züricher, Herr Jacques, has harmless adolescent delusions of grandeur. He wants to be an original
genius, but his godfather, who cannot envisage him in such a role,
relates the five stories to show what constitutes genuine and spurious
originality.

Hadlaub, the son of a Swiss peasant living in mediaeval times,
was able by virtue of his exceptional gifts of intellect and imagination
to rise from his humble milieu to fame as a *Minnesänger* and win the
hand of a noble lady. He was originally commissioned by his aristocratic patron, Rüdiger Manesse, to compile a fine manuscript
collection of all examples he could find of the *Minnesang* before they
were lost. In the course of conscientiously performing this service
Hadlaub discovered his own poetic vein, and found a young lady
to adore. She was Fides, the illegitimate daughter of the Lady
Abbess of Zürich by the Bishop of Constance. Against the wishes
of her family and friends Fides returned Hadlaub's love, and in due
course they were married and set up house in Zürich, where their
family lived for many generations. Hadlaub had originally aspired
to do far less than he was capable of, unlike Herr Jacques, who had
imagined himself to be a far more wonderful person than he was.
Hadlaub, like Gottfried Keller, was a poet, but unlike his creator
Hadlaub found happiness and fulfilment in love. *Hadlaub*, a wish-
fulfilment story, is not unlike *Pankraz der Schmoller* in a late mediaeval
setting.

Der Narr auf Manegg warns Jacques of the dangers of trying to
seem to be what one is not. Buz Falätscher, an illegitimate descendant of the Manesses, is never content to accept the kind of work or
station in life to which he is suited by birth and ability. The *Novelle*,
a very slight one, tells how, preoccupied with grandiose and fruitless
schemes, he loses one opportunity after another in life of making
good in a humble way, and finally becomes mad and perishes
miserably. He goes to live in Burg Manegg, the half-ruined ancestral
castle of the Manesses and sets himself up as a *Minnesänger* with the
aid of the Manesse *Liederhandschrift* which he has managed to steal.
The theft is discovered, and Buz dies of fright when a crowd of
young patricians and noblemen march on the castle and demand
the surrender of the manuscript. He has paid the penalty for having
pretended to be what he was not.

Der Landvogt von Greifensee concerns a genuine original, Salomon
Landolt, who lived in and around Zürich in the late eighteenth
century. Keller closely follows a biography by David Hess of the
famous *Landvogt*. But Keller's hero is also in various respects a
reflection of his creator. Landolt, magistrate of Greifensee, lives
by the lake of that name in an ancient castle, waited upon by an

old dragon of a housekeeper. An amateur painter and musician, a confirmed bachelor, a man of taste and good judgment, he is well able to administer justice even in matrimonial disputes. Once he invites to his castle all the five women whom he had loved, and spends a happy day surveying these gracious ladies, who had all for various reasons rejected him. The work is a most effective justification of the bachelor form of existence. What Salomon Landolt once regarded as a bitter cross to bear he now recognizes as a blessing. This work contains a wealth of unobtrusively introduced local colour, for Keller was well versed in the history of eighteenth-century Zürich and was learned in its literature. The ladies whom Landholt had loved are all depicted as having more or less recognizable characteristics of Keller's own loves; Hess says little about this aspect of Landolt's life, so that Keller was able to improvise freely and credibly from his own experience. *Der Landvogt* stands out as the most artistically satisfying of the *Züricher Novellen*.

In *Das Fähnlein der sieben Aufrechten* the Seven are elderly tradesment of strong democratic convictions who have for years regularly met round a *Stammtisch*. They decide to march together to the Federal Marksmen's Competition with a banner they have had made and present a prize for the best marksman. A certain coolness has arisen between two of their number because the son of the poor tailor Hediger wishes to marry the daughter of the rich joiner, Frymann. On the day of the contest none of the Seven is prepared to speak in public for the group when they hand over their trophy to the chairman of the competition. Karl Hediger appears at the crucial moment, takes over this task and makes an effective little speech about his country's free institutions and the principles for which the old men have always stood. Karl's words reflect Keller's satisfaction with the constitutional improvements achieved in Switzerland in 1848. Then Karl goes off, and with Frymann's daughter aiding and abetting him wins high credit in the shooting competition. The Seven unanimously agree that the young couple should be allowed to marry. If we think of the *Eidgenössisches Schützenfest* as an event comparable in Switzerland to a Test Match in this country we may be able to summon up some sympathy for this frankly didactic little work.

Ursula, a story of the Reformation wars, tells how Hans Gyr, a peasant farmer, returns to his native Bachtelberg to find the populace there in the grip of sectarian delusions. His fiancée Ursula, is also affected by the false beliefs proclaimed by the *Winkelpropheten*, and he leaves the region again for the wars, intending to marry Ursula if and when she recovers her sanity. Hansli's wanderings and his eventual reunion with Ursula are interesting from the historical point of view, with accurate descriptions of the prevailing religious moods of that age and district, but the spectacular and sudden cure of Ursula's mental abberrations is hard to swallow.

VIII

Das Sinngedicht, first conceived in the 1850s, was not completed till 1883. The epigram in question was Friedrich von Logau's:

"Wie willst du weisse Lilien zu roten Rosen machen?
Küss eine weisse Galatee; sie wird errötend lachen." (4)

Reinhart, a young scientist, having strained his eyesight by overwork, goes out in search of a wife by way of relaxation. Following Logau's advice he seeks a girl who will both blush and laugh when he kisses her; after a few casual encounters he decides that his quest will not be easy. But then he comes across Lucia, the very person (the name is symbolical) who is calculated to bring sweetness and light into the life of a man who has become involved in scientific experiments to the exclusion of human interests.

Lucia is amiable and intelligent, rich, beautiful and extremely independent in outlook. Reinhart, having reached her country house late in the day, has to stay the night there, and the couple, along with Lucia's aged uncle, tell one another stories to pass the time. All the stories are concerned with love and marriage, relationships between the sexes and what factors can disturb or completely destroy a marriage.

Lucia begins with the story of Salome, a handsome inn-keeper's daughter whom Reinhart had just met on the way to her house. Salome had become engaged to a young townsman of good family, but, lacking a common background and having no shared interests at all to lend content to their relationship, they had become thoroughly bored with one another and quarrelled violently. That was the end of Salome's hopes of marriage.

Reinhart instances *Regine* in support of his contention that differing social backgrounds need not constitute an absolute bar to happiness in marriage. A rich young American of German descent goes to Germany in search of a wife. Having tried in vain to find one among young women of his own class, he finally marries Regine, a beautiful servant girl. By native intelligence, tact and adaptability Regine is well qualified to fulfil her new role with distinction, but foolish pride on Erwin's part prevents him from taking home his bride to Boston until she has lived longer in good society. Regine, left to her own devices while her husband returns to America, makes one or two comparatively harmless social mistakes, has some troubles with her own family, and, when Erwin after many months takes her

to Boston, feels thoroughly insecure and miserable. Through a series
of misunderstandings Erwin has lost confidence in Regine and she
takes her own life. This tragedy is not due to her inability to make
him a good wife, but to his failure to show confidence in her and
provide her with sufficient moral support.

Die arme Baronin, also related by Reinhart, has a happier outcome.
Hedwig von Hohenhausen has had a hard life and is forced to let
rooms for a living after the collapse of her marriage and the loss of
her child. Soured by her misfortunes, she has the reputation of a
throughly unpleasant woman. Her lodger, Brandolf, brings affection
and material prosperity back into her life and restores the foundation
of wellbeing and happiness. Her character now improves out of all
recognition. When she and Brandolf marry we are confident that
theirs will be a sound and happy marriage. One element in this
Novelle jars somewhat, namely Brandolf's revenge on Hedwig's
rascally husband and brothers; in this incident Keller gives free
rein to his love of grotesque fantasies, and we feel that it is in poor
taste.

Lucia's uncle, who now joins in the conversation, contributes
Die Geisterseher, an improbable story of a young woman, who, being
unable to choose between two admirers, decided to test their
courage by staging a mock haunting of their bedrooms. The man
whose rational faculties remained unimpaired married her; he
was Reinhart's father; the unsuccessful suitor was Lucia's uncle.
The point made is this: A man worth his salt will not easily allow
himself to be intimidated into forsaking the use of his reason.

Reinhart's long tale of *Don Correa* falls into two sections. The first
tells of Admiral Don Correa's first marriage to a rich Portuguese
noblewoman; he does not reveal his identity to her, and she takes
him for a person of no consequence. As long as he complies with
her wishes they get on very well, but as soon as he develops a mind
of his own she is angry with him. Don Correa finds himself in the end
presiding over the trial and execution of his own wife, because
Donna Feniza in her pride of birth and wealth has assumed that a
husband ought to be merely an accommodating chattel. Don
Correa's second marriage reminds us of the story of Regine. In
perfect humility and docility Zambo-Maria leans on her rescuer,
educator and protector; in return he saves her from servitude
and savagery and makes of her a free human personality. The closing
scene of this *Novelle* is very impressive. Reinhart is clearly anxious
to establish the superiority of the male in matters of marriage, but
his Don Correa takes a rather broad view of a husband's liberty
by modern standards.

Lucia is stung into rebellion by the masculine view of the matrimonial estate expressed in *Don Correa* and relates *Die Berlocken,* in which an unscrupulous young Frenchman is firmly put in his place by a pretty Red Indian girl. M. de Vallormes had collected a series of trinkets for his watch-chain from ladies young and old whose affection he had managed to win, generally by thoroughly unethical means. Arriving in North America with Lafayette's army he fell sufficiently in love with the attractive Quoneschi to give her his trinkets, imagining that by doing so he had won her heart. Alas, she passed them to her Indian lover and quickly disappeared. De Vallormes, who had behaved in exactly the same way towards many women as Quoneschi towards him was more than a little taken aback to discover what it must have felt like to be one of his victims.

The last chapter of *Das Sinngedicht* is taken up with the story of Lucia's and Reinhart's reconciliation and rapprochement in idyllic country surroundings while the shoemaker sings Goethe's *Mit einem gemalten Bande* wih great feeling. At the climax of the song the lovers kiss and Reinhart observes that Lucia is blushing and laughing all at once. And so she has fulfilled the condition laid down in Logau's epigram.

This summary gives little impression of the ripe wisdom and practised art of *Das Sinngedicht.* A little artificial the work certainly is, with its elaborately stylized setting and the constantly recurring symbolism of the epigram, but it has a charm and polish all of its own. In this work Keller shows himself to be not merely a profound writer, but also extremely accomplished. *Das Sinngedicht* is the greatest work of Keller's old age, as *Der grüne Heinrich* is the greatest work of his youth.

IX

Martin Salander is a noble failure. Influenced by the later realists and not unaffected by the rising Naturalist school, Keller tried to write a book which would take into account the changing literary climate of the age. Alas, his genius was by now drying up, largely because his life had become arid and disappointing. His sister, Regula, was dying, his own health was failing, he disliked the flat to which they had just moved, and all these miseries of old age are reflected in the book. It concerns a typical Swiss citizen of the *Gründerzeit.* Martin Salander goes to Brazil to make money and returns home. There he loses all and has to go abroad again. He once more makes his fortune and comes home. His daughters make very unsatisfactory marriages with Julian and Isidor Weidelich, the twin sons of an ambitious washerwoman. It comes almost as a relief to Salander and his wife when both Julian and Isidor are convicted of embezzlement and sentenced to long periods in prison. It then becomes possible to dissolve the two girls' marriages. Martin

Salander himself is not a very satisfactory figure for the hero of a novel. With his naive trust in human nature which causes him twice over to entrust his money to the rascally Wohlwend, his susceptible heart, which very nearly causes him to make a fool of himself with Wohlwend's beautiful but stupid sister-in-law, and his excessive faith in democratic politics, he is a strangely unimpressive successor to Keller's earlier heroes. His son Arnold, at one time intended as the principal character of a second volume, is too priggish and clear-sighted to be altogether agreeable. The novel represents an unsuccessful attempt by an ageing writer to come to terms with the new literary idiom introduced by the Naturalists.

X

Gottfried Keller's *oeuvre* is the most distinguished that has emerged from German Switzerland. Although not a very prolific writer he had a lively artistic conscience, and even when, as often, he badly needed money, he always observed the highest standards of which he was aware. As a result all his work bears the unmistakable imprint of genius, though it is not, as we have seen, of altogether even quality. In spite of its weaknesses *Der grüne Heinrich* will always be regarded as a very great *Bildungsroman*, and in particular as one that shows a true appreciation of the difficulties of the child and adolescent. Each of his cycles of short stories has its own peculiar merits, and taken together they represent a valuable contribution to German and European literature. Keller was never content to relapse into a cosy and comfortable Swiss-ness; his work compares very favourably with anything that was being produced in Germany in his generation.

TRANSLATIONS

1. Here I feel a connection
   With the One and All.
2. The coarsest and most trivial art in the world to pull the shifts off over the heads of the female characters."
3. Seldwyla means according to the older language a delightful and sunny place, and indeed the little town of this name, which is situated somewhere in Switzerland, is just that. It is still confined within the same old town walls and towers as it was 300 years ago, and so it is still the same old hole; the original deep purpose of this siting is confirmed by the circumstance that the founders of the town stuck it a good half hour's journey from the nearest navigable river, as a manifest sign that nothing would ever become of it.
4. How will you make white lilies into red roses?
   Kiss a white Galatea; she will blushingly laugh.

BIBLIOGRAPHY

The standard edition of Keller's works is:
Sämtliche Werke, edited by Julius Fränkel and Carl Helbling, 24 vols.
Berne, 1926–54.
The standard edition of the letters is:
Gesammelte Briefe in 4 Bänden, ed. Carl Helbling. Zurich, 1954.
The following collections of letters have been published separately:
Storm-Keller Briefwechsel, ed. A. Köster. Berlin, 1904.
Keller-Heyse Briefwechsel, ed. Max Kalbeck. Berlin, 1919.
At present available in English translation are:
Green Henry, translated by A. M. Holt. John Calder, London, 1960.
A Village Romeo and Juliet, translated by P. B. Thomas. 1955.

WORKS ABOUT KELLER

ACKERKNECHT, E. *Gottfried Kellers Leben, Berlin,* 1939 (a very full biography, not including the works).

ERMATINGER, E. *Gottfried Kellers Leben.* Zürich, 1950 (The standard critical biography).

ROWLEY, B. A. *Keller: Kleider machen Leute* (an interpretation). E. Arnold, London, 1959.

SCHAFFNER, PAUL. *Gottfried Keller als Maler.* Zürich, Atlantis, 1942.

See also the relevant sections of:

BENNETT, E. K. *The German Novelle.* Cambridge, 1960.

PASCAL, R. *The German Novel.* Manchester, 1956.

Conrad Ferdinand Meyer

Conrad Ferdinand Meyer

by w. e. yuill

IT would be difficult to imagine men more different in character, upbringing, taste and even appearance than the two celebrities who, as Meyer put it, occupied opposite ends of the literary see-saw in Zürich between 1870 and 1890. On one end perched Keller—a small, pugnacious figure, Bohemian in his habits, a Swiss patriot to the backbone; on the other end sat Meyer—large, lymphatic, neurotically reserved and punctilious, a convinced cosmopolitan. Little wonder that they disliked each other, that Keller complained of the other's "unnötiges Wesen und Sich-mausig-machen," [1] while Meyer accused Keller of rudeness and lack of "Bildung." The relations between them were tenuously sustained by Meyer out of a sense of propriety which even prompted him to visit Keller on his death-bed. One thing, it is true, they might seem to have in common with each other (and with the other great Swiss writer of the nineteenth century, Jeremias Gotthelf): the long struggle to realize their poetic vocation. Even here, however, there was a significant difference. Keller struggled against the handicap of poverty—and an obstinate misapplication of his talents; Meyer spent nearly the first forty years of his life in overcoming a paralysis of the creative faculty. His were obstacles invisible to the onlooker: nothing could have seemed more propitious than the circumstances of his youth in a respected patrician family, nothing more natural than that he should continue a tradition of public service. Instead, his youth and early manhood were passed in a twilight dream:

> "Ich war von einem schweren Bann gebunden,
> Ich lebte nicht. Ich lag im Traum erstarrt." [2]

This was Meyer's later view of a youth spent in neurotic seclusion, so complete at one point that he was rumoured to have died. Amongst a people devoted to ideals of hard work, efficiency and success he lived a life tortured by a sense of inadequacy, tormented by vague ambitions. The early death of his father left him too much under the influence of his mother, a woman of somewhat morbid religiosity, given to referring to her son as "poor Conrad" and to praying for his salvation. While Keller took an active part in the hectic political events of the 1840's, Meyer was absorbing himself in lonely pursuits—fencing, rowing, walking in the mountains—and feeding his brooding melancholy on the Romantic works of Tieck, Lenau, Novalis and Victor Hugo. By the age of twenty-seven he had so lost contact with the outside world that he was sent to the mental hospital of Préfargier. To a similar refuge he was forced to return some forty years later. Between these withdrawals from the world Meyer built for himself a personality of precarious equilibrium and a series of brilliantly executed works of literature.

This emancipation was, however, relatively slow. His removal from the oppressive atmosphere of Zürich to French Switzerland and the consequent necessity of absorbing himself in another language was undoubtedly a first step. After a short stay in Préfargier Meyer went to Lausanne, where he was taken in hand by a friend of the family, Louis Vulliemin. Meyer remained grateful throughout his life for the benevolent influence of this man, to whose nobility of mind he has paid a tribute in the figure of Rohan in *Jürg Jenatsch*. Not only did Vulliemin discipline Meyer's literary ambitions by making him apply himself to translation from French, he also introduced him to the study of history, which was to become the indispensable element of this writer's art. By doing this he opened up for Meyer, who was incapable of effective action in the world around him, a world of the imagination in which he was given the possibility of creating a substitute for real experience. The other essential feature of Meyer's art, linguistic virtuosity, came to him in the long labour of translating Augustin Thierry's *Récits des Tempts Mérovingiens*.

In 1856 Elisabeth Meyer committed suicide after her growing melancholy had led her to the same asylum which four years previously had received her son. In a sense her death represented a further stage in the liberation of the latter from the inhibitions of his youth. The freedom which the breaking of this bond entailed was further augmented by the inheritance of a modest fortune which enabled Conrad to travel to Paris and then, with his sister Betsy, to Italy. It was on these journeys that his eyes were opened to the contrast between the Latin and the Germanic cultures that forms such a frequent theme in his work. The contact with the Latin mode of life and the experience of Classical and Italian art seem to have turned his mind from a preoccupation with ethical matters and given the final impetus to his emergence as a poet: by 1860 he had compiled a collection of ballads, and although it was not published until 1864, his new life had begun.

This emergence from the dark cell of the mind, the change from an ascetic to an aesthetic attitude, from contemplation to the release of energy is reflected and magnified in Meyer's work. He sees an image of his experience in the growth of bright new foliage over the old:

> "Eppich, mein alter Hausgesell,
> Du bist von jungen Blättern hell,
> Dein Wintergrün, so still and streng,
> Verträgt sich's mit dem Lenzgedräng?
>
> 'Warum denn nicht? Wie meines hat
> Dein Leben alt und junges Blatt,
> Eins streng und dunkel, eines licht
> Von Lenz und Luft! Warum denn nicht?' " [3]

In the notion of the flight from the cloister this experience occupies a very prominent place in his works. The identification of the cloister with moribund states of mind and the association of religion with the sufferings of his youth are no doubt the psychological basis of the anti-clericalism, and particularly the anti-Catholicism, that are for long a feature of his stories. The hero of one of Meyer's earliest works, the Reformer, Ulrich von Hutten, is inspired by Luther's escape from the cloister:

> "Ein sächsisch Mönchlein aus der Kutte schloff.
> Da, Ritter, habt Ihr einen guten Stoff!" [4]

The verse epic, *Engelberg*, revolves round this theme, as do the unfinished stories, *Clara* and *Die sanfte Klosteraufhebung*; Jürg Jenatsch exchanges the sword of the spirit for that of the soldier; Hans, the narrator in *Der Heilige* is a runaway monk; *Die Hochzeit des Mönchs* contains, either in the "framework" or in the main story, no less than four such figures: Manuccio, Helene Manente, Astorre and Brother Serapion. The conflict of clerical and worldly values is perhaps clearest of all in *Plautus im Nonnenkloster*. Yet the opposition here is not between the cloister and the court, but between the cloister and the hearth. Poggio Bracciolini, with his "feine Lüge" and his blasphemous identification of Pallas Athene and the Virgin Mary, is not the true hero of the story. He, no less than Brigitte, is a type of clerical degeneracy:

> "Die Verweltlichung des hohen Klerus . . . der wahre Typus des Humanisten: Geist, Leichtsinn, Nachäffung und übertriebene Schätzung der Antike, Unwahrheit, Rachsucht. . . , Diebstahl und Bettelei." [5]

Meyer, who was often enough criticized by his pious countrymen as a mere "artist" and hence as immoral, is concerned that his views should not be identified with those of Poggio:

" . . . au fond et malgré la gaité du récit je méprise cet humaniste, ce Poggio qui voit dans son fils devenu brigand ou peu s'en faut, sa facilité de vivre dégénérer en crime et ignominie.' Ce n'est pas pour rien que j'ai mis cela au commencement de mon récit."

It is not the sophisticated paganism of the Renaissance humanist that Meyer sets against the superstition and fanaticism of the Church but the simple philosophy of Gertrude. She may stand for a pagan way of life, but it is an earthy paganism with its own roots: "Was mir taugt," she cries, "ist Sonne und Wolke, Sichel und Sense, Mann und Kind . . ." [6] This is the same affirmation of the idyllic life to which Meyer gives expression in such poems as *Veltliner Traube*, *Der Hengert* and *Bacchus in Bünden*—although, as in the last example, he often uses the figures of Classical mythology to express the thought.

In *Der Heilige* the change is from the worldly life to the life of asceticism. But in interpreting Becket's development from the man of the world to a saintly figure Meyer is simply substituting irony for direct attack. Becket's piety is the subtlest of attacks on the King, as Bertram de Born points out in the story:

"Du stiller, langsam grabender Mann, du duldest wie dein Meister, und lässest dich töten wie er. Du glaubst der Liebe zu dienen, aber der Haß ist der mächtigere, und dein Tod, wie der deines Gottes, ist die Verdammnis der Menschen." [7]

This is clear, too, from Meyer's comment on his hero:

"Dieser—eine geistig überlegene, fast modern humane, aber der Roheit des Mittelalters gegenüber wehrlose Natur—bedient sich ohne gläubig zu sein—die Legende und der Dichter geben ihm orientalisches Blut—der Kirche als einer Waffe." [8]

For all that he glorifies energy and vitality in so many of his works, Meyer is haunted by the spectre of death. He spoke to Keller of "the insecurity of life," and was well aware of a fundamental difference in outlook between himself and the author of such stories as *Kleider machen Leute* and *Spiegel, das Kätzchen*:

"Keller hat der Menge gegenüber vor mir den Vorteil, daß er im Grunde Optimist ist. Daher ist er für die Menge. Denn so sind die Leute: sie drängen sich um den Brunnen des Lebens und sind froh, wenn sie mit ihrem Becherchen wenigstens ein Tröpflein auffangen. Die finden nun ihre Rechnung bei Keller, der alles gut enden läßt. Er kennt keine tragischen Ausgänge. Das ist ein Mangel, denn der Reiz des Daseins vollendet sich erst in beiden." [9]

Meyer's fault, if it is indeed one, lies in the opposite extreme—he rarely achieves a happy ending. His taste was for the tragic and he shows very few signs of a sense of humour: "Mir individuell hinterläßt das Komische einen bittern Geschmack," he writes, "während das Tragische mich erhebt und beseligt." [10] Keller, himself by no means always free from a subtle form of sadism, thought this quality pre-eminent in his compatriot's work:

> "Meyer hat eine Schwäche für solche einzelnen Brutalitäten und Totschläge. Wenn er so was hört oder liest, so sagt er: Vortrefflich! So hat jeder seinen Zopf." [11]

For Meyer death frequently represents the dramatic climax of life, the crown of passion fulfilled: Jenatsch is struck down by Lucrezia at the feast which celebrates his triumph: Astorre, plunged into life like a glowing splinter into a stream of oxygen is consumed in a blaze of passion, united with his lover in death; "Komme, Tod, und raub mich, Tod, im Kusse!" [12] cries a girl at her lover's breast (*Der Kamerad*); the harvesters toil beneath the threatening storm and

> "Von Garbe zu Garbe
> Ist Raum für den Tod;" [13]

the victor in a duel, although his life is forfeit, revels in his triumph:

> "Ich besitze den Kranz und verdiene den Tod."
> (*Der Ritt in den Tod*.) [14]

Leubelfing, Gustav Adolf's page, chooses the motto "Courte et bonne" and longs for the hour of glorious life that culminates in death:

> "Ich wünsche mir alle Strahlen meines Lebens in ein Flammenbündel und in den Raum einer Stunde vereinigt, daß statt einer blöden Dämmerung ein kurzes, aber blendendes helles Licht von Glück entstünde, um dann zu löschen wie ein zuckender Blitz." [15]

The flash of lightning invoked here frequently has symbolic value in Meyer's work as the mark of a climax.

For Keller, Meyer was no doubt an inhabitant of that grisly borough of Ruechenstein, with its garland of gallows and execution blocks. In only one of his stories does he appear to breathe the more congenial air of Seldwyla. Mythikon, an imaginary village on the Lake of Zürich, is indeed "ein wonniger, sonniger Ort." The whole story is suffused with a warm, Southern light:

> "Eine warme Föhnluft hatte die Schneeberge und den Schweizersee auf ihre Weise idealisiert, die Reihe der einen zu einem

einzigen stillen, großen Leuchten verbunden, den andern mit
dem tiefen und kräftigen Farbenglanz einer südlichen Meerbucht
übergossen, als gelüste sie eine bacchische Landschaft, ein Stück
Italien, über die Alpen zu versetzen." [16]

It is perhaps significant that this story was written not long after the
poet's marriage, at the age of fifty, to Luise Ziegler. At last he seemed
to have achieved full maturity. Although the story is set in the seventeenth century, it is more closely linked, through its location and
through the relationship between Pfannenstiel and Rahel, with the
circumstances of Meyer's personal life than any other of his prose
works. The story illustrates the development in its shy hero of a
comfortable sensuality; its message is not that of death in ecstasy
or in triumph, but Keller's message of reconciliation with one's lot.
Rahel reproves Pfannenstiel for his desperate plan to become
chaplain to a regiment stationed in the Balkan wilds:

"Ihr wolltet aus Eurer eigenen Natur heraus, und er hat
Euch heimgespottet . . . Warum auch? Wie Ihr seid, und gerade
wie Ihr seid, gefallt Ihr mir am besten." [17]

Meyer was aware of this rare affinity with Keller and feared that
he might be thought a mere imitator of the *Züricher Novellen*:

" . . . die Vortrefflichkeit von Keller's Züricher Novellen (wird)
mich sicher in Schatten stellen und vielleicht gar ungerechter-
weise als Nachahmer erscheinen lassen." [18]

In spite of the comic dénouement, however, in spite of the cheerfulness and the mild irony at the expense of the narrow-minded
clergy and parishioners, there is a shadow on the sunlit landscape
of the story—the shadow of Jürg Jenatsch, for, as Meyer pointed out,
the story is, through the figure of Wertmüller, a continuation of the
novel. Even here there is an element of the morbid: Wertmüller's
dream of Jenatsch and himself as both dead. And Wertmüller
himself is a problematic figure, a forerunner, in his scepticism and his
traffic with the exotic, of Becket and of the figure who haunted
Meyer's mind without ever emerging on the scale which the poet
wished—the Hohenstaufen emperor, Frederick II. It is in such
figures, rather than in Pfannenstiel, that Meyer expressed his inner
nature. "Im *Jenatsch* und im *Heiligen* . . . ist in den verschiedensten
Verkleidungen weit mehr von mir, meinen wahren Leiden und
Leidenschaften als in dieser Lyrik," [19] he wrote to Louise von
François. Into such men of destiny he projected a taste for power
which he could never indulge in reality. There are many variations
on the theme of the leader—Jenatsch, the ruthless; Rohan and

Gustav Adolf, the saintly; Becket the subtle; Stemma, the sinful; Pescara, the loyal. Of these perhaps Becket is closest to Meyer's heart and exerts the most compulsive power over his imagination:

"Ich habe den Heiligen fast unbewußt, besessen, im Rausch geschrieben, weil ich ihn los werden mußte, er lag mir quälend auf der Brust wie ein Alp." [20]

Becket has the fastidiousness, the suavity, the subtle sense of superiority along with a certain lack of manliness that were characteristic of his creator. "Eines aber . . . mangelte dem Kanzler: das Ungestüm und die Schärfe eines männlichen Blutes." [21] There is something here of the poet described by Adolf Frey:

"Leidenschaftslosigkeit war ein Grundzug seines Wesens. Ich sah ihn niemals zornig und vermochte mir ihn auch nur schwer so zu denken." [22]

The analysis of motive in the enigmatic situations and figures of history and the infusion of his own modes of feeling into these figures constitute the most remarkable features of Meyer's use of historical material He looks upon himself not as a rival to the historian but as his coadjutor; his aim, as he describes it in an unpublished story, is to represent the psychological processes which gleam like fish through the wide meshes of the historian's net. By and large, Meyer realizes this aim without giving too much offence to the historian's conscience and justifies his claim: "Ich behandle die Geschichte souverän aber nicht ungetreu." [23] If anything, his stories are too richly embroidered with cultural reference, there are traces of "Möbellust," an antiquarian relish, in his recreation of the past. Occasionally, too, he is guilty of falsifying the spirit of an age—in *Das Leiden eines Knaben*, for instance, there is evidence both of an informality and a middle-class sentimentality that were hardly characteristic of the court of Louis XIV.

The interest in historical themes was, as we have seen, first dictated by objective considerations; it was in any case something which lay in the air. Meyer lived in an age of great historians— Mommsen, Ranke, Gregorovius, Burckhardt—an age when antiquarian interest was strong. The pervasion of this interest with his own feeling was not something that was given him straight away. His early ballads have the stiffness of historical vignettes. It is only gradually that he came to realize both the relevance of the past to contemporary political events that inspires *Huttens letzte Tage* and the advantages of historical themes as a mask for his own views and feelings. This function of the historical narrative he clearly states in a letter to his friend Felix Bovet, written in January 1888:

"Je me sers de la forme de la nouvelle historique purement et simplement pour y loger mes expériences et sentiments personnels, la préférant au 'Zeitroman' parce qu'elle me masque mieux et qu'elle distance davantage le lecteur. Ainsi sous une forme très objective et éminemment artistique, je suis au dedans tout individuel et subjectif."

It is this alienation, to use a current term, which prompts Louise von François to describe Meyer as a "Telescopisten," as compared with Keller, whom she calls "einen Microscopisten der Gegenwart." The "très objective et éminemment artistique, je suis au dedans tout" use of a theatrical term is not inappropriate, because Meyer, who long toyed with the notion of writing dramas, tends to look upon history as a stage. Of many of his works it might be said, as of the sermon heard by Gustav Adolf, that they "compare life with a stage, with men as the actors, the angels for an audience and death as the producer who rings down the curtain."

But even the historical remoteness of the theme is not sufficient protection for the author: in many of his stories Meyer strives to dissociate himself from his work through the technique of the narrative. The use of the "framework" is characteristic:

"Die Neigung zum Rahmen dann ist bei mir ganz instinktiv. Ich halte mir den Gegenstand gerne vom Leibe oder richtiger gerne so weit als möglich vom Auge, und dann will mir scheinen, das Indirekte der Erzählung (und selbst die Unterbrechungen) mildern die Härte der Fabel." [24]

This device, clumsily used in *Das Amulett*, reaches a climax of refinement in *Die Hochzeit des Mönchs*. Altogether, this is a bravura piece, a self-conscious work of art. For once the story is presented, not as an account of authentic events experienced by the speaker, but as a piece of invention by the master, Dante. "Es schien mir," wrote Meyer to his sister, "Dante müsse erfinden, nicht erzählen." [25] The narrator weaves the characters and the relationships of his listeners into the story, selects and constructs with deliberate artistry: "Seine Fabel lag in ausgeschütteter Fülle vor ihm; aber sein strenger Geist wählte und vereinfachte." [26] The author indulges in a degree of elaboration here which subsequently seemed excessive even to him:

"Hier freilich wird der Verschlingung von Fabel und Zuhörer zu viel; die Sache wird entschieden mühsam. Ein non plus ultra! M'en voila guéri!" [27]

And cured he was, for this is the last of the stories in which the technique of the "Rahmen" is used.

Die Hochzeit des Mönchs demonstrates admirably not only Meyer's objectivity as a writer, but also the plasticity of his style. These were qualities first learned through the writings of F. Th. Vischer and confirmed by what Meyer saw in France and Italy, qualities which are summed up for him in the notion of "gesture":

"Kurz, was ich vom Romanischen bekommen habe, ist der Sinn für die Gebärde, Geste. Es ist mir nicht zu entbehrendes Bedürfnis geworden, alles nach außen hin schaubar, sichtbar zu gestalten, auch in der Sprache." (28)

In this Meyer consciously turned away from the traditional attributes of German poetry: its capacity for reflection, its musical quality and its power to evoke atmosphere. He once remarked to Hermann Friedrichs:

"Ja, wissen Sie, . . . ein paar stimmungsvolle Verse bringt schließlich jeder Backfisch zu Stande, der Heine, Geibel, Ritterhaus . . . verschlungen hat; aber in balladenartiger Form, ich möchte sagen, plastisch greifbare Gestalten hervorzuzaubern und sie handelnd auftreten zu lassen, das ist eine Kunst, die nur verschwindend Wenigen gegeben ist." (29)

On another occasion he criticized the lack of visual sharpness in most German writers:

"In der deutschen Literatur empfinde ich einen Mangel: das ist nicht scharf genug gesehen, nicht sinnlich herausgestellt, es ist unbildlich verschwimmend. Die Gleichnisse und Bilder im Deutschen sind schwach, sie erhellen und beleuchten nicht. Dagegen die Ariosts sind immer, wenn auch übertrieben grotesk, so doch scharf gesehen, erleuchtend . . ." (30)

This sharpness of definition is evident in almost every aspect of Meyer's work—in the rapid, unreflective narrative of his early stories (which owe a good deal to Mérimée), in the concise similes: "So redete Victoria aufwallend und überquellend wie ein römischer Brunnen"; "Das Spiel seiner Natur war ehrlich wie ein Stoß im Hifthorn und überquoll wie der Schaum am Gebiß eines jungen Renners." (31) Contrasts of faith, outlook, national idiosyncrasy or destiny are embodied in figures placed in dramatic opposition: Schadau and Boccard, the grave Calvinist with his belief in Predestination and the gay, superstitious Catholic; Jenatsch and Rohan, the unscrupulous Gewaltmensch and the gentle Gewissensmensch; Becket and Henry II, the fastidious intellectual and the gross sensualist; Lucrezia and Angela Borgia, as Meyer said, "zu wenig und zu viel Gewissen." And across the span of the poet's work as a whole something of the same contrasts: Jenatsch pursuing unrepentant a career of crime and apostasy, Stemma succumbing to the perennial pressure of conscience and judging herself as she had judged so many others; Becket avenging himself ironically through his death for the injury done him by his sovereign, Pescara refusing in the presence of death, to avenge a like injury. The increasing prominence of conscientious scruples in such contrasts represents a significant development in Meyer's attitude.

This striving for the concrete, for the visual effect permeates the texture of the works. Thought and feeling are expressed in gesture: Otto von Gemmingen sketches Hutten's fate in a graphic sign (*Die Gebärde*); the Emperor Otto pardons his brother with a gesture (*Der gleitende Purpur*); Jenatsch utters not a word of grief at the murder of his wife, he is *seen* as "dieses Nachtbild sprachlosen Grimms und unversöhnlicher Trauer." [32] Events and relationships are epitomized in objects or gesture: "Drei Hindernisse erschwerten eine Brautfahrt: die hohen und oft finstern Brauen Dianas, die geschlossene Hand ihres Vaters und die blinde Anhänglichkeit ihres Bruders Germanos an den Tyrannen" [33]; ". . . die weggeschleuderte Kutte des Mönchs . . . die vereinigten Hände Dianas und Astorres." [34] Posture can be the clue to the soul: "Ich sehe, wie er sitzt und sinnt," says Michelangelo of Julianus Medici, "und kenne seine Seele" [35] (*Il Pensieroso*)

The affinity of Meyer's descriptions with painting and sculpture is clear: his masters are Titian and Michelangelo. Everywhere he reveals a love of the sumptuous and the statuesque—and nowhere more than in those scenes where the actors are frozen by death or grief: Lucrezia posed with the body of Jenatsch beneath the figure of Justice, Becket prostrate by the body of his daughter:

"Ich schaute in das Halbdunkel der Burgkapelle. Aber da war kein Kruzifix und kein ewiges Licht und statt eines heiligen Leichnams unter dem Altare lag in einem Schrein vor demselben, ebenso reich geschmückt, die tote Gnade. Ein Lichtstrom, der durch das einzige, hochgelegene Fenster sich ergoß, beleuchtete ihre überirdische Schönheit. Ihr Haupt ruhte auf einem Purpurkissen und trug ein Krönchen von blitzendem Edelgestein. Der zarte Körper verschwand in den von Goldstickerei und Perlen starrenden Falten ihres über die Wände des Schreins ausgebreiteten Gewandes. Die kleinen durchsichtigen Hände lagen auf der Brust gekreuzt und hielten keusch den schwarzen Schleier ihres Haares zusammen, der vom Scheitel fliessend die zarten Wangen einrahmte, und die zwei Wunden des Halses bedeckend, sich unter dem blassen Marmorkreuz ihrer Arme wieder vereinigte.

"Neben dem lieblichen Todesantlitz aber lag ein anderes hingesunken, von demselben Sonnenstrahle gebadet, lebloser und gestorbener als das der Leiche, ein Antlitz, über das die Sterbenot der Verzweiflung gegangen und von dem sie, nach getanem Werk, wieder gewichen. Es war der Kanzler, der mit zerrauftem Haar und aufgerissenem Gewande neben dem Sarge lag, die Arme aud den Rand desselben stützend.

"Lautlose Stille herrschte. Nur ein Laubgeflüster regte sich im offenen Fenster und leichte Blätterschatten tanzten über das Purpurkissen und die beiden Angesichter." [36]

This description does not depend for its effect on the musical quality of the language, on richness of metaphor, on overtones or the evocation of associations, but on the creation of an individual, objective, visual impression in the mind of the reader. It is essentially plastic rather than musical: its statuesque quality emerges even in expressions like "starrend" and "Marmorkreuz."

This predilection for the visual can seem artificial and mannered, particularly when it leads Meyer to attempt a reproduction in words of the painter's or sculptor's work, as in the poem, *Das Joch am Leman*, or when it prompts him to see a landscape or a human situation through the prism of art (*Auf Goldgrund; Venedig*). This occasional artificiality is perhaps most noticeable in the lyric where a certain spontaneity and musicality are normal. The rigid, tense, often staccato rhythms and the lapidary expression of Meyer's lyric suggested to poets of a more fluid idiom that he lacked spontaneity of feeling, and hence the authentic lyric voice. Storm wrote to Keller:

"Ein Lyriker ist er nicht; dazu fehlt ihm der unmittelbare, mit sich fortreißende Ausdruck der Empfindung, oder auch wohl die unmittelbare Empfindung selbst." [37]

Meyer himself was of a very different opinion and deplored "a sentimental streak which I recognize in myself and despise but which appears as a matter of course in my lyric." In support of Storm it must be admitted that there is often enough in Meyer's lyric a strange discord between mood and form. A striking instance is the poem, *Stapfen*, where the nostalgic and sentimental theme— the sight of the beloved's footprints in the snow—is oddly at variance with the terse style. In the absence of a direct expression of emotion, however, this disparity vanishes, and Meyer is capable of achieving —often by a process of refining and filing that extended over years— a perfection of form, a coincidence of rhythm, sound and image that has rarely been surpassed in German. The qualities of Meyer's lyric at its best are shown in what is perhaps his most famous poem, *Der römische Brunnen*, a refinement over the years of a diffuse first version twice as long:

> "Aufsteigt der Strahl und fallend gießt
> Er voll der Marmorschale Rund,
> Die, sich verschleiernd, überfließt
> In einer zweiten Schale Grund;
> Die zweite gibt, sie wird zu reich,
> Der dritten wallend ihre Flut,
> Und jede nimmt und gibt zugleich
> Und strömt und ruht." [38]

From the energetic opening to the dark, restful vowels of the last line, the poem traces the motion of the fountain; its pauses mark the contrast of rest and flow; the combination of dark and light vowels seems to suggest the solidity of the stone and the fluidity of the water; the whole epitomizes in the images of giving and receiving, of rest and motion a cosmic process. It is a poem of perfect "objectivity."

Something of the same objectivity appears in poems describing the Lake of Zürich, e.g. (*Schwarzschattende Kastanie* and *Im Spätboot*). Elsewhere, the picture has a symbolic value—the Bacchic reapers saving their sheaves from the threatening storm in *Erntegewitter*, or the gondolas in *Auf dem Canal grande*, whose rapid passage through a band of evening sunlight symbolizes the brief span of human life:

> "Eine kleine, kurze Strecke
> Treibt das Leben leidenschaftlich
> Und erlischt im Schatten drüben
> Als ein unverständlich Murmeln." [39]

But amongst these poems, uniformly controlled and epigrammatic, there are some which hold fast a moment of intense feeling or a mood of profound melancholy. It was not the case, as the poet claimed in the verses which open a section of his collected lyric, that "It was all a game." *Eingelegte Ruder*, although it is again the product of many revisions, describes a despondency none the less genuinely felt. In *Schwüle* there is a suggestion of panic as the poet scans the sky for the first stars, the symbol of hope which will deliver him from the dark fascination of the depths beneath, the depths in which his mother had found her end:

> "Fern der Himmel und die Tiefe nah—
> Sterne, warum seid ihr noch nicht da?" [40]

Against such despair, against the havoc wrought by passion and the torment of moral misgivings, Meyer's talisman was the concept and the practice of art. Art represents a timeless, passionless world. The Medici envies the statues of Michelangelo: "Leidlose Steine, wie beneid ich euch," [41] and the master himself apostrophises his creations:

> "Ihr stellt des Leids Gebärde dar,
> Ihr meine Kinder, ohne Leid!" [42]

Art is the escape from mortality; its element is eternity:

> "Den Augenblick verewigt ihr,
> Und sterbt ihr, sterbt ihr ohne Tod.
> Im Schilfe wartet Charon mein,
> Der pfeifend sich die Zeit vertreibt." [43]

At the peak of his career, between 1875 and 1885, Meyer seems to be sustained by this faith in art, moral issues are subordinate to aesthetic considerations. Not only does the author dissociate himself from his creations, the tone of the stories is fatalistic. Even the pious Gustav Adolf succumbs momentarily in Wallenstein's presence to a sense of fatality, while Ezzelino in *Die Hochzeit des Mönchs* is the very personification of fate. The characters, particularly in this Novelle, are driven on by circumstance and overpowering passion. Once Astorre has taken the decisive step of leaving the monastery he is blind to all sense of obligation, to everything but the love which possesses him entirely. The problem of guilt hardly enters into the work. With *Die Richterin*, however, a new phase seems to begin in Meyer's development. A moral problem, the problem of guilt and atonement occupies the foreground. Meyer pointed to the parallel with *Crime and Punishment*, which he described as "a pathological masterpiece":

> "Meine *Richterin* hat ein verwandtes Motiv, doch als mittel-alterliche Burgfrau stärkere Nerven als das russische Student-chen." [44]

Instead of being driven simply by instinct, the characters here are torn by an inner struggle; a conflict such as is elsewhere embodied in two opposing figures is compressed into the person of Stemma. There is indeed a pathological element in the story, and certain emotional problems in the mind of the author do not yield as formerly to the discipline of art. The suspected incestuous relation-ship between Wulfrin and Palma seems to hint at some psychological disturbance in the poet and might be taken as a belated echo of the long and intimate association with his sister Betsy that preceded his marriage. The turmoil of emotion in the characters is matched by the wild and fantastic scenery of the Alps. These landscapes are not objectively described, they represent symbolically the feelings of the characters, they are externalizations of mental states: the idyllic setting of the pool into which Wulfrin and Palma gaze, the savage gorge through which Wulfrin passes, believing that he lusts after his own sister—these are powerful images of psychological conditions. *Die Richterin* stands out among Meyer's Novellen as being entirely his own invention, and it may well be that it springs more immediately from psychological sources than his other stories. He hints at something of the kind when he writes to Louise von François: "(ich) schloß klüglich die Augen und ließ das Saumroß . . . meiner Einbildungskraft den Fuß setzen, wie es für gut fand." [45]

His next work, *Die Versuchung des Pescara* (1887) shows Meyer back on more familiar ground with a historical theme from the Italian Renaissance. Here, again, there is a moral problem, Pescara's choice of loyalties between the Imperial cause and the cause of Italian unity. It never becomes a real problem, however, for the hero is doomed by a mortal wound. Death in *Pescara* is for once not a sudden and brilliant climax, but something which paralyses action and makes choice vain, an insidious enemy who can only be met with resignation. In spite of all its glowing scenes the story is pervaded by melancholy and an abhorrence of death that springs more from fear than fascination. Meyer felt an alien element creeping into his work, "a mystical or phantom element à la Kleist," and in the midst of creating he was visited with intimations of mortality:

> "Wenn ich sehe, welche Arbeitskraft mir noch zu Diensten steht, wenigstens an schönen trockenen Tagen und bei offenen Fenstern, könnte ich versucht sein, große Pläne zu entwerfen, doch ich fühle zugleich die Ungewißheit menschlichen Glücks. Zwei Jüngere als ich, nahe Bekannte, sind mir in den letzten Wochen weggestorben." [46]

The sombre note grows deeper in the last of the Novellen, *Angela Borgia*, a story heavy with foreboding and full of nightmare and hypnotic states. Its gloom is not entirely relieved, as Meyer claimed, by an ending which is "conciliatory, almost idyllic." The blinding of Don Giulio epitomizes the turning of the poet's gaze inwards, a narrowing of his world, an incipient withdrawal to the cloister of the mind. Humility and renunciation are the virtues of which Angela Borgia bears the symbolic cross on her brow, imprinted there by the bars of Don Giulio's prison; spiritual poverty is the lesson preached by Father Manette to the sightless Don Giulio in a favourite image of the poet's:

"Werdet arm und ärmer, damit Ihr empfangen und geben könnt, wie ein Brunnen, der Schale um Schale überfließend füllt." (47)

The gaiety, the energy and brutality of the Renaissance is overlaid with the spirituality of Tolstoy; irony gives way to faith.

It may be the more intensely personal nature of this work which leads to a relaxation of the strict form which Meyer customarily imposed on himself: the two figures of Angela and Lukrezia, although they form a pattern, tend to divide the work into phases, and hence to disrupt its unity, the narrative is episodic, even the language is less plastic, more haunting and lyrical. There is a slackening of control; in fact, the author found it difficult to achieve the necessary concentration, and managed to complete the work only by an effort of the will: "*Angela Borgia* is finished, if not a work of art, at least a powerful act of the will."

It was his last creative achievement. Ill-health heralded a return to the neurotic condition of his youth, he slipped back into the twilight world. In the summer of 1892 he once more entered a mental hospital—this time in Königsfelden—his condition diagnosed as "senile melancholia." A little over a year later he was able to return to Kilchberg, but he never fully recovered and his poetic voice was silenced for ever. In November 1898 there came to an end a career which he himself described as "incredibly remarkable." Remarkable it was as an example of a double life, not only in its successive phases, but also in the contrast between the man and his art, between the tranquil, withdrawn, uneventful life of the Swiss villa and the restless, brilliant, savage life of the stories and ballads. C. F. Meyer's art is essentially a mask and a substitute for real experience. What saves it from appearing mere fantasy is its visual quality, its full-bloodedness, its linguistic discipline and its psychological truth. Although he works with settings remote in time and space and describes events and emotions of which he can have had only an imaginative experience, nevertheless Meyer can claim to be a realist: "I go to bed every evening more realistic than I rose," he wrote to Spitteler. His aim is not "to make the poetic real," but "to make the real poetic." Where Keller realizes poetic themes of universal validity in familiar Swiss settings, Meyer seeks to evoke, by imaginative interpretation, the inner, poetic truth of recorded history. These are very different approaches, but both writers might be described as "poetic realists." There is little point in assessing the merits of one against the other; as far as popularity with his fellow-countrymen goes, the see-saw will probably always come down in favour of Keller. There is never likely to be a *Jürg*

Jenatsch restaurant in Zürich to rival *Der grüne Heinrich*. It may be, however, that Meyer's appeal is more universal. Nor is he without successors: his irony, his morbidity and his use of symbols are carried into the twentieth century by Thomas Mann, another offspring of a patrician race who found salvation in his art.

TRANSLATIONS

1. All his carry-on and hoity-toity ways.
2. I lay in bondage to a heavy spell,
   I did not live. I lay as in a trance.
3. Ivy, my old house-mate
   You gleam with young leaves.
   Your wintry green, so grave, austere,
   Does it well consort with the riot of spring?

   "Why not? Like mine,
   Your life has leaves both old and new,
   One grim and dark, one bright
   With spring and air. Why not?"
4. A petty Saxon monk did doff his habit.
   There, Sir Knight, you have a splendid theme.
5. The secularization of the higher clergy . . . the authentic type of the humanist: wit, frivolity, emulation and exaggerated respect for antiquity, insincerity, vindictiveness . . . theft and mendicancy.
6. What I need is sun and cloud, sickle and scythe, husband and child . . .
7. You silent man, working slow subversion, you are long-suffering like your master and you encompass your own death as he did. You believe that you are serving charity, but hatred is the stronger and your death, like the death of your God, is the damnation of men.
8. This man—an intellectually superior nature, humane almost in the modern way, but defenceless in the face of mediaeval barbarity—this man uses the Church as a weapon without being himself a believer—legend and the poet both endow him with Oriental blood.
9. As far as the majority of the people are concerned, Keller has the advantage over me that he is at heart an optimist. That is why he is a man for the masses. People are like that: they crowd round the spring of life and are pleased if they catch at least a drop in their little cups. In Keller they find what they are looking for, because he always contrives a happy ending. Tragic dénouements are a thing unknown to him. That is a fault, for to have its full charm existence must include both.
10. As far as I personally am concerned, the comic leaves a bitter taste in my mouth, whereas the tragic elevates and inspires me.
11. Meyer has a weakness for particular brutalities and slaughters of this kind. Whenever he hears or reads about this sort of thing he says: Excellent! Everyone has his eccentricities.

12. Come, death, and bear me off, death, in the fervour of a kiss.

13. From one sheaf to another
    There is space for death.

14. I have gained the palm and merited death.

15. I want all the rays of my life to be joined in one blaze of fire and in the space of a single hour, so that instead of a senseless gloom there might be generated a brief but blinding light of rapture which would vanish like a fleeting flash of lightning.

16. A warm southerly breeze had idealized the snow-capped mountains and the Swiss lake in its own manner, blending the chain of the former into one vast, serene luminosity, submerging the latter with the deep and vividly glowing colours of a Southern bay, as though eager to transport a Bacchic landscape, a portion of Italy, across the Alps.

17. You were trying to divest yourself of your own nature and he sent you about your business by making fun of you . . . And why? I like you best of all as you are, and just as you are.

18. . . . the excellence of Keller's *Züricher Novellen* will certainly put me in the shade and even make me look, quite unjustly, like an imitator.

19. In *Jenatsch* and in *The Saint* there is far more of me in various disguises, my true sufferings and passions, than in these lyric poems.

20. I wrote *The Saint* almost without knowing it, obsessed and intoxicated, because I had to get rid of it, it lay on my chest like a tormenting nightmare.

21. But one thing, however, the Chancellor lacked: the energy and asperity of a manly temperament.

22. Impassivity was a fundamental feature of his character. I never saw him angry and could not even easily imagine him so.

23. I treat history in a sovereign manner, but not inaccurately.

24. The propensity for the framework is quite instinctive in me. I like to keep my subject at a distance, or rather as far as possible from my eye, and, again, it seems to me that the indirect nature of the tale (and even the interruptions) mitigates the harshness of the plot.

25. It seemed to me that Dante must invent and not narrate.

26. The plot lay in scattered profusion before him; but his astringent mind chose and simplified.

27. Here, admittedly, there is too much intertwining of plot and listener: the whole thing becomes decidedly tiresome. A non plus ultra! I am cured of it!

28. In short, what I have gained from the Romance world is a sense of gesture. For me it has become essential and imperative to shape everything so that it is outwardly observable, visible, even in language.

29. Yes, you know . . . when you come to think of it, any flapper who has read Heine, Geibel, Rittershaus . . . can put together a few lines full of atmosphere; but to conjure up in ballad-like form what I might call plastic and substantial figures, and to make them appear in action, that is an art that is given to an infinitely small number of people.

30. I feel a lack in German literature; it is not keenly enough observed, not made obvious to the senses, it is abstract and blurred. The similes and metaphors in German are feeble, they do not shed light and illuminate.

Ariosto's, on the other hand, even although they are exaggeratedly grotesque, are nevertheless sharply observed and illuminating.

31. So Victoria spoke in surging and overflowing words like a fountain of Rome.

The motion of his nature was as honest as a blast on a hunting-horn and overflowed like the foam on the bit of a young charger.

32. This nocturnal phantom of speechless wrath and inconsolable grief.

33. Three obstacles hindered a match: the high and often sombre brow of Diana, the close fist of her father and the blind attachment of her brother Germano to the tyrant.

34. ... the cast-off habit of the monk, the linked hands of Diana and Astorre.

35. I see how he sits and ponders and I know his soul.

36. I looked into the semi-darkness of the castle chapel. But there was no crucifix there and no eternal lamp, and instead of a holy corpse beneath the altar, in front of it and just as richly decked there lay in a coffin the body of Grace. A flood of light that poured through the one window high in the wall, lit up her ethereal beauty. Her head rested on a purple pillow and wore a coronet of glittering gems. Her slight body was hidden in the folds of her dress, which, stiff with pearls and gold embroidery, spread over the sides of the coffin. Her small, transparent hands lay crossed on her breast and modestly held together the black veil of her hair which, flowing down from both sides, made a frame for her delicate cheeks, and covering the two wounds in her neck, was joined again beneath the marble cross of her arms.

By the side of the lovely dead face, however, reclined another, bathed in the same shaft of sunlight, more lifeless and more dead than that of the corpse, a countenance across which the mortal pang of despair had passed, leaving it again after its work was done. It was the Chancellor who lay with disordered hair and doublet torn open by the side of the coffin, resting his arms on its edge.

Complete silence reigned. Only a whisper of foliage stirred by the open window and the light shadow of leaves danced across the purple pillow and the two faces.

37. A lyric poet he is not; he lacks the immediate and compulsive expression of emotion, or probably even the emotion itself.

38.   Up springs the spray and falling fills
The marble basin's curving rim
That, veiled in water, ceaseless spills
To reach a second basin's brim;
The second sheds its lapping swell
To flood the third one as it goes,
And each one takes and gives as well
   And rests and flows.

39.   One brief little space
Life drifts on in passion,
And dies away in the shadows yonder
As an indistinct murmur.

40. Far the heavens and the depths are near—
    Stars, why are you not yet here?
41. Passionless stones, how I envy you.
42. You shape the gesture of grief,
    You my children, who know not grief.
43. The moment is by you eternalized
    And when you die you know not death.
    While in the sedge old Charon waits for me
    And whistling whiles the time away.

44. My *Richterin* has a related motif, but as a mediaeval chatelaine she has stronger nerves than the little Russian student.

45. I closed my eyes prudently and let the pack-horse of my imagination pick its way as seemed best to it.

46. When I see what energy is still at my disposal, at least on fine dry days and with open windows. I might be tempted to make great plans, but I feel at the same time the uncertainty of human happiness. Two younger men than I, close acquaintances have been taken from me by death in the last few weeks.

47. Become even poorer, that you may receive and give, like a fountain, which fills one basin after another as it overflows.

BIBLIOGRAPHY

WORKS

Sämtliche Werke, hrsg. von R. Faesi. Th. Knaur Nachf., Berlin, 1926. 4 vols., with an essay condensed from Faesi: *C. F. Meyer*, Frauenfeld, 2nd ed., 1948.

Sämtliche Werke, Droemersche Verlagsanstalt, Th. Knaur Nachf., München, Zürich, 1959.
One volume, with an account of Meyer's life and works by Hans Schmeer.

Sämtliche Werke, Dieterich Verlag, Leipzig, 1956.
Two volumes, with a long introduction and (rather elementary) notes by Chr. Coler.

Sämtliche Werke. Historisch-kritische Ausgabe. Besorgt von Hans Zeller and Alfred Zäch, Benteli-Verlag, Berne, 1959.
Vols. 10 and 11 have appeared so far.

LETTERS

Briefe C. F. Meyers. Nebst seinen Rezensionen und Aufsätzen. Hrsg. von A. Frey. Leipzig, 1908. 2 vols.

C. F. Meyers Briefwechsel mit Luise von François, hrsg. von A. Bettelheim. Berlin, 1905 (2nd ed., 1920).

C. F. Meyer. La crise de 1852–6. Lettres de C. F. Meyer et de son entourage, ed. by R. d'Harcourt. Paris, 1913.

BIOGRAPHY AND COMMENTARIES

BEHARRIEL, F. J. "Conrad Ferdinand Meyer and the origins of psycho-analysis" (*Monatshefte für den deutschen Unterricht,* xlvii, 3, 1955).

HENEL, H. *The Poetry of Conrad Ferdinand Meyer*. Univ. of Wisconsin Press, 1954.

HOHENSTEIN, L. *Conrad Ferdinand Meyer*. Bonn, 1957.

MEYER, B. *C. F. Meyer in der Erinnerung seiner Schwester*. Berlin, 1903.

OBERLE, W. "C. F. Meyer: ein Forschungsbericht." (*Germanisch-Romanische Monatsschrift*, xxxvii, 3, 1956).

WIESMANN, L. *Conrad Ferdinand Meyer, der Dichter des Todes und der Maske*. Berne, 1958.

Theodor Fontane

Theodor Fontane

by H. B. GARLAND

IT is probably true that good novels are usually written by men of maturity and experience. Jane Austen, as a woman, could manage *Pride and Prejudice* at twenty-one. But most of the English writers and more of the Germans have entered upon novel writing in their thirties and forties. No novelist of rank, however, has been such a tardy beginner as Fontane. When his first novel appeared in 1879, he was in his sixtieth year, widely known as poet, travel writer and journalist, and his work in these various fields had given no hint of the sudden burgeoning of talent in works which were to raise him from a background figure of German literature to one of its outstanding representatives. His novels were perfectly matched to the movement of their age, and yet they have stood the test of passing time and fading fashion, the astonishing achievement of an ageing man between his sixtieth and his eightieth year.

Fontane has sketched out many phases of his life for us with a simplicity and unpretentiousness which inspire credence and with a magic touch which brings the past to life as only the autobiographer at his best can do it. He was born in Neu-Ruppin, in Brandenburg on 30 December 1819, the eldest son of the owner of the *Löwenapotheke*. Both of Fontane's parents were of French descent, late off-shoots of the Protestant immigration of the seventeenth century. Louis Fontane, the apothecary of Neu-Ruppin, was in the practical affairs of life an amiable failure. A Micawber-like character, of insouciance, bonhomie and charm, he could not overcome a passion for cards and steadily lost money throughout his life. Fontane's portrait of him in *Meine Kinderjahre* (1894) conceals none of his faults, yet manifests such affection and appreciation that a sense of worth of personality emerges through all the weaknesses and failings. And indeed Fontane *père*, in his irregular, spasmodic and anecdotal manner of instruction made history live for Theodor; and in doing so he did more than orient him in the past; from this vivid realization of the lives of others before his day stems Fontane's own awareness of the lives of others who are his contemporaries. Without the slightest intention Louis Fontane laid the first foundations for the novelist of fifty years later.

When Fontane was seven the family moved to Swinemünde on the Baltic, the environment and atmosphere of which re-appears not only in *Meine Kinderjahre*, but also in *Effi Briest*. The casual education carried on by Fontane's father and occasional tutors gave way in 1832 to a regular schooling away from home at the gymnasium of Neu-Ruppin. Hardly had this begun than the father changed his mind and in September 1833 Theodor was sent to the *Klödensche Gewerbeschule* in Berlin. Leaving school in 1836 he was apprenticed to an apothecary in the capital, and here he spent almost four years, being released from his indentures late in 1839. He remained for a further year with the apothecary in Berlin, spent then three months in a position in Burg near Magdeburg, was next in Leipzig and later in Dresden in the calling for which he had been trained. There followed in 1844–5 his military service, spent as a one-year volunteer with a Guard Regiment. Simultaneously he found entry to a Berlin literary club with a wide and distinguished membership, the *Tunnel über der Spree*. The *Tunnel* widened and deepened his literary interest, and it perhaps prematurely fixed his attention upon the ballad, which could be publicly recited at meetings.

The year 1848 came and when revolution broke out on 18 March, the apothecary took for an hour or two to the barricades, but his enthusiasm soon cooled. He was by temperament no revolutionary. Two years later Fontane suffered a second access of political passion; this time patriotic. Defeat of the German nationalists by the Danes at Idstedt in 1850 sent him hotfoot to Altona to enlist in a "free corps." But once again enthusiasm was easily deflated. Fontane accepted an offer from the "Literarische Bureau" of the Ministry of the Interior. On the strength of his new prospects he got married. Six weeks later, a political re-shuffle left him jobless.

Fontane never returned, however, to dispensing. From 1850 on, journalism was his livelihood. In 1852 and from 1855 to 1859 he was in England as a newspaper correspondent. His scattered comments and especially *Ein Sommer in London* (1854) characterize the mid-Victorian English scene with detachment and fairness.

Fontane's first publications fall in the 'fifties. A volume of poems appeared in 1850 and others in the following years. In the 'sixties he explored a new field, geographical description and historical recollection of his native land, Brandenburg. The four volumes of *Wanderungen durch die Mark Brandenburg* appeared between 1862 and 1882. In the autumn of 1870 Fontane travelled to France as a free-lance war correspondent. While visiting Domremy, the birthplace of Joan of Arc, he fell into the hands of francs-tireurs, was treated as a prisoner of war and spent two months in various military prisons.

He published a vivid, truthful and scrupulously fair account of these experiences under the title *Kriegsgefangen, Erlebtes, 1870.*

From 1871 to 1889 he worked as dramatic critic for the *Vossische Zeitung* displaying notable understanding for Ibsen. The sixty-nine-year old Fontane was also one of the very few who saw the first performance of Hauptmann's *Vor Sonnenaufgang* with an impartial eye and open-minded judgment.

His shrewd level-headedness and his readiness for new impressions were remarkable enough. But the most surprising thing about the last two decades of Fontane's long life is the series of novels which unexpectedly began with *Vor dem Sturm.* No fewer than eight novels appeared in the eighteen-eighties, culminating in the masterpiece *Irrungen, Wirrungen* of 1889. And in the years 1890 to 1898 there followed seven more, including three outstanding works, *Frau Jenny Treibel* (1892). *Effi Briest* (1895) and *Der Stechlin.* To this astonishing productivity of an Indian summer must be added *Mathilde Möhring,* almost finished in 1891 but laid aside and not published till ten years after Fontane's death, and the autobiographical writings, *Meine Kinderjahre* and *Von Zwanzig bis Dreissig.*

By 1890 Fontane's reputation was established. His conservatism and his humanity had won for him one half of the public, his realism delighted the younger generation. Worn in body, but mentally fresh and alert to the last, he died of heart failure on 20 September 1898.

Fontane first thought of himself as a poet. In his old age he wrote a number of lyric poems, brief and often moving expressions of sadness, grief and resignation, expressed in an idiom belonging to an earlier generation. Derivative though they are in style, they have the honesty and unpretentiousness of the mature Fontane, and though they have disappeared from currency, these slightly faded, modest miniatures can still afford pleasure to the connoisseur.

The young Fontane, however, was a ballad writer. A thorough acquaintance with Schiller's ballads was one of the few intellectual possessions which he brought with him to the Neu-Ruppin Gymnasium at the age of twelve. His father had encouraged in him an anecdotal knowledge of history, and had made the striking episode and the striking phrase live for him. History was something real and vivid for him, and as with Bergengruen's *Rittmeister* what mattered in it was not a process of development but a series of graphic and epigrammatic climaxes.

Yet even in the ballads Fontane of the novels is present. The theatrical gesture, which is almost an inevitable feature of the patriotic ballad, is rare in Fontane. And his patriotism is wide; firmly Prussian, and within that framework an indisputable "Märker" (that quintessence of the Prussian), Fontane can understand love of country wherever he finds it; in France, in England, and, most frequently of all, in Scotland. And so it comes that the one ballad which is all that usually represents Fontane in anthologies is *Archibald Douglas*. And it is characteristic that this ballad is not concerned with battle, murder or sudden death, but with the ineradicable love of home and homeland.

"Der ist in tiefster Seele treu,
Wer die Heimat liebt wie du." [1]

In Fontane's ballads war has its place, especially in the crystallization of well-known anecdotes from the time of Frederick the Great, as in the Seydlitz or the Grenadier poems. But many, though set in war, are elegiac, like *Prinz Louis Ferdinand*, *Das Trauerspiel von Afghanistan*, or *Admiral Herluf Trolles Begräbnis*. And a whole host of them have as their theme the times of peace, moments of catastrophe like *Die Brück' am Tay* or of calm consummation like *Waldemar Atterdag* or *Herr von Ribbeck*. Attractive and arresting though some of these ballads remain, they are relics, echoes, last descendants of Bürger, Herder, Schiller, Walter Scott and Thomas Moore. Many stem from the admiration of Fontane for a heroism which he knew to be foreign to himself. They represent a compensation in which he does not fundamentally believe—it was not for nothing that he quizzically wrote in *Ein Sommer in London*.

"Man darf Heldentaten nicht in der Nähe betrachten." [2]

More essential to the man are the ballads of peace such as *Archibald Douglas* and *Herr von Ribbeck*. Terseness and relevance and sobriety are the qualities of these ballads, and these, though attractive qualities of the man Fontane, are not enough to make living poetry.

Between the early period in which Fontane was journalist and ballad writer and the later novels come the *Wanderungen durch die Mark Brandenburg*. For the reader with patience and leisure they can still offer attractive reading. First conceived in Scotland the work was intended, Fontane tells us, to bring home to the Brandenburger the scenic and historical wealth of his homeland, which were in his view not less than those of Scotland, so fashionable as a touring-ground since Walter Scott. From this slightly irritated beginning arose four desultory volumes, accounts of actual journeys in Brandenburg, by train where possible, but mostly by carriage or cart, in which Fontane sets forth topography, landscape, architecture and history in the sober, factual, yet personal and living fashion which is his special gift. It was a gift, which required development, and it is in these four volumes of travels that Fontane evolved the style which appears so casual and incidental and yet is both precise and evocative. And not only did Fontane's style evolve in these years; the close and intimate acquaintance with Brandenburg was to be an essential component of the novels. Rheinsberg and Stechlin, Lübbenau and Treptow are real backgrounds because Fontane knew them well, because he had studied them with an eye both curious and affectionate. It is on these journeys, too, and in the writing of these books that the intimate union between place and past, the awareness of Brandenburg history in the visual scene, the sense of "rootedness" develops, which, unobtrusive though it is, pervades even the non-historical novels of Fontane.

The importance of the *Wanderungen* as a phase of preparation and transition is emphasized by the specifically historical character of the early novels. Of the first seven novels, five have historical settings, ranging between the early seventeenth century for *Grete Minde* to the time of Fontane's own childhood in *Unterm Birnbaum*. The first of these novels is by far the longest. *Vor dem Sturm* is set in East Brandenburg in the winter of 1812–13 and has as its background the gradual revelation of Napoleon's failure in Russia and the crystallization of Prussian resistance. Only in two brief inserted narrations do the great events of war appear. Fontane's interest lies in the unheroic, the everyday, even the apparently trivial. The historical climax of the book is the abortive and ill-organized attack upon the French in Frankfurt (Oder), in all its futility and with its mixture of muddle, misunderstanding and courage. It is much more characteristic of Fontane's focus than any famous set battle-piece. His approach was totally unromantic. The age without a name meant more to him than the crowded hour of glorious life. His story unfolds accordingly. Almost two thirds of it is past before the first private event, the elopement of Kathinka, is reached; the rest is background, political, social and literary climate, the things that in Fontane's eyes make up the greater, and perhaps more important part of life. Dinners, balls, skating parties, family and house parties fill the greater part of this book. There are conversations on literature, politics, social life and religion, on the problems of the Pole in Prussia, on the behaviour of the occupying French, on Napoleon's defeat and Yorck's change of sides at Tauroggen. The main characters, Bernd von Vitzewitz and his son and daughter, Ladalinskys, and Bininsky and General Bamme are drawn from the aristocracy, but a whole host of additional figures, from the poet Hansen-Grell to the grotesque rural figure of Hoppenmarieken, can give it a justified claim to be a comprehensive survey. And that is clearly what Fontane sought. It was his aim to recreate a society to show, not the deliberations of statesmen, but how the wide variety of common men spoke, thought and acted, how they spent their lives and how they responded to the momentous tidings which were reaching them. It embodies a conception of history and a sense of values which is eminently humane. Even in the shadow of great events the little things in life continue, and as they do so they are accompanied by Fontane's sympathy. He has written the history which the historians cannot remember unless, ceasing to be historians they become novelists instead. Out of his patriotism and his interest in local history and topography has grown, with the help of his fairness, his balance and his moderation, a vivid evocation of the Prussian scene in the winter before the great war of 1813.

Certainly *Vor dem Sturm* has faults. Its immense material seems not to be fully organized; the book is congested and the multitude of retarding elements brings it at times virtually to a standstill. The long period spent by Fontane over this novel was a sign of tentativeness and uncertainty. He was learning a new métier and moreover at a time when he was occupied with the journeying and writing of the *Wanderungen durch die Mark*, which of necessity inclined to discursiveness. That the lesson was learned was a consequence of Fontane's independence and originality. He wrote already in 1866 of this novel: "Ich habe mir vielmehr vorgenommen, die Arbeit *ganz nach mir selbst*, nach meiner Neigung und Individualität zu machen, ohne jegliches Vorbild." [3] It is this freshness of approach which maintains the attractiveness of *Vor dem Sturm* despite its theoretical shortcomings.

As the writing of this historical novel was completed, Fontane busied himself with a series of short works, which he frequently referred to as "Novellen." Of these *Grete Minde* was published in 1880, *Ellernklipp* in 1881, but *Schach von Wuthenow* was delayed and did not appear until 1883. In a letter written to Mathilde von Rohr (15 May 1878), who supplied him with the material for *Schach von Wuthenow*, Fontane outlined his conception of these shorter works: "Es kommt immer auf zweierlei an: Auf die Charaktere und auf ein nachweisbares oder poetisch zu mutmaßendes Verhältnis von Schuld und Strafe." [4] The ethical problem, in fact, plays a much greater part than in *Vor dem Sturm*. It is a complex problem, for Fontane's honesty, balance and impartiality debars him from the simple solutions obtained by darkening the shadows and heightening the light spots. In *Grete Minde* the injustice suffered by the heroine in the loss of her inheritance leads her to an act of vengeance which is disproportionate to the injuries she has suffered. The burning of Tangermünde is not without a certain poetic justification, since the municipality, executing its own unjust laws, has refused Grete her rights. Grete's act recalls that of Michael

Kohlhaas, but her deed springs from an overwrought spirit, not from a fanatical sense of right.

The father who in his jealousy kills his son in *Ellernklipp*, succumbs at last to conscience; and the conclusion, with its somewhat self-conscious note of harmony, underlines Fontane's social approach. From the broodings of the Heidereiter the attention is directed to the greater world, to the service of which his widow henceforth devotes herself.

In *Schach von Wuthenow*, Fontane returns to Berlin and gives on a more modest scale a picture of manners recalling that of *Vor dem Sturm*. Its sub-title is of similar type "Erzählung aus der Zeit des Regiments Gensdarmes"; the year is 1806, in the summer immediately preceding the Prussian disaster. But *Schach von Wuthenow* is at least as much a study of guilt and punishment as a historical portrayal of manners. Schach himself is a man of character and qualities, whose virtues are neutralized by an inordinate vanity, so that sooner than face the world with a wife whose once pretty face is pock-marked, he shoots himself. It is characteristic that Fontane, commenting on this story should write, "Die Furcht vor dem Ridikülen spielt in der Welt eine kolossale Rolle," [5] for Fontane is pre-eminently the historian of man in his world and conscious of his environment. He is a social novelist in the sense that he portrays a society and its manners.

None of these stories is filled with the life which Fontane breathes into his best novels, but a fourth story of this type stands on a higher plane. *Unterm Birnbaum* (1885) is set, like all Fontane's best work, in his native Brandenburg and within a generation of his own time. The inn-keeper, Hradschek, in pecuniary straits, murders a wine-traveller. With desperate adroitness he repeatedly averts suspicion, only in the end to lose his life while trying to remove the incriminating remains from his cellar. A plain moral story, it might seem, ending with the punishment of guilt, "Es ist nichts so fein gesponnen, 's kommt doch alles an die Sonnen." [6] *Unterm Birnbaum*, however, is more subtle than that. Fontane creates an extraordinary tension and suspense, not from the question "Who did it?"—We all know that Hradschek murdered the traveller—but from the question, "Will it be brought home to Hradschek?" And in this excitement and anxiety the reader is brought into a balance of sympathy and repulsion. The fluctuating tide of *pro* and *contra* here is the stuff of real life.

Affiliated to this group of shorter works are three novels, separated in time but all three set against backgrounds which Fontane knew superficially or not at all. *Graf Petöfy* (1884) plays in Vienna and the plains of Hungary; *Quitt*, (1891, but written in 1885–6) is set partly in Silesia, where Fontane had spent a holiday, and partly in America, which he knew only through Bret Harte and Mark Twain; *Unwiederbringlich* (1891) has Holstein and Denmark as its background. In these three novels Fontane takes real pains to make his milieu abundant and convincing; only in *Unwiederbringlich* is he successful. The remoteness of the setting has thrust upon him a different type of character portrayal. His human figures normally belong to their environment, their surroundings are made to reveal all the facets of their make-up. In these three novels Fontane has to adopt, at least partially, a more direct method which was less congenial to him. The difficulties were augmented in *Graf Petöfy* by the necessity of portraying a profound passion, never Fontane's strong suit, and in *Quitt* by the symmetrical balance of guilt and atonement which was more suitable to a Novelle than to the scale of this work. If in *Graf Petöfy* a somewhat pale novel results, and *Quitt* is a merely competent piece of story-telling with a too insistent motif of moral order and balance, *Unwiederbringlich* is a remarkably successful study of a marriage and its eventual failure, not through easily assessable guilt, but through minor flaws of character. Count and Countess Holk are an obviously well-matched pair and equally obviously in love; but slight differences of temperament and outlook become inflated until the marriage breaks down completely, and an attempted restoration of it ends catastrophically with the Countess's suicide. Here, as in all the best of Fontane's novels, we are more concerned with "what people are like" and "how things happen" than with an apportionment of blame or responsibility.

Of the five novels and stories published by Fontane between 1878 and 1883 all but one has been historical. The one exception, *L'adultera* (1882), is the forerunner of Fontane's later work, set in his own day and in Berlin and the surrounding country he knew so well. As with many of his novels, the action, if taken in isolation, seems banal. The young wife of a wealthy financier, irritated by her husband's vulgarity, runs away with a rich young man. She is unhappy in her new environment until loss of fortune brings to her new responsibilities. The ethical problems certainly interest Fontane; and his attitude is a mixture of the traditional and the progressive. He does not, in theory, approve of Melanie van Straaten's desertion of her husband. No doubt Melanie's unhappiness after her divorce and re-marriage is to be seen in part as an inevitable consequence of her flouting the established conventions of society. But it is, as Fontane portrays it, a natural, and not a moral, consequence. Moreover, Melanie recovers as soon as she readjusts her values, turning her back on the idleness of a "society" life, and accepting real responsibilities. Fontane's independence and individualism colour his view of society.

The essence of Fontane's work lies in the reflection of a society. His ethical attitude, which may be summarized as acceptance in general, and criticism in detail, provides a necessary footing, without which the view of society would lack stability. But it is the presentation in description and dialogue which makes up the special quality of his Brandenburg novels, of which this is the first.

A picture of a society is not convincing unless it is localized. Fontane's Berlin is detailed and circumstantial, the excursions into the country have as their scene restaurants and cafés which really existed (Löbbeke's Kaffeehaus or later in *Irrungen Wirrungen* "Hankels Ablage," where Fontane himself stayed in May 1884); the décors of the houses and flats are detailed and authentic. Most important of all, however, is the human material. Fontane's chief characters do not move in a vacuum, they are not on a larger scale than their fellows, they form part of a group; the composition of the group fluctuates, but it is itself constant. And this group is itself not in isolation.

Through the conversations, of which he is so great a master, Fontane brings his small group into relationship with society at large. At the dinner parties, receptions and outings, the talk ranges through politics, touches Bismarck, war-scares or current legislation, passes to art or the theatre, glances for a moment at current scandal or current fashion, all the time in a tone and with an emphasis corresponding to the character and outlook of the speaker; the ball is continuously in play; though those seated at the table differ, they all clearly belong, usually without giving the matter a further thought, to the society of their day, sharing a common background. The portrayal of the society in Berlin and the Mark is one of the most important aspects of Fontane's work, which in its conversational technique is highly original. For with Fontane dialogue is not an adjunct but staple material. In their dinner-table conversations the parties portray the world in which they live and, unconsciously, themselves. And the same double revelatory use is made of their comments on each other.

Fontane's cycle of Berlin novels consists of five serious novels or "Novellen," and four comedies; in addition to the somewhat Ibsenist *L'adultera* there are among the serious or tragic novels *Stine* (1890) *Cécile* (1887), *Irrungen Wirrungen* (1888) and *Effi Briest* (1895). *Stine* is the earliest of these, and the slenderest. Fontane refers to all his stories except the longest as "Novellen." Many of them are undoubtedly novels (Romane), but with *Stine* none would question his designation. Yet its theme is broader than that of *L'adultera* which played within a single class, the wealthy bourgeosie on the fringe of the aristocracy. *Stine* portrays the sexual diversions of the nobility, showing us a count with a mistress far lower in social standing, but nevertheless well able to look after herself. It is a relationship in which both parties see to their own interests. The mistress, however, has a sister and the count a nephew, and these two lack both the mercenary bias and the frivolity of their elders. They fall in love and Graf Waldemar plans to marry Stine in spite of the social difficulties. But society with its conventions is too much for them.

One sees in *Stine* how easily Fontane's method can degenerate if the author loses touch. In spite of many deft touches it is a "Novelle" on a par with hundreds of others in its age, a story in which reality is arranged, adapted and titivated and simultaneously the claim of realism made for it. Though Fontane was an economical writer the sparseness of form in *Stine* imposed restrictions which hampered him too severely. For the social novel needs a certain irreducible minimum of room and leisure in which to display its background.

Cécile is a tragic novel which moves along the periphery of high society. Its central figures are the beautiful sensitive, neurotic former mistress of a prince, the ruthless, straight-shooting duellist of an ex-officer who has married her, and a reckless civil engineer and reserve officer who involves himself and her in disaster. And this tragedy arises, as Fontane sees it, because all these figures, in one way or another, are untrue to the society, whose conventions they acknowledge. *Cécile* has a twofold background, the Harz around Thale and Berlin. Fontane portrays less the landscape of the holiday resort than the social life of the hotel guests. Conversation at the table d'hôte offers the possibility of a wide range of character portrayal through speech, and he grasps the opportunity of satirizing a number of incidental characters, above all the scholar Eginhard aus dem Grunde, a minor masterpiece of caricature, based on a real figure.

The characters of *Cécile*, while admitting the claims of society, choose to disregard them in their actions. Those of *Irrungen Wirrungen* not only respect society but act in accordance with its exigencies. This is the first of Fontane's novels to avoid everything sensational, to portray the rule rather than the exception. There is neither duel, divorce nor suicide. It is a realistic novel in theme as well as in treatment. A young officer strikes up a casual acquaintance with a working-class girl and the acquaintance ripens to love on both sides. His family press him to marry a cousin with money. He does so, and is neither happy nor unhappy in the marriage. Lene, the girl he has loved, marries a man of her own class. The scars heal on both sides, but they do not disappear.

The basic theme of this novel, the love affair between the man of rank and the poor girl is a sufficiently familiar one from *Faust* through Lenz and H. L. Wagner to Schnitzler and Hartleben. How easily it can lend itself to false rhetoric and pathos is all too evident in Hartleben's *Rosenmontag*. Fontane's temperamental aversion to pose preserved him easily from such perils. The scrupulous fairness, the meticulous avoidance of any sort of distortion are outstanding features of *Irrungen Wirrungen*. Every character has his due, and since all the characters are genuine human beings, some may be ridiculous, some superficial, but all are such that the reader can see in them something of his own humanity.

The novel, as its theme demands, has a dual structure; before and after the parting. Its earlier stage is concentrated upon Botho von Rienacker and Lene Nimptsch. Its tenderness is accentuated by the certainty that an end will come, which is never far from the mind of either, though Lene is more ready to face the thought. With great skill Fontane reveals the unbridgable social gulf between the lovers by his portrayal of Lene's environment, old Frau Nimptsch and Frau Dörr, the portly gardener's wife. The remarkable feature of this is the friendliness, even the affection, with which these figures are treated. And yet, though Fontane here, as elsewhere, shows himself the inventor of an irony which makes its object attractive rather than repellent, the environment is clearly one into which the cavalry officer, for all his good nature and good manners, cannot possibly fit. Fontane demonstrates the false position into which the two lovers have drifted on the second day of the outing to "Hankels Ablage," when mess comrades appear with their mistresses who treat Lene as one of themselves. It is a symbolical scene, done with complete realism and unaccompanied by any comment.

This abstention from sermonizing, commenting, or even underlining must be reckoned one of Fontane's major virtues. He lets his characters and events speak for themselves and credits the reader with ability to see what is obvious.

The second half of *Irrungen Wirrungen* is more complex. Botho's marriage leads to a counterpoint, in which the further life of the two lovers (who do not meet again) is pursued. The silliness of Botho's wife is revealed, though not without a hint that he would have been less perceptive of it if he had never met Lene Nimptsch; and the qualities of character in Lene are shown in her outspoken honesty to her husband-to-be. But there is never a suggestion that any other solution was possible. Through the mind of Botho himself the inevitability of the development is made explicit, firstly in the side on which he makes up his mind, and secondly when he gives his comrade Rexin advice for a similar situation. It is here, in an implied and penetrating analysis of his own position that he indicates the tragedy which underlies this book: "Denn alles hat seine natürliche Konsequenz, dessen müssen wir eingedenk sein. Es kann nichts ungeschehen gemacht werden und ein Bild, das uns in die Seele gegraben wurde, verblasst nie ganz wieder, schwindet nie ganz wieder dahin. Erinnerungen bleiben und Vergleiche kommen. Und so denn noch einmal, Freund, zurück von Ihrem Vorhaben, oder Ihr Leben empfängt eine Trübung, und Sie ringen sich nie mehr zu Klarheit und Helle durch. Vieles ist erlaubt, nur nicht das, was die Seele trifft, nur nicht Herzen hineinziehen und wenn's auch bloss das eigne wäre." [7]

Fontane's preference for discretion, self-restraint, under-statement, detectable throughout this novel, is perhaps most characteristically seen in the form in which Botho, already married some years, acknowledges his love for Lene; on learning of the death of Frau Nimptsch he hires a cab, drives out to the cemetery and fulfils a promise of laying a wreath upon her grave. And this funeral occasion is for him as well as for the reader, a symbol for the ending in decency and respect, of his and Lene's love. In this episode, one of the most attractive in this book, Fontane turns what appears to be a digression, a self-indulgence, into a purposeful symbol and a significant component.

The conversation which is so outstanding a feature of Fontane's work achieves a widening here. The speech of the uneducated is done with realism and conviction, and a new note appears in Botho von Rienacker, the ease and friendliness with which the gentleman can converse with those below him in rank. Though Fontane criticizes by implication Botho's action, his speech and his thought (which here appears as monologue of the same tone and quality as the speech) show him to be a man after Fontane's own heart in his freedom from snobbery, vanity or conceit, his honesty and unpretentiousness, and his gift for easy expression which puts others at ease.

Effi Briest is perhaps better known than *Irrungen Wirrungen*. It is possibly in some ways a better novel. Its lights and shadows are stronger, its action has a sensational climax; *Irrungen Wirrungen*, in its paradoxical combination of half-tones and firm drawing is a new achievement. *Effi Briest*, on the other hand, is an admittedly fine example of a more conventional type of novel. The environment of this novel is again that of the Prussian military and administrative upper class, and the "lower orders" disappear. Effi Briest is married at seventeen to an ex-officer civil servant of thirty-eight. The young bride joins her husband in a small provincial town on the Baltic coast. Left much alone by her husband she falls in her boredom to an experienced philanderer. Some years later, when the affair is a thing of the past, the husband discovers it, shoots the former lover and divorces his wife. It is noteworthy that Innstetten, in shooting Crampas and dismissing his wife, obeys simply a formal code. He has no feeling of hatred, he experiences no urge for revenge. The conventions of society control his actions, and though he after-wards never ceases to question the rightness of his actions, Effi on her deathbed accepts and confirms his standpoint. Fontane himself does not praise or blame; he is filled with compassion, sympathy and understanding.

Effi herself is Fontane's fullest portrait of a young woman. It is not a fixed portrait; for the events of this novel embrace years of development. Effi appears first as little more than a schoolgirl; she dies as a woman of twenty-eight. It is the only novel of Fontane in which such a process is attempted and the result is not only convincing but also endearing. Her death at the close of the book is, in its reticence, more deeply moving than most of the deaths of young women which occur so abundantly in nineteenth-century fiction.

Effi Briest was Fontane's last tragic work. His serious novels occupy in the main the decade 1880–90. In his seventies there appear a series of comedies in novel form, works of subdued tone and polished irony, which, scherzo-like, complement the "tragedies." *Die Poggenpuhls* (1896) traces a pattern of decayed gentility putting a brave face on things. Fontane exposes pretentions, and laughs at foibles, portraying the Poggenpuhls in their mean apartment with an irony which is both gentle and delicate. So even is the tone that an unaccustomed eye may overlook the subtlety and find the presentation dull. *Mathilde Möhring*, written in 1891 and never revised by Fontane, was published posthumously in 1908. It resembles *Die Poggenpuhls* in portraying the struggle of respectability against poverty. Mathilde, however, is no aristocrat, but a determined young person of humble descent who forms her plan, pursues her end, marries her man, makes a success of his career and survives with undiminished energy his early demise. The irony is once again wedded to admiration and sympathy. Though we laugh at Mathilde we cannot help liking her.

Fontane's finest comedy, however, is *Frau Jenny Treibel* (1892), which portrays the woman who has risen in the world. Frau Jenny is in essence a common enough type, but Fontane has endowed this example with the belief that she has aspirations for "das Höhere" and a dminisarg ignorance of her own real nature. Frau Jenny does not, however, stand alone; she is surrounded by a whole gallery of rich characters, her Hamburg daughter-in-law with her English snobbery, the unpractical schoolmaster whom she nearly married, and his determined daughter who very nearly puts the cat among the Treibel pigeons in her misguided intention to marry the younger Treibel son. It is one of Fontane's most successful and most rewarding portrayals of society. And the three comedies together make up a fascinating triptych presenting various aspects from middle and lower middle class regions.

Fontane's last novel is almost as long and as discursive as his first. *Der Stechlin* has the slenderest plot of all his novels and yet is a richer work than any. In action it is no more than the history of a wooing unimpeded by any obstacle. In essence it is a picture of society. Moreover, Fontane, journalist as he was, can hear the movement of the times. His portrait of a society has historical bearings, he is sensitive to new developments. Through the refracting medium of his characters, yet clearly discernible, social democracy impinges upon the feudal structure of Brandenburg-Prussia, progressive and reactionary circles interlock among the nobility, the Christian Social party makes its appearance in Lorenzen, the nouveau-riche in Gundermann and the integrating influence of the Prussian schoolmaster is embodied in Krippenstapel. Characters act as symbols and, simultaneously, as commentators. In all this diversity a unity is imposed fundamentally by Fontane's own honesty and impatience of shams and pose. The symbol of this unity is the figure of Dubslav von Stechlin. Old Stechlin is a character in every sense of the word. A whimsical humorist, full of prejudices, yet aware of his bias and ready to admit it and laugh at it. Open-minded in conversation, ready to touch any subject with irony yet without malice, Dubslav is the most winning of all the men portrayed in Fontane's novels. Clearly he is very close to Fontane's heart; indeed he derives many of his attractive features from Fontane's own father.

This figure of the whimsical, unpractical, unpretentious and shrewd old man, who clearly knows his own limitations, and is neither proud of them nor ashamed of them, is a symbol of the preoccupation of the ageing Fontane with his own father and his own childhood. He first appears in Schmidt, Corinna's father, in *Frau Jenny Treibel*, and reappears in Herr von Briest, and then, undisguised, as Fontane's father in *Meine Kinderjahre* (1894) which deserves in its simplicity, warmth and vividness, to rank as one of Fontane's best narrative works. In the episode which narrates Fontane's last visit to his father in Neu-Tornow all the tenderness and affection can be felt which makes *Der Stechlin*, for all its slow tempo and discursiveness, so lovable a book.

The novels of Fontane have a flavour which no other German novels have. They derive it from a rich and unique personality. Fontane could only give himself as he was. The gift of self-inflation was, fortunately, denied him. In *Aus den Tagen der Okkupation* he writes of a colleague "Seine Entrüstungssprache liegt jenseits meiner Kraft." [8] This incapacity for moral indignation is a part of the independence of the man but also of his dislike of ostentation, of affection or of pomposity, whether of bearing or of word. His strongest dislikes are for the shams, for Cujacius and Gundermann in *Der Stechlin*, or for Espe in *Quitt*, and in lesser degree for pretentiousness, in Eginhard aus dem Grunde (*Cécile*), and above all in *Frau Jenny Treibel*.

Nevertheless, where it is at all possible he balances his contempt or mockery with respect for other characteristics, for the genuine learning which Eginhard possesses, and the robust and determined character of Frau Jenny. This is the secret of Fontane's character drawing, that faults cannot blind him to qualities. He does not make a calculation of plus and minus ending with a positive or negative result, but allows the good and the bad, the attractive and the repellent, the endearing and the irritating to exist side by side as they do in life. His tolerance is a true tolerance, not a form of indifference. It can function because it is based on a recognition of human qualities and a refusal to dispose of them by dropping them into ready-made categories. His irony sees human foibles but he never forgets that he himself is subject to similar weaknesses. The irony is a sympathetic irony which bridges gaps. This is what distinguishes him from that other great ironist Thomas Mann who, with all his sympathy, remains on a plane above his characters. Fontane has nothing like Mann's intellectual power but he surpasses him in warmth.

Fontane has not only balance and tolerance but also humour. Perhaps the other qualities could not exist, or at least not express themselves, without the humour. It is not a common trait in German literature. But Fontane can create characters who are humorists as well as portray them with humour.

The web of social life is conversation, and any novelist who seeks to portray a society must be an adept at catching the tone of it. Fontane renders all forms of conversation, whether pretentious and pompous, witty and satirical, downright and rough, tender and intimate. Whatever the character and his station, whatever the situation, the speech matches. He could catch this tone with such infallible accuracy because he himself loved conversation. "Ich bin . . . ," he wrote, "im Sprechen wie im Schreiben ein Causeur." [9] But he was not the kind of "causeur" who is only willing to listen to himself. His modesty and his fairness made him love the give and take, the ebb and flow of talk. He has caught it and fixed it in his novels in a range of conversations which can rank with Jane Austen's.

The dualism of Fontane's outlook is part and parcel of his fairness and his balance. The reverse of a doctrinaire, he liked life as he found it, yet his open mind could welcome new ideas and see through prejudices and obstinacies. He was conservative and progressive at one and the same time. He could rouse enthusiasm for the Prussian idea and the Prussian army and yet appraise with an unprejudiced eye the Gerhart Hauptmann of *Vor Sonnenaufgang*. This broad perception of change with an unwavering focus on stability makes of him the kindest of moralists. He himself in a letter to Frau Stephany summed up the drift of *Irrungen Wirrungen* as: "Die Sitte gilt und muss gelten. Aber dass sie's muss, ist mitunter hart." [10] There, in a nutshell, is the polarity of Fontane's outlook. There, too, is the human sympathy which never deserts him.

There have been many German writers, who have written one, two perhaps three outstanding novels. But there are scarcely any German novelists, as we understand novelists; writers who portray men and manners, rather than discuss and propagate ideas; writers who in a long series of works build up, piece by piece and facet by facet, a solid, coherent, three-dimensional world. Fontane is the German equivalent to Trollope. He falls short, it is true, of Trollope's extraordinary fertility, and he nowhere rises to the Shakespearean level of such passages as the death of Mrs. Proudie; but he possesses, in compensation, a deeper humanity and a more independent spirit and in his combination of urbanity, irony and warmth of feeling, he has achieved something unique. Fontane's personal modesty, his respect for others' personalities, his delight in their talk, his pleasure in their environment has made of him a master of appearances, of the surface of the world, which he renders with such exactness and perception that the treatment of the surface implies a depth. The painter of social scenes becomes, almost unwittingly and unwillingly, an interpreter of life.

TRANSLATIONS

1. He who has such love of his homeland as you, is true in the depth of his heart.

2. Acts of heroism ought not to be closely examined.

3. Rather have I set out to write the work in my own fashion, as my own inclination and personality dictate, without heed to any model.

4. There are two things that matter: the characters and a demonstrable or poetically plausible relationship between guilt and punishment.

5. Fear of ridicule plays an enormous role in the world.

6. Nothing is ever so finely spun, but it comes at last into the sun.

7. For everything has its natural consequences; that is something we must never forget. We can not undo anything we have done; and any image which is graven on our heart will never be quite erased, will never quite fade. Memories remain and comparisons force themselves upon us. And so, my friend, once more, drop your plans or your life will be tinged by it and you will never get back to serenity and balance. Many things are allowed but we must keep clear of what strikes deep; keep hearts out of it, even if it were only your own that is involved.

8. His capacity for indignation is outside my scope.

9. In writing as in speech I'm a *causeur*.

10. Morals prevail, must prevail; but that they must, can sometimes work out very hard.

BIBLIOGRAPHY

FONTANE, TH. *Sämtliche Werke*, 1959 (up to 1961 13 volumes issued).

FONTANE, TH. *Meisterromane*, 1928. 4 vols.

FONTANE, TH. *Ausgewählte Werke*, 1922. 6 vols.

WANDREY, C. *Theodor Fontane*, 1919.

HAYENS, K. *Theodor Fontane. A Critical Study*, 1920.

MANN, TH. In *Rede und Antwort*, 1920.

KRAMMER, M. *Theodor Fontane*, 1922.

SEIDEL, H. W. *Fontane*, 1940.

PASCAL, R. In *The German Novel*, 1956.

Gerhart Hauptmann

Gerhart Hauptmann

by H. F. GARTEN

IN most European countries, the second half of the nineteenth century saw the emergence of Realism in literature. This was in the first place a reaction against the Romantic movement which had dominated the first half of the century. It also was the result of the growing application of scientific methods, the deepening interest in psychology, and the ever increasing awareness of the social and material factors determining human life.

In Germany, where the impact of Romanticism had been particularly strong, the change of outlook, as reflected in literature, was somewhat retarded. Two distinct phases may be observed: the first, generally known as Poetic Realism, still retained some of the magic and aloofness of Romanticism. Its main exponents—Droste-Hülshoff, Stifter, Gottfried Keller and Storm—though realistic in the loving observation of external detail, still shrank from coming to grips with reality in all its aspects. They still "escaped"—though not into an unreal world of dream and fancy, but into the tranquillity of country life, far from the squalor and bustle of the growing cities. Their realism was still softened by a poetic shimmer, and a nostalgia for the past. More important still, they were in harmony with the society in which they lived. In their writings, they extolled the accepted values of the middle class, the *Bürgertum*, to which they belonged, and for which they wrote. For all its individual conflicts and tragedies, life was good, and all was right with the world.

It was only in the last decades of the century that the full force of Realism broke on German writing, adopting the name of Naturalism. This of course was not only a German phenomenon. All over Europe, during the 1880s and 90s, a new spirit made itself felt in the field of creative writing. Outwardly, there seemed to be no particular reason for this change. It was a period of comparative stability, of steadily growing wealth, of dynamic optimism. The teething troubles of the Industrial Revolution seemed a thing of the past, and the ruling middle classes more secure than ever before. Yet there was everywhere a growing doubt and unrest. This unrest was closely linked with the rise of the working classes, which found expression in the Socialist movement. In Germany, this intellectual revolt

237

seemed particularly unwarranted. For here the newly founded empire of Bismarck was in the full flush of power and prosperity. Yet behind the glittering façade there was a growing sense of dissatisfaction and frustration, carried by an intellectual élite. It was this opposition that now came to the fore.

In the preceding twenty years, German literature had reached an impasse. With the death of Hebbel, in 1863, the line of great dramatists which had started with Lessing had come to an end. The spirit of Weimar Classicism had petered out in spurious imitators. The only outstanding genius of the period, Richard Wagner, combined the last flights of romantic imagination with the new national self-assertion. But now, in the early 1880s, a fresh wind stirred the stagnating waters of German literature. The impulse came from three different quarters. First of all from France, where the doctrines of Hippolyte Taine, who saw man as a mere product of heredity and environment, were realized in the social novels of Zola. Secondly, from Russia, where the great prose epics of Tolstoy and Dostoevsky explored new fields of human experience. Their realism was not based on any aesthetic theories but was deeply rooted in Russian life, and suffused with Christian mysticism. Tolstoy saw in the poor and humble the true bearers of the Christian message. And Dostoevsky said of himself: "I am a realist in the full sense of the term, that is, I describe all the depths of the human soul." The third, and probably most important, impulse came from Scandinavia, above all from Ibsen, whose social plays inaugurated a new form of drama. It was in Germany, where he spent most of his voluntary exile, that Ibsen reaped his first resounding successes in the early 1880s.

These, then, were the three main streams which fertilized the ground for the literary revolution known as the Naturalist movement. In keeping with the German predilection for logical consistency, the new artistic doctrines were carried to extremes. Zola's famous formula, "Une oeuvre d'art est un coin de la création vu à travers un tempérament," which still allows for the subjective approach of the artist, was capped by the dictum of Arno Holz, the first full-fledged German Naturalist: "Die Kunst hat die Tendenz, wieder Natur zu sein" [1] which eliminates the subjective element and sees art as an impersonal process.

For the time being, however, Germany had no outstanding creative writer to match the great figures of the European scene. A newly-founded Munich periodical, Die Gesellschaft, published, along with critical essays, model specimens of the new writing in translation, as for instance, a chapter from Zola's Germinal, which was acclaimed as "die künstlerische Bibel des Naturalismus."

The main interest was at first focused on prose writing. In 1889, Arno Holz and Johannes Schlaf published, under the pseudonym Bjarne P. Holmsen, their volume *Papa Hamlet*, a collection of short stories in which the naturalist method was carried to extremes. Here they introduced what became known as *Sekundenstil*—the precise reproduction of speech and thought processes, which led to the well-known "stream-of-consciousness" technique. A year later, they applied this method to the theatre in their play *Die Familie Selicke*, which stands as the very model of naturalist drama, depicting, in minute detail, the life of a poor family in the East End of Berlin. All the principles of Naturalism are here carried to the point of absurdity. The action as such is negligible; instead, there is the typical *Zustandsschilderung*—a detailed depiction of a state of things, a given social "milieu." The dialogue reproduces with phonetic accuracy the mannerisms and inconsistencies of everyday speech. There is no "hero," since the characters are determined by the laws of heredity and environment. What "guilt" there is has shifted on to society and circumstance. The total effect is deadening as the work lacks human interest and genuine poetic imagination. It needed a real dramatist to infuse the new form with these indispensable qualities; this dramatist was Gerhart Hauptmann.

The year before, in 1889, the venture which was to carry the Naturalist movement to victory was launched in Berlin. Modelled on André Antoine's *Théâtre Libre* in Paris, a group of writers and critics founded *Die Freie Bühne*, a theatre club dedicated to the production of new plays. The leading mind was Otto Brahm who, with this venture, was to inaugurate a new epoch of the German theatre. In a manifesto published in the first issue of a weekly review *Freie Bühne*, he defined his programme: "Eine freie Bühne für das moderne Leben schlagen wir auf. Im Mittelpunkt unserer Bestrebungen soll die Kunst stehen, die neue Kunst, die die Wirklichkeit anschaut und das gegenwärtige Dasein ... Der Bannerspruch der neuen Kunst ... ist das eine Wort: Wahrheit; und Wahrheit, Wahrheit auf jedem Lebenspfade ist es, die auch wir erstreben und fordern." [2] *Wahrheit*, in this context, did not apply merely to the faithful and unadorned depiction of reality in all its aspects: it embraced every social, moral and religious issue of contemporary life.

Die Freie Bühne opened, in September 1889, with a performance of Ibsen's *Ghosts*. Then, as the second production, came the first play of an unknown German author, *Vor Sonnenaufgang*, by Gerhart Hauptmann. It caused a public uproar; but the final outcome was a triumph for the new dramatist, and for a new type of drama. Hauptmann, who was then twenty-seven, had first tried his hand as a sculptor and studied at the art school in Breslau. As a young married man, he settled in a lakeside village near Berlin, where he made contact with a group of writers and social reformers, such as Wilhelm Bölsche, Bruno Wille, Arno Holz and the brothers Hart. In a literary club, named *Durch!*, the theories of naturalist art were fervently discussed. It was in this circle that Hauptmann delivered a talk on Georg Büchner, whose work had been all but unknown during the past fifty years. In the dramatic fragment *Woyzeck* he recognized a lone forerunner of the modern social drama he was striving for.

Hauptmann's own first ventures in naturalist writing were two prose stories, *Fasching* and *Bahnwärter Thiel*. Both were set in the environment of Berlin and were drawn from immediate life observation. In these stories, the principles of Naturalism were for the first time fully applied. Both deal with common people—the first with a sailmaker and his family, who find their death in the frozen lake, the second with a signalman who is driven, by inexorable circumstances, to murder his wife and child. Both are, in form as well as in substance, far removed from the poetic-realistic *Novellen* of Storm, Heyse or Raabe, which preceeded them. These two stories remained the only strictly naturalist *Novellen* in Hauptmann's large number of epic writings. But their themes were taken up in some of his dramatic works.

In the last chapters of his autobiography, *Das Abenteuer meiner Jugend*, which covers the first twenty-five years of his life, Hauptmann has given a vivid account of the ideas that inspired him and his fellow-writers at this crucial turning-point. As in a sudden flash, it occurred to him that German literature had lost touch with the people. "Die Dichterwerke reihten sich horizontal, meinethalben wie Perlen an einem Faden sich reihen. Eine vertikale Ausdehnung hatten sie nicht." [3] From this insight sprang the realization of his own "weite und tiefe Lebensverwurzelung," from which his work could draw nourishment. He acknowledges his indebtedness to Tolstoy: "Als ich *Die Macht der Finsternis* von Leo Tolstoi gelesen hatte, erkannte ich den Mann, der im Bodenständigen dort begonnen, wo ich nach langsam gewonnener Meisterschaft im Alter aufhören wollte." [4] Hauptmann's adoption of Naturalism was thus not the result of theoretical speculation but an instinctive realization of his true powers. "Was ging das Geschwätz vom Naturalismus mich an? Aus Erde ist ja der Mensch gemacht, und es gibt keine Dichtung, ebensowenig wie eine Blüte und Frucht, sie sauge denn ihre Kraft aus der Erde!" [5] Following this insight, a whole world of childhood memories came to life again: his parental home, the peasants and weavers of the Silesian foothills, the years at the Breslau art school.

To these were added the impressions of the years he lived in the
neighbourhood of Berlin. In fact, these two settings, his native
Silesia and the countryside round Berlin, provide the background
and the characters of nearly all his naturalist plays. A further result
of this decisive turn was the introduction of dialect into serious
drama. This had nothing to do with its occasional use in the local
Volksstück or in the prose stories of the so-called *Heimatdichter*, where
it served mainly picturesque or humourous purposes. For Hauptmann, dialect was the natural form of expression and the logical
conclusion of his new insight. It was equivalent to the *Hochdeutsch*
of great drama, and to the verse of Goethe or Schiller. "Ich wollte
dem Dialekt seine Würde zurückgeben." [6]

To Hauptmann, Naturalism was thus never a mere technique,
still less an aesthetic theory, as it was for his lesser contemporaries.
To him it was no more than a convenient form in which he could
develop what was his greatest gift: the creation of living characters,
each with his own atmosphere, his idiosyncrasies, his subtle mannerisms of speech and gesture. He discarded the naturalist method as
soon as it no longer served his purpose. Only his first play, *Vor
Sonnenaufgang*, and his masterpiece, *Die Weber*, can be called
naturalist in the strict sense of the term. Though separated by two
plays of a very different kind, they spring from the same source—his
childhood memories—and have the same aim: the portrayal of a
whole social milieu, the farmers and the weavers of Silesia respectively, without regard to individual characters and conflicts. *Vor
Sonnenaufgang* still shows signs of immaturity and uncertainty of
touch. First of all, there is an element of moralizing, totally absent
from Hauptmann's later work. The central character, Loth, is a
social reformer and idealist—the very epitome of a naturalist
doctrinaire, who tries to impose his ideas on a family of Silesian
farmers utterly demoralized by suddenly acquired wealth. The
farmer's daughter, Helene—the only member of the family unsullied
by the corruption around her—falls in love with the newcomer.
Loth, fearing that the laws of heredity and environment may affect
their future children, abandons the girl, who kills herself in despair.
The play stands as the very model of naturalist drama. Yet, as the
action proceeds, the emphasis gradually shifts: the hero, who at first
appears as the apostle of the naturalist creed, and who no doubt
voices the author's own ideas at the time, in the end stands revealed
as a prig: the real human tragedy is played out by the girl who has
simply obeyed her natural instincts. The irrationality of life proves
more important than any rational theory. In the artless love-scene,
set against the background of the awakening farm at dawn, the
genuine Hauptmann tone is heard for the first time. Helene is the

first in a long line of female characters who follow unreflectingly their
womanly impulses and are crushed by the force of circumstance.

The aims of naturalist drama are most fully achieved in *Die
Weber*, which is a drama without a hero, portraying as it does the
futile rising of the famished weavers during the 1840s. Here the
only dramatic impulse is given by the very momentum of the mass
movement which gathers force, reaches a climax, and subsides.
Yet the whole vast picture is composed of thousands of minute
traits, like strands in a huge tapestry. Though it has often been
exploited for propagandist purposes, this play is in fact a human
tragedy, inspired by compassion for the poor and suffering, and
overshadowed by inexorable fate.

If *Die Weber* is the fullest realization of naturalist drama, *Der
Biberpelz*, which appeared one year later (1893) is its comic counterpart. The period is the last years of Bismarck's rule, at the time of
the anti-socialist laws, which form the background of the play.
In no other work has Hauptmann indulged to such an extent in
direct social satire. His district-counsellor von Wehrhahn is the very
epitome of Prussian militarism and bureaucracy. Yet even here the
emphasis is laid not on social criticism but on the subtle delineation
of character, above all in the central figure of the washerwoman
Mutter Wolffen, who with her natural craftiness outwits her judge.
Once again, a whole social milieu is brought to life, drawn from
immediate observation.

The two plays separating *Vor Sonnenaufgang* and *Die Weber*, *Das
Friedensfest* (1890) and *Einsame Menschen* (1891), are of a different
kind. Firstly, they are middle-class plays; both are set in a country-
house near Berlin. Then, they concentrate on a small set of characters and observe the classical unities of time and place. Never did
Hauptmann come closer to Ibsen, in whose shadow he had grown
up, and as whose "*Erfüller*" he was hailed by Theodor Fontane.
There are obvious parallels between *Das Friedensfest* and *Ghosts*, on
the one hand, and between *Einsame Menschen* and *Rosmersholm*, on
the other. Yet it soon became evident that Hauptmann's dramatic
technique, and indeed his very essence, was very different from
Ibsen's. In contrast to Ibsen's analytic method, which from a
final situation gradually unravels the past, Hauptmann shows his
characters in the full process of life. While Ibsen (at any rate in the
plays of his middle period) points a moral, Hauptmann is never
concerned with social or moral concepts. His characters are at no
time embodiments of ideas but all-round human beings who live
out their destiny. This—the building-up of characters and their
reactions upon one another—is the very essence of Hauptmann's
dramas. Plot and action are merely subservient, or rather, they

spring inevitably from the conflict of characters. Thus, the plays grow as it were of their own accord, like living organisms. "Ein Drama muss sich selbst bewegen, nicht vom Dichter bewegt werden," Hauptmann notes in one of his reflections on dramatic art. "Der Ursprung seiner Bewegung muss, wie der Ursprung des Lebens, allen verborgen sein." [7] Hauptmann's drama has been called "vegetative" or "biological." Its essential quality is not the precise reproduction of surface reality but an intuitive recreation of life from deeper layers of the mind. It is this quality which raises it far above the works of the lesser naturalist playwrights, such as Sudermann, Halbe or Hirschfeld.

A further important fact distinguishing Hauptmann from Ibsen is that his social range transcends the middle classes, Ibsen's exclusive domain, and includes the lower classes. In fact, he was the first (after the solitary precedent of Büchner's *Woyzeck*) to raise the poor and humble to the dignity of tragedy. His greatest, and probably most enduring, plays are those centring on the inarticulate tragedies of common people—*Die Weber*, *Hanneles Himmelfahrt*, *Fuhrmann Henschel*, *Rose Bernd* and *Die Ratten* (and, of course, his comic masterpiece, *Der Biberpelz*).

What drew Hauptmann to the poor and underprivileged was not only the awakening of social conscience, a common feature of the age. It was a deep sympathy with human suffering, wherever he encountered it, and an awareness of the dignity of man, even in its humblest forms. In fact, social oppression plays a part only in *Die Weber*, and even here it is by no means the dominant theme. More important than the need for material improvement is the inarticulate urge for a higher and fuller life. "A jeder Mensch hat halt 'ne Sehnsucht"—these words of a wretched rag-and-bone-man have often been cited as a *leitmotif* not only of this drama, but of Hauptmann's entire work.

More and more, as Hauptmann matured, his delineation of a social milieu gave way to the creation of human characters pure and simple. The foremost instances (within the range of "proletarian" plays) are *Fuhrmann Henschel* (1898), *Rose Bernd* (1903) and *Die Ratten* (1911). All these sprang from personal experience: the first from childhood memories, the second from the case of a Silesian peasant girl he had heard as a juryman, the last from his intimate knowledge of the Berlin East End. Though all three employ the naturalist technique in every detail, the emphasis is not on the faithful reproduction of a milieu but on the delineation of characters, with their inescapable tragedies. "Im rauhen Gewand volkstümlich-realistischer Gegenwart eine attische Tragödie" [8]—this is how Thomas Mann has characterized *Fuhrmann Henschel*.

Like all true drama, Hauptmann's mature plays are tragedies of fate. But for him fate is not outside or above man; nor is it in social factors (though these play, at any rate in the beginning, a certain part): it is within man, rooted in his character, and therefore all the more inescapable. Hauptmann sees all life as drama. "Schliesslich werden alle Gedanken dramatisch gedacht, wird alles Leben dramatisch gelebt," [9] he notes in one of his reflections. Hauptmann's underlying philosophy is deterministic: however man struggles, he cannot escape his fate, which is born with him. There is thus no interaction of guilt and atonement; for where there is no free will there cannot be guilt in the accepted sense. Hauptmann's dramas are dramas not of action but of suffering, and of the ultimate loneliness of man. This sense of isolation is most poignant where it is inarticulate, that is, among the primitive and unreflecting common people. No expression of loneliness can be so telling as silence, or inadequacy of words. "Schlecht bin ich geworn, bloss ich kann nischt dafier," says Henschel, feeling himself to be hopelessly ensnared in the meshes of fate. "Ich bin ebens halt aso 'neingetapert." [10] And Rose Bernd, in her predicament, cries out: "Wenn ma bloss nich aso alleene wäre! Ma is zu sehr alleene hier uff d'r Erde!" [11] Their deepest tragedy lies in their incapacity to communicate, their *Verstocktheit*. "Ein Wort bloss! Ein Wort mit ihm reden! Ein Wort! das hätte ja alles wahrscheinlich gewendet," [12] says Michaline in *Michael Kramer*, when her brother's tragedy has run its course. This is true of most of Hauptmann's central characters.

It has often been observed that there are no villains in Hauptmann's plays, only men misguided or conditioned by their upbringing and surroundings. Even those who, by design or mere coincidence, contribute to the tragedy, do so not with evil intent but compelled by their own character and by circumstances. The true, indeed the only tragedy lies in the interrelations of men, and the closer these are, the deeper the tragedy. Man, for Hauptmann, is both hunter and hunted. This basic view is illuminated in the final situations of his plays. In almost every instance, the central character (the term "hero" or "heroine" would be quite inadequate) finds himself driven into a corner from where he sees no escape but death. The idea of a hunt is, either explicitly or implicitly, often touched on towards the end of the play: "Wenn Schilling wirklich geflohen ist . . . nein, nicht mehr . . . nicht mehr wie die Jagdhunde nachlaufen!" [13] (*Gabriel Schillings Flucht*). "Sie haben ihn mir zu Tode gehetzt. Erschlagen . . . wie so'n Hund," [14] says Michael Kramer over the body of his son. "Das sind die Verfolger! Das sind die Hetzhunde!" [15] cries Inken in *Vor Sonnenuntergang* when the family close in on their victim. Even in the historical drama *Florian Geyer*, the final scene shows the knight entrapped by his enemies, and his killer "fällt über den Toten her wie über ein erlegtes Wild." [16] The examples could be multiplied.

The most frequent solution in this tragic predicament is suicide. Of Hauptmann's principal characters, nearly half take their own lives. The striking incidence of suicide is not a sign of a moral defect. No stigma attaches to an act which is the logical outcome of Hauptmann's particular type of drama. It illustrates better than anything the "passive" nature of his heroes, whose "guilt" lies not in a flaw of character, or a breach of the moral law, but rather in a heightened susceptibility to the exigencies of life. Instead of hurting others, they do away with themselves. Far from debasing them morally, their self-inflicted death raises them high above the others: the defeated stands in the end as the true victor.

It is no mere coincidence that Hauptmann was attracted again and again to the figure of the artist. In the artist, he saw the outstanding instance of a man endowed with an excess of sensibility, in contrast to the coarse and unimaginative philistines around him. However, Hauptmann is far removed from any romantic glorification of the artist. On the contrary: all his artists are failures, either in life or in their work, or in both. In *Kollege Crampton*, his earliest comedy (1892), and *Peter Brauer* (1910), this theme is treated humourously, though verging on the tragic; in *Michael Kramer* (1900) and *Gabriel Schillings Flucht* (1906), it emerges with the full force of tragedy. These two last plays rank among the most poignant and intensely personal of Hauptmann's works. Though outwardly naturalist in the minute depiction of setting and character, they transcend the realistic plane and enter into a higher realm which belongs to an altogether different aspect of Hauptmann's creative world. In *Michael Kramer*, after three naturalist acts, the closing fourth act rises to a transcendental level on which the individual story assumes universal significance. Even the language imperceptibly falls into a rhythmical pattern. In this drama two artists, father and son, are confronted—the one a failure in his art but a great and sincere personality, the other a genius but a failure in life. *Gabriel Schillings Flucht*, on the other hand (the only one of Hauptmann's realistic plays set not in Silesia or near Berlin, but on an island in the Baltic) is suffused with a peculiar mysticism linked with the ever-present sea. The theme of this play—a man torn between two women—echoes that of the early *Einsame Menschen*. But now it is shorn of any doctrinal and tendentious components and centres on the deadly clash of characters.

All Hauptmann's naturalist plays deal with contemporary life,

with the single exception of *Florian Geyer*. This was his only attempt
to apply the naturalist technique to historical drama (*Die Weber*
is in its subject-matter too close to Hauptmann's own time and to
his personal childhood impressions to be really "historical").
Florian Geyer, which at its first appearance in 1896 proved a complete
failure, gradually came to be recognized as one of his greatest
achievements. An entire past age, the age of the German Peasants'
War, is brought to life. In contrast to *Die Weber*, there is an individual hero—the knight who turns his back on his own class to
become a leader of the revolt. But his fate merges with that of the
peasants; virtually, it is no less than *Die Weber* the drama of a mass
movement. Similarly, it is composed of a multitude of minute
touches which together build up a vast panorama of an entire
revolutionary movement. All external action is relegated to the
background; what we see is merely the effect it has on the peasants,
their initial triumph and their ultimate failure. Yet, despite the
minutely observed detail, a poetic undercurrent runs through the
whole drama. More essential than the realism of speech and
character-drawing is the evocation of atmosphere and mood, which
gives the play the power of a ballad. It is this quality that foreshadows, even in this early work, Hauptmann's later move towards
poetic drama.

The last play of Hauptmann which can strictly be called naturalist
is *Die Ratten*, of 1911. It not only shows once more his genius for
realistic portrayal but also contains a theoretical discussion of the
principles of Naturalism. A young student-actor (a portrait of the
author in his younger days), who takes lessons in acting from a retired theatre director, upholds the tenets of naturalistic art against
the latter's stubborn defence of classical tragedy. He insists that
"ein Barbier oder eine Reinmachefrau . . . ebensogut ein Objekt der
Tragödie sein könnte als Lady Macbeth und König Lear." [17]
His argument culminates in the sentence: "Vor der Kunst wie vor
dem Gesetz sind alle Menschen gleich." [18] This statement is
poignantly illustrated by a real tragedy which runs its course before
our eyes: a humble woman's desperate fight for her adopted child.
The drama shows, in a juxtaposition of several plots, a cross-section
of German society at the eve of the first world war. The Berlin
tenement in which it is set symbolizes the whole social structure,
whose very foundations are undermined by "the rats." *Die Ratten*
is the last of a line of plays in which Hauptmann shows himself
a trenchant critic of Wilhelmine Germany—a line which includes
the comedy *Der Biberpelz* and its sequel, *Der rote Hahn*. Together,
these three plays present a consummate picture of German society
in progressive disintegration. They reflect clearly the social and

political criticism which was so vital an aspect of the whole Naturalist movement.

Die Ratten was in fact a late-comer, for Naturalism as a movement had lost its force by the turn of the century, when it was superseded by its very opposite, the emergence of poetic and symbolist drama, known as Neo-Romanticism. Hauptmann himself had undergone this significant change at a very early point in his development. Along with his naturalist plays, he turned again and again to a very different type of drama, which drew its subjects from history and folklore, clothing them in rich and florid verse. However, what at first seemed like inconsistency or yielding to a change of fashion, was gradually recognized to be a natural process of creative growth. It was, in fact, the same impulse that informed his naturalist as well as his symbolist and poetic plays. In several instances, the two forms are fused in one and the same work, as, e.g. in *Hanneles Himmelfahrt*, *Schluck und Jau* and *Und Pippa tanzt*! In these plays, a minutely depicted reality rises almost imperceptibly to a symbolic and poetic plane. But even in his most strictly naturalist plays, there is an undercurrent of mysticism which flows from deeper sources of his creative mind. For Hauptmann, the visible world is surrounded by mystery; the borderline between the two, between reality and dream, is fluid. It is this sense of mystery, this absorption in the universal and timeless questions of human existence, which carried him to regions far beyond the realistic portrayal of contemporary life. More and more, as he grew older, he was drawn into the orbit of Goethe. Another vital impulse came from his contact with Greece and Greek tragedy, which had a lasting effect on his later work and completely changed not only his dramatic form but his whole conception of drama.

Nothing could illustrate this change better than the three realistic plays he wrote in his sixties, that is, between 1922 and 1932, *Dorothea Angermann*, *Vor Sonnenuntergang* and the uncompleted *Herbert Engelmann*. Though portraying realistic characters in a realistic setting, the language of these plays has a literary quality which distinguishes it from the colloquial diction of his naturalist plays. Hauptmann, by that time, had evidently lost that intuitive sense of the rhythms of everyday speech which was his outstanding faculty. Instead, his creative mind developed along lines which eventually led him to forms far removed from his beginnings.

Viewing Hauptmann's work as a whole, one can observe a clear caesura round about 1912, that is, in his fiftieth year. All his naturalist plays belong to the earlier part of his life. Without attempting any critical evaluation, it can be said that with these plays he has made his most lasting contribution to German drama.

It is these plays that are most fully alive on the German stage today. This is not only because their closeness to everyday life has a more immediate appeal to the public at large. It is because in them Hauptmann succeeded in bringing German drama down to earth. More essential than his mastery of the naturalist technique is the fact that, after a long period of stagnation and intellectual aloofness, he rooted the drama deep in the soil of his country.

TRANSLATIONS

1. Art has the tendency to revert to nature.

2. We are setting up a free stage for modern life. Our aspirations shall centre on art, the new art which looks at reality and contemporary life . . . The battle-cry of this new art is the one word—truth! And it is truth, truth in every path of life for which we are striving, and which we demand!

3. The poetic works were strung horizontally, as it were like pearls on a thread. They had no vertical dimension.

4. When I had read *The Power of Darkness* by Leo Tolstoy, I recognized the man who had begun in the soil where I, after slowly gaining mastership, meant to end up in old age.

5. What did I care for the babble about Naturalism? Why, man is made of earth, and there is no work of literature, any more than there is a blossom or a fruit, but draws its strength from the earth.

6. I wanted to restore dialect to its dignity.

7. A drama must move by itself, and not be moved by the author. The origin of its movement, like the origin of life, must be hidden to all.

8. An Attic tragedy in the coarse guise of the popular-realistic present.

9. After all, all thoughts are thought dramatically, all life is lived dramatically.

10. I've turned bad, but I can't help it. I've just stumbled into it.

11. If only one wasn't so alone! One is too alone here on earth!

12. Just a word! To talk a word with him! A word! That might have changed everything!

13. If Schilling has really fled—no—let's not run after him like blood-hounds!

14. They've hunted him to death. Slain, like a dog.

15. There are the pursuers! There are the bloodhounds!

16. Falls on the dead man as on a slaughtered quarry.

17. A barber or a charwoman . . . could just as well be a subject of tragedy as Lady Macbeth or King Lear.

18. Before Art, as before the Law, all men are equal.

BIBLIOGRAPHY

ARNOLD, R. F. *Das moderne Drama*. Strasbourg, 1912.
BEHL, C. F. W. *Wege zu Gerhart Hauptmann*. Goslar, 1948.

BENOIST-HANAPPIER, L. *Le drame naturaliste en Allemagne.* Paris, 1905.

BERG, LEO. *Der Naturalismus.* Munich, 1892.

CONRAD, M. G. *Von Zola bis Hauptmann: Erinnerungen zur Geschichte der Moderne.* Leipzig, 1902.

FECHTER, PAUL. *Gerhart Hauptmann.* Dresden, 1922.

GARTEN, H. F. *Gerhart Hauptmann.* Cambridge, 1954.

GREGOR, JOSEPH. *Gerhart Hauptmann. Das Werk und unsere Zeit.* Vienna, 1952.

LESSING, OTTO E. *Die neue Form. Ein Beitrag zum Verständnis des deutschen Naturalismus.* Dresden, 1910.

MANN, THOMAS. *Gerhart Hauptmann.* Gütersloh, 1953.

SINDEN, M. *Gerhart Hauptmann: The Prose Plays.* Toronto-London, 1957.

SOERGEL, ALBERT. *Dichtung und Dichter der Zeit.* 19th ed. Leipzig, 1928.

STOCKIUS, A. *Naturalism in recent German Drama. With special reference to Hauptmann.* New York, 1903.

TANK, K. L. *Gerhart Hauptmann.* Hamburg, 1959.

ZIEGENFUSS, W. *Gerhart Hauptmann. Dichtung und Gesellschaftsidee der bürgerlichen Humanität.* Berlin, 1948.

Hugo von Hofmannsthal

Hugo von Hofmannsthal

by BRIAN KEITH-SMITH

HUGO von HOFMANNSTHAL, son of a bank director, was born in Vienna on 1 February 1874. His heritage, which included grandparents of Austrian, Italian, Jewish and Swabian blood, was as cosmopolitan as Vienna itself, and from his earliest days he was aware of the influence of foreign landscapes and cultures. His love for Italy stemmed from family connections and from the link between Austria and the Vatican. Vienna had been as important a seat of government and progress as any other within the Holy Roman Empire. It has been the farthest west that the invading Ottoman armies had been, and it continued to be a centre of Italian, Southern Germanic and Slav cultures. Like Venice, Vienna was a meeting-place of East and West, which was to have great significance in Hofmannsthal's thought.

Hofmannsthal was brought up in the world of the Viennese aristocracy, and was able to witness all the cultural activities that he wanted with no material restrictions, He was a child of abnormal intelligence, whose mind by the age of twelve was as inquiring and receptive as that of a normal intelligent twenty year old. By twelve years of age he had read and understood the works of Goethe, Schiller, Kleist and Grillparzer. Three years later he had extended this to Homer, Dante, Shakespeare, Voltaire, Browning and Byron. By eighteen years of age he had added to this list Plato, most of the great Russian and Scandinavian writers, the French philosophers, Keller, Nietzsche and the more important works of his contemporaries throughout Europe. He is said to have then been able to write in five languages and read in eight. While still at school, he started to publish poems and essays in periodicals, writing under pseudonyms, the most famous of which was Loris. Through one of these early essays he became acquainted with a group of young intellectuals mostly some five to ten years older than himself, who met in the Café Griensteidl to discuss artistic creation, literature and philosophy. He was soon accepted as their leader, not only because of his astonishing powers of memory and conversation, but also because of his growing reputation as a writer.

His first lyrical dramolet *Gestern* (1891) already shows some of the

253

themes and problems that will interest him in many of his later works. Andrea, a self-confessed aesthete, tries to control everyone and everything with which he comes into contact—the very lives of his friends, their pasts, presents and futures; but he is made to change from the illusory life of an aesthete into a full awareness of an existence which he does not entirely control.

It was into such a dictatorial aesthetic system that Hofmannsthal refused to be drawn by the young German poet Stefan George, who visited Vienna in the winter of 1891. George was fascinated by the brilliance and potential artistry of this schoolboy, and hoped to start a relationship with him which would re-create Hofmannsthal as a writer after George's own image. Hofmannsthal was greatly impressed by the intensity of George's poetry, but he would not be drawn into a relationship which promised no independence and a contact with life only through the expressions of an aesthetically sheltered world. He saw George as a possible negative influence on his personality, and broke with him after only a few weeks acquaintance. He continued to admire George's poetry, contributed to his *Blätter für die Kunst*, met him occasionally later in his life, and dedicated *Das Gerettete Venedig* (1904) to him: "in Bewunderung und Freundschaft."

In 1892 Hofmannsthal became a student at Vienna University, where he studied Law and Romance languages and literatures. He also went to the lectures of Ernst Mach, the fashionable philosopher of the day, whose philosophy was based on interpreting human existence as a sum of the sensory impressions of which the individual is conscious. Mach's attempt to explore the common fields of physics, psychology and thought was typical of Viennese intellectual interests of the time. In the summer of 1892 Hofmannsthal went on holiday to France, Provence and Northern Italy and was immediately impressed by the colours of their landscapes and the richness of the culture of their peoples. Later in his life he often spent some three months in the summer travelling over Northern Italy and the Riviera, usually stopping for a few days at Venice. Venice was the town of adventure for him, and five of his works have a Venetian setting. Venice he represents as the hunting ground for the Don Juan type adventurer, the Casanova, standing for all that is sensual and irresponsible. The development of his attitude towards the adventurer is reflected in his growing dislike for Venice in later life. In 1894 he did his military service in the cavalry, and while taking part in exercises in the Hungarian part of the Austro-Hungarian Empire kept up his voluminous reading. By 1898 he had written a thesis on the language of the Pléiades and a longer dissertation on Victor Hugo. Professorial rejection of this made him give up his

plans of becoming a lecturer in Romance Languages, and he finally
determined to become a full-time writer. In 1900 he spent a month
in Paris where he met many celebrated men of letters, but being by
nature retiring, he did not make many friends. He learnt to admire
the work of Rodin the sculptor, and was deeply impressed by the
quiet temperament of the Belgian poetic dramatist Maeterlinck. In
1901 he married and settled down in a country house at Rodaun
near Vienna, which remained his home for the rest of his life. His
marriage was peaceful, and there were two sons and a daughter.
Outwardly at least he was able to live peacefully in the style of the
English gentleman, whose manners he so much admired.

The peace that Hofmannsthal found in his family life was not
enough to still the hypersensitivity of his mind and spirit. His
marriage was a partial solution to a crisis in his whole being both
as an artist and as a man whose roots may be traced back in his
earliest works. The seven dramolets which he wrote between 1891
and 1897 were nearly all written in monologue style having the
general theme of the transience of life and the denial of the dangerous and decadent way of life of the aesthete. They show that man is
subject to the law of change, that life and dying are not static conditions, but preparatory developments in the progress of a soul.
Hofmannsthal was intellectually aware as a young man of such
concepts, but he had not yet experienced enough in his personal life
to be able to examine them against the touchstone of his own
existence. The best known of these dramolets is *Der Tor und der Tod*
(1893). Here Claudio, a nobleman and aesthete, whose life is empty
of meaning, has no human contacts, and is isolated from everything
but his works of art and his books. The figure of Death enters, not as
a skeleton in the dance of death tradition, nor as a messenger of God
calling man to judgment, but as a great God of the human soul. He
introduces to Claudio the figures of his dead mother to whom
Claudio never listened, a young girl whose love he eventually
denied, and a friend whom he let down, all because he wished to
remain uncommitted to enjoy a world of his own. Faced now with
his own death, Claudio realizes how useless his life has been—an
"Erstarrensein." In this moment he realizes and recognizes the
value of every moment and the true inner meaning of relationships
and things. For him it is the moment of his dying, but he is no longer
afraid because he has achieved a feeling of fulfilment for his existence.
So he asks Death to become his life, for he knows that his soul in
dying will take on a new and more meaningful form of existence:

"Da tot mein Leben war, sei du mein Leben, Tod!
Was zwingt mich, der ich beides nicht erkenne,

Dass ich dich Tod und jenes Leben nenne?
In eine Stunde kannst du Leben pressen [1]
. . ."

In *Der Tor und der Tod*, as in the other dramolets, the main characters
have to find a way to intensify every moment of their lives, to find a
meaning for their lives, to find their correct place in the hierarchy
of the universe. The characters in *Das kleine Welttheater* (1897) are
sub-titled "Die Glücklichen." They are fortunate because they are
aware of a hierarchical pattern of the universe. They all have varying
degrees of insight into their situations, culminating in the madman,
whose direct contact with the whole of the universe is formless and
not tied down by a style of living or expression like those of the gardener or poet. He is Hofmannsthal's Homunculus, an attraction
and warning to those who have their place in life, and know but
deny the desire to break with this and take up the office of the
madman. The madman's pleasure comes from his ability to mock
at the other Glücklichen:

> "Was aber sind Paläste und Gedichte:
> Traumhaftes Abbild des Wirklichen!
> Das Wirkliche fängt kein Gewebe ein:
> Den ganzen Reigen anzuführen,
> Den wirklichen, begreift ihr dieses Amt?
> Hier ist ein Weg, er trägt mich leichter als der Traum.
> Ich gleite bis ans Meer. . . .
> . . .
> Bacchus, Bacchus, auch dich fing einer ein
> Und band dich fest, doch nicht für lange." [2]

The finding of a place in life and the acceptance of a fate is one
of the roots of the crisis through which Hofmannsthal went as a
young man. In the autobiographical tract *Ad me ipsum* (1916)
we are given fragmentary insights into his Weltanschauung and the
problems which he faced as an artist and man. The quotation which
he places at the head of this from Gregor von Nyssa, a fourth century
Latin Saint:

> "Quocirca supremae pulchritudinis amator quod jam viderat
> tamquam imaginem eius quod non viderat credens, ipso frui
> primitivo desiderabat." (*Vita Mosis.*)[3]

Hofmannsthal may have taken from Konrad Burdach's work *Faust
und Moses*, where the argument is concerned with the "Verhältnis
des strebenden Menschen zur Natur," and this is the basic theme of
Ad me ipsum. Hofmannsthal tries to find a connection between the

mortal and immortal parts of human existence. He examines stations of the soul, the first of which is "Präexistenz," which he calls a "glorreicher aber gefährlicher Zustand." It is glorious because in this state the individual spirit has sovereignty over the universe, and dangerous because it can detect only totalities; as if in a climbing aeroplane, it can make out the patterns of the fields of life below, but it cannot pick out the individual details. The soul in Präexistenz is not committed to any philosophy or religion or person or responsibilities, and has not yet taken its place in the human hierarchy. All life lived as an approximation to human standards and traditions is damaging to the purity of Präexistenz, and birth itself is a releasing of the soul from pure Präexistenz into a gradually decaying Präexistenz. Certain positions in society seem to recapture this state, for instance the ruler, who by a turn of his hand can alter the lives of all his peoples, but cannot control the details of their daily lives; or the madman who is not tied down by convention but lives in a world of his own making; or the boy or girl who have not yet given away their independence in marriage. But this is against the demands of change made by mortal life. A soul in Präexistenz seeks for perfection by self-criticism, by trying to recapture those parts of Präexistenz that have not yet been made impure, or by seeking a mirror of pure Präexistenz in another soul. Once it understands that all souls have to lose their Präexistenz in human life, then it longs for a release from the illusion of purity and for a fateful life. In accepting a fate it tries to keep as much power as it has had over the universe as is possible. Hofmannsthal thus states the problem:

"Verknüpfung mit dem Leben. Durchdringen aus der Präexistenz zur Existenz . . . zum Sein. [4]

He goes on to consider Verschuldung and calls it "ein halb verlorener Zustand der Präexistenz." This involves the acceptance by the soul of its subordinate role in the universe. Having seen this desire to enter into Existenz, he tries to find ways into it. The first he finds is through introversion, the mystic way. But this way proves false; many (as shown in the Chandos Letter) take this way without any mysticism. The mystic way is based on a belief that a parallel of the universe lies within the human soul—the doctrine of macrocosm and microcosm. Introspection should lead to a complete identification of the two. The other way which Hofmannsthal finds into Existenz is the non-mystical way, or the "Weg zum Sozialen." This is achieved in three ways—through Tat, Werk or Kind. For Hofmannsthal "Tun ist sich aufgeben"—and what is important is not the deed itself but the acceptance which is implied of the Treue to follow. Once one has acted, then one must accept the results and remain faithful to them as they are part of the act. There follows "Identität von Treue und Schicksal." Passive introspection denies the taking on of a fate, and merely maps out a course which strangles development of the soul. It is retrogressive because it is always looking inside itself for a mirror image of what is rapidly fading away all the time, and this is a development of the Spiegelung found in Präexistenz. Hofmannsthal sums this up in *Das Gespräch über Gedichte* as "Draussen sind wir zu finden, draussen." The adventurer or philanderer seeks himself in so many others that he eventually loses sight of himself. Too much knowledge of himself brings him to a situation where he is identified with a formless universe. Where the madman is intoxicated by not being held down in the hierarchical system, the philanderer no longer experiences any significance in the act of love, because all individuality is lost in an abstracted event. Werk and Kind are the expressions of Treue and are implied by Tat. Hofmannsthal sees the necessity for man to accept an allomatic element, the influence of others. The attempt to live isolated from human contact and to supply one's own fate he calls automatic. The search for oneself by the non-mystical way implies the changing of oneself. In *Die Frau ohne Schatten* the acceptance of a fate leads to the birth of children who will become magical mirror images of their parents, and representatives of that state of Präexistenz to which the parents once belonged. The parents become aware of the spiral found in the repetition of stages in life. Finally we see (as in *Reitergeschichte*) the motif of the Doppelgänger, where the individual meets his double before he dies. The individual can see himself *in toto* in another. He is aware of the whole human personality of his soul and of the pattern in the cosmology of the universe. Death is no longer approached with anxiety, for it offers an opportunity to return to a state of pure Präexistenz. Death means the shedding of a long fate and the refreshment of a new spell in Präexistenz. The false values of the world make it possible for the soul to be led astray and never be able to view the cosmological position in which it stands. Therefore death can also be an imponderable.

Although we may see obvious reflections of his crisis in for example the different styles and solutions shown in 1899 by *Das Bergwerk zu Falun, Die Hochzeit der Sobeide* and *Der Abenteurer und die Sängerin*, Hofmannsthal's crisis is most clearly stated in the famous Chandos Letter. This is written as an answer from Philip, Lord Chandos to Francis Bacon, and describes a parallel situation to one in *Ad me ipsum* described as "Die Situation des Mystikers ohne Mystik, dazu zuviel Weltfrömmigkeit. Der Anstand des Schweigens als Resultat." In struggling with the meaning and nature of symbols, Hofmannsthal began to realize that he might not always be able to see clearly the hidden relationships between things in the universe, and that as a result of this his critical and selective powers might disappear. It is typical of his honesty of thought and strength of faith in life, that he did not accept this in silence but tried to capture it in writing, and thereby be able to use this concrete expression of the crisis as a means to overcoming it. Only by overcoming this could he then continue to develop his literary form and turn later to drama. Chandos describes how his soul could not be tied down to a definite style of living, and that the works which he had already written appear strange to him. They are strange to him because his soul is always changing, and the as yet unwritten works of the future remain unwriteable, as he has to change again. Plans, and presumably also works of art, are no longer the expression or property of himself, for he has given part of himself in them:

"Jedweder vollgesogen mit einem Tropfen meines Blutes, tanzen sie vor mir wie traurige Mücken an einer düsteren Mauer, auf der nicht mehr die helle Sonne der glücklichen Tage liegt." (5)

He has arrived at an awareness of non-possession which leaves a feeling like that experienced by Roquentin in Sartre's *La Nausée*. In a sort of inebriation Chandos sees the whole of the universe as one great entity based on a system of polarity between "höfisches und tierisches Wesen, Kunst und Unkunst, Einsamkeit und Gesellschaft." These were held in harmony by nature, which he saw in "den Tölpelhaftigkeiten junger Bauern nicht minder als in den süssesten Allegorien." In countless forms of nature he finds himself. Paradoxically he wants to find values not tied down by a particular style, and also in this to find a style or personality which is the full expression of himself. Even religious faith becomes a sublime allegory (Hofmannsthal as a young man saw religions as "schöne Mythologien"); but Chandos is torn between accepting the enticement of the rainbow-like mirage of peace in faith and the more positive offerings of human values. He finds it impossible to pass judgment on any everyday occurrence, and even finds that contacts with his family are all on a "white-lie" level which may be contrary to the sensitivity of his soul. Anecdotes have been told of Hofmannsthal's own sudden disappearances from his family circle when he no longer felt it possible to live in direct contact with humans living with values in discord with his own sensibility. Nor can Chandos find order in the models of classical authors such as Seneca and Cicero—a situation in which Hofmannsthal also found himself. Finding that his description of his inner soul as a scene of rats dying from poison arouses in him Mitleid, he achieves again a moment of contact with the whole of the universe:

"Es war viel mehr und viel weniger als Mitleid: ein unge-heueres Anteilnehmen, ein Hinüberfliessen in jene Geschöpfe oder ein Fühlen, dass ein Fluidum des Lebens und Todes, des Traumes und Wachens für einen Augenblick in sie hinübergeflossen ist— von woher?" [6]

Similarly when one evening he watches a water-boater flit across from one dark side of a watering-can to another, he becomes aware of the "Nachgefühl des Wundervollen." "Gegenwart der Liebe" which he experiences in such moments gives to him a sense of throbbing life in every organic and inorganic thing in the universe:

"In diesen Augenblicken wird eine nichtige Kreatur, ein Hund, eine Ratte, ein Käfer, ein verkrümmerter Apfelbaum, ein sich über den Hügel schlängelnder Karrenweg, ein moos-bewachsener Stein mir mehr, als die schönste, hingebendste Geliebte der glücklichsten Nacht mir je gewesen ist. . . . Es ist mir dann, als bestünde mein Körper aus lauter Chiffern, die mir alles aufschliessen. Oder als könnten wir in ein neues, ahnungsvolles Verhältnis zum ganzen Dasein treten, wenn wir anfingen mit dem Herzen zu denken." [7]

Chandos reaches a state where he must either have such moments or be completely out of touch with the world. The only language he can now use is the cipher language of his own direct empathy dormant in his soul.

Die Briefe des Zurückgekehrten (1901), five letters which describe the feelings of an Austrian who returns home after twenty years in South America, reveal Hofmannsthal's position of utter loneliness in the German way of life was replacing its old foundations of Menschlichkeit with those of avarice and self-consciousness. The twentieth-century European appeared to snatch haphazardly at different values and lose himself, delighted and fascinated in abstracts. The water jug, which in its function and associations became for Hofmannsthal a connection with all other human beings, becomes representative of too much—perhaps a Freudian symbol, even a political device—and thereby loses its original associative value. Man becomes a machine or a statistical nonentity, and Hofmannsthal, like Ortega y Gasset and Rudolf Kassner, sees that once this happens Menschlichkeit will turn into barbarity. He de-velops from this a sense of responsibility towards his contemporaries. He writes either to emphasize Menschlichkeit and soulfulness, the importance of the individual and the particular moment, and the importance of human contact—the necessity for society to rebuild its values on a common humanity; or else he writes to reveal the advent of barbarity. From this he gradually works out a system for an integrated Europe, an answer to the fragmenting effect on human life of twentieth-century values, which he expressed in his lecture *Das Schrifttum als Geistiger Raum der Nation* (1927):

"Der Prozess, von dem ich rede, ist nichts anderes als eine konservative Revolution von einem Umfange, wie die europäische Geschichte ihr nicht kennt. Ihr Ziel ist Form, eine neue deutsche Wirklichkeit, an der die ganze Nation teilnehmen könne." [8]

Before Hofmannsthal became fully aware of the impending collapse of Menschlichkeit, he wrote nearly all of his lyrical poems between 1890 and 1901. They are creations of his own Präexistenz, but although they are intensely lyrical in that they are concerned with the relationship between the poet and the universe, Hofmannsthal himself rarely appears in them. They are Ich-Gedichte with no direct mention of the Ich. Even in the earliest poems we are shown that the correct way of life is not a lone one (automatic) but a mixing and meeting with the world and the steering of a course through its maze. Hofmannsthal described the problems of his poetry as follows:

"Zwei Antinomien waren zu lösen: die der vergleichenden Zeit, und der Dauer—und die der Einsamkeit und der Gemeinschaft." [9]

In his essay *Gespräch über Gedichte* (1903) Hofmannsthal sums up the essence and function of a poem:

"Wovon unsere Seele sich nährt, das ist das Gedicht, in welchem, wie im Sommerabendwind, der über die frischgemähten Wiesen streicht, zugleich ein Hauch von Tod und Leben zu uns herschwebt, eine Ahnung des Blühens, ein Schauder des Verwesens, ein Jetzt, ein Hier und zugleich ein Jenseits, ein ungeheueres Jenseits. Jedes vollkommene Gedicht ist Ahnung und Gegenwart, Sehnsucht und Erfüllung zugleich." [10]

Every perfect poem excites a "Schwingung der Seele," is a vessel in whose contents and form we have a cipher for the relationships between all created things in the universe. We have only to look at the vessel, and we shall momentarily recreate a relationship. The poem represents a particular event or situation, encapsulates the intensest meaning and connotation of that event—is Gegenwart; it also reveals what place that event has in the cosmology of the universe, shows the universal significance to be seen behind the particular moment—is Ahnung; it also awakens the presentiment in the reader that there is such a significance—is Sehnsucht; and finally it is a permanent proof of the existence of this hidden cosmological status of the particular event—is Erfüllung. The soul is refreshed by the poem bringing together and laying bare before it particular event and universal significance. This leads to a way of finding a meaning to one's own existence. Man at birth and death is actively brought into contact with different stations of existence, and it is perhaps man's desire to understand these that makes him create poetry. Hofmannsthal finds that the symbolic dying of the man who plunges his knife into the throat of a ram—this re-enacting of a transformation in the universe—is the root of all poetry.

Hofmannsthal's poetry is full of such moments: a boy who creeps back home after his first night of love catches a glimpse of a new person in the mirror; a passer-by looks back at a scene of peace where an old man sings, a young woman feeds her child and other children play; a boy looks across at his new life on the unknown bank of a stream; a youth recognizes a spider as a challenge to enter life. Other poems describe how close Hofmannsthal felt himself to his ancestry and cultural heritage. In *Terzinen über Vergänglichkeit Nr. 1* he feels his ancestors as close to him as his own hair; and in *Manche freilich* . . . he says:

> "Ganz vergessener Völker Müdigkeiten
> Kann ich nicht abtun von meinen Lidern,
> Noch weghalten von der erschrockenen Seele
> Stummes Niederfallen ferner Sterne.
>
> Viele Geschicke weben neben dem meinen,
> Durcheinander spielt sie alle das Dasein,
> Und mein Teil ist mehr als dieses Lebens
> Schlanke Flamme oder schmale Leier." [11]

These ecstatic moments in his poetry are examples of the erotic as Hofmannsthal describes it in *Die Wege und die Begegnungen* (1906):

> "Mich dünkt, es ist nicht die Umarmung, sondern die Begegnung die eigentliche entscheidende erotische Pantomime. Es ist in keinem Augenblick das Sinnliche so seelenhaft, das Seelenhafte so sinnlich, als in der Begegnung. Hier ist alles möglich, alles in Bewegung, alles aufgelöst. Hier ist ein Zueinandertrachten noch ohne Begierde, eine naive Beimischung von Zutraulichkeit und Scheu. Hier ist das Rehhafte, das Vogelhafte, das Tierischdumpfe, das Engelsreine, das Göttliche. Ein Gruss ist etwas Grenzenloses . . . Dies Irgendwo, dies Unbestimmte und doch leidenschaftlich

Begehrende, dies Schreien des Fremden nach der Fremden ist das Gewaltige. Die Begegnung verspricht mehr als die Umarmung halten kann. Sie scheint, wenn ich so sagen darf einer höheren Ordnung der Dinge anzugehören, jener, nach der die Sterne sich bewegen und die Gedanken einander befruchten." [12]

This precarious balance at the moment of meeting when everything is possible is given more extensive treatment in *Andreas, oder die Vereinigten* (written in 1907 and 1917–18, published 1932), Hofmannsthal's unfinished novel. Here the style of harsh realism and Romantic Märchenwelt is embodied in the double and disassociated personality of Maria-Mariquita. The interweaving of the simplest and most intensely symbolic and spiritual shows us the development of a young man's education to life and the basic psychological patterns of human behaviour. It has been called "ein österreichischer *Wilhelm Meister*" and is a novel as perplexing and revealing as Novalis's *Heinrich von Ofterdingen*. Andreas finds the integration of his personality in love, and from the love he has for Romana he sees in her a way not only to self-possession, but also to possession of the secrets of the universe.

Lyrical form cannot hold an extension of such intense moments of "Schreien des Fremden nach der Fremden," for it involves change or at least looseness of identity. There can be no "automatic" orientation from such ecstatic moments, and the portrayal of the allomatic demands dramatic form. Clearly monologue is unsuitable, but Hofmannsthal when he reached this point in his artistic development had not found the formula by which he could express on the stage the "Geheimnis der Konfiguration," the interaction of one character on another. So he turned to the Novelle form. In *Reitergeschichte* (1898) the looseness of identity of the rider Lerch is evoked by the way in which the reader is helped by the prose style to experience the action through the consciousness of both Lerch and his horse. The absence of dialogue makes the only words spoken seem like steps leading from one level of existence to another. In *Buch der Freunde* (1922) (a book of maxims, etc.) Hofmannsthal writes:

> "Niemand ist von Haus aus weniger Psychologe als der Novellist. Er betrachtet die Charaktere als das Allgemeine und die Situation als das Besondere." [13]

In both *Reitergeschichte* and *Das Erlebnis des Marschalls von Bassompierre* (1900), the characters are no more than ciphers set in certain situations. We are interested in their fates not because of themselves, but because they represent typical qualities in humans, and we become interested in the forces unleashed by those qualities. In *Das Erlebnis des Marschalls* . . . the woman becomes "das Weiblich-Sinnliche"; in *Reitergeschichte* Lerch becomes the fated warrior. The situations develop a power of their own into which these figures have to fit.

In *Elektra* (1909) Hofmannsthal combines his interest in psychology with his skill for developing the powers of a situation. Before writing it he read Freud's study on hysteria; and in it he shows Elektra as the embodiment of one overruling passion—revenge on her mother. She is unable to kill Klytämnestra herself, but when her brother Orest does so, she experiences complete fulfilment of her being. As there is no other function for her existence, she too has to die; and the opera closes with her dance of frenzy into death.

Hofmannsthal first met Richard Strauss in 1900, but it was not until after Strauss had set *Elektra* to music that Strauss pegged Hofmannsthal down to the demands of musical form. This was a discipline which was perhaps necessary for Hofmannsthal's sensitive and shaken spirit's search for adequate means of expression. Like Chandos, he went on the search for classical models to give him a sense of form and find situations and descriptions of human behaviour which would be of striking interest and educative value for him and his contemporaries. For some years Hofmannsthal was unable to find fresh inspiration from his own imagination for new plots and characters, so he turned naturally to the art of translation and adaptation. His models were the French comedies, Greek tragedies (particularly the Ödipus legend) and English Elizabethan dramas (such as Thomas Otway's *Venice Preserved*). He also found suitable material in the Everyman legend which he knew mainly through the English mediaeval morality *Everyman* and Hans Sachs's *Comedi eines reichen sterbenden Menschen*.

Realizing that the Everyman theme could have a universal application to all ages, Hofmannsthal wrote his version *Jedermann* (1911). Here he tried to reconcile the Roman Catholic and Protestant solutions to human life, which had found in this legend a vehicle for inter-denominational warfare. Today most productions of *Jedermann*, including the one at Salzburg, emphasize the Roman Catholic or Protestant elements in the play, and neglect or play down the opposing viewpoint. This does not prevent the work from being a most compelling invitation to lead a Christian life, but it takes away from the play the originality and purpose for which it was first written. Jedermann, a rich and still young man, is surrounded with all that money can buy. He does not think about the time when he will have to face God's judgment, and treats others according to the ways in which they are useful to him. In the middle

of a banquet at which he is most unlikely to be thinking of anything
but the superficial enjoyment of the moment, Death appears as
God's messenger to call him to judgment. One by one, Jedermann's
friends, relatives and riches leave him. The figure of his works,
Werke, a cripple, implores him to take her as a companion to
judgment. She is unable to help him without her sister Glaube,
whose words of compassion and call to humility before God finally
win over Jedermann, who wilfully accepts her, takes the last sacra-
ments and descends into the grave to appear before God's judgment.
Jedermann suffers in the realization of the falseness of his former
outlook and enters into a new existence. He is reborn before us on
the stage—a change which is effective mainly because of the
spiteful nature of Death and the emphasis laid on Jedermann's
loneliness.

In 1911 Hofmannsthal and Strauss finished writing their most
famous and successful comedy for music Der Rosenkavalier. The
letters written between them at this time give the detailed working
out of an intricate and sophisticated work of art. Here for probably
the first time in history composer and librettist worked together
jointly on the creation of an opera. High comedy in a Molière style,
opera buffa in the spirit of Mozart, and a commentary on the manners of Viennese society are fused into a new operatic form. As in
Wagner's operas, and in particular in Die Meistersinger, every detail
of score, libretto and production is combined into a Gesamtkunst-
werk of polished originality. Not only is the whole plot an original
extravaganza, but the characters are not types but fully dimensional
and develop as the work proceeds. The themes of love, time and
fidelity are shown from many different viewpoints, and these also
develop. There are moments of deepest tragedy or Wehmut for the
Marschallin, moments of uproarious comedy with Baron Ochs, and
moments of the intensest emotion and feeling especially between
Octavian and Sophie in the final Act. The particular events are
clearly representative of universal truths, and throughout there is a
note of bitter sweet irony which makes the opera quite unique as a
work of art and as an entertainment. The curtain opens on a
boudoir scene in which the Marschallin, experienced in love and
life, is about to take breakfast with her young lover Octavian.
They are interrupted by the arrival of her country cousin Baron
Ochs, who wants her advice on how to find a suitable cavalier to
present the traditional silver rose to his fiancée Sophie, daughter of
a rich parvenu Faninal. Disguised as a lady's maid, Octavian
excites the amorous advances of Ochs, but the scene changes
into the Marschallin's levee, after which she moans over her fleeting
youth. In Act 2 Octavian (as the knight of the rose) presents the

rose to Sophie, and these two fall in love on first meeting. Ochs appears, a quarrel breaks out, and he is slightly wounded in a duel with Octavian. Octavian sends him a note signed as the lady's maid arranging a rendezvous with him; and on this Ochs sings lecherously of the delights to come. In Act 3 the rendezvous takes place in an inn where Octavian has arranged a series of practical jokes to be played on Ochs. Uproar follows, ending with the arrival of the police, followed by Sophie and her father and later the Marschallin. Ochs leaves hurriedly, and the Marschallin renounces Octavian so that he can find his happiness with Sophie.

Hofmannsthal's association as a librettist with Strauss continued for the rest of his life. The detailed story of this is told in their correspondence which gives deep insights into the joint composition of a series of operas including among others *Elektra* (1909), *Der Rosenkavalier* (1911), *Ariadne auf Naxos* (1912) (which was to be performed after Molière's *Bürger als Edelmann*, and which appeared in a second version in 1916), *Josephslegende* (1914), *Die Frau ohne Schatten* (1919), *Die Ägyptische Helena* (1928), and *Arabella*, whose first performance took place four years after Hofmannsthal's death. It has been the custom to underestimate the achievement of Hofmannsthal as a librettist, probably because the rhapsodic quality of Strauss's music hides the intricately worked out devices by which words and music are interwoven. It is easier to appreciate immediately the use of leitmotif in music than the recurrent use of key-words and images in the libretto. Strauss's musical phrasing develops together with themes in the plot and also with key-words in the libretto acquiring more and more associative value. The same care for detail was exercised by them both in the presentation of the operas, in their décor, stage-movements, etc.

During the war, Hofmannsthal wrote several political essays behind which there is a deep grief for the collapsing Austro-Hungarian Empire and a growing realization that after the war there would be an age no longer interested in the former values of European civilization. Hofmannsthal called to the Germans to look back at the "Geist der Antike." This he describes in *Vermächtnis der Antike* (1928):

"Es ist der Mythos unseres europäischen Daseins, die Kreation unserer geistigen Welt (ohne welche die religiöse nicht sein kann), die Setzung von Kosmos gegen Chaos, und er umschliesst den Helden und das Opfer, die Ordnung und die Verwandlung, das Mass und die Weihe." [14]

The Salzburg Festival, and in particular Hofmannsthal, Strauss and Max Reinhardt their stage director, set out to reintegrate the spiritual life of the Bavarian-Austrian people, as is stated in *Festspiele in Salzburg* (1921):

"Musikalisch theatralische Festspiele in Salzburg zu veranstalten, das heisst: uralt Lebendiges aufs neue lebendig machen; . . . es heisst: den Urtrieb des bayerisch-österreichischen Stammes gewähren lassen, und diesem Volk, . . . den Weg zurück finden helfen zu seinem eigentlichen geistigen Element." [15]

Through the Festival it was hoped to bring together people of all races and classes in common appreciation of works of art which displayed humanity and to pay homage to Mozart's genius. Hofmannsthal's own works which have been performed at the Festival include most of the operas he wrote with Strauss, *Jedermann*, *Das Salzburger Grosse Welttheater*, *Der Schwierige*, *Der Tod und der Tod* and *Der Turm*. *Das Salzburger Grosse Welttheater* (1922) adapted from Calderon's play, shows the hierarchy of human life in allegorical form. The King, rich man, peasant, beggar, Wisdom and Beauty are all part of a tradition found in the mediaeval mystery plays. Hofmannsthal has recast the figure of the beggar as an active character set against the rest of the world. He represents "die Drohung des Chaos an die geordnete Welt," and, by raising his axe against the rest of the world, symbolically threatens the whole tradition of European civilization. But at this very moment, Hofmannsthal allows Wisdom to pray for the beggar's redemption. He is moved by some mysterious force to drop his axe, and falls on his knees. This action is the decisive one of his life, and through it he overcomes the desire for power, and goes to his death as an almost saintly figure.

Hofmannsthal's interest in comedy is for him an exploration of a way to human contact in life, of the "Weg zum Sozialen," this aspect primarily interesting him in his earlier comedies such as *Silvia im "Stern"* (1907), *Florindo* (1907) and *Cristinas Heimreise* (1908); it is also a challenge to portray the decay of civilized society, which he sets in everyday scenes particularly in his later comedies. Misunderstandings of ambiguous meanings in conversation are shown to lead to amusing and disastrous consequences. *Der Schwierige* (1921) shows the possibilities and limits of human society in its central character Karl Bühl. He is both the self-conscious representative and sharpest critic of the society in which he lives; but in his passivity lies an insight into the weaknesses of his environment which eventually involves him in its most intricate entanglements. Bühl represents the cultured conservative Austrian who believed in Menschlichkeit and bygone values, whereas Neuhoff, his opposite figure, is typical of the new cultured man after the first world war, unbalanced between the demands of his reason and his ambition. But in the new environment Neuhoff is less of a problem than the simple retiring Bühl, who finds some unshifting values in his marriage to Helene, as he is made to face up to keeping a definite style of living not always of his own choice. Perhaps the least appreciated of Hofmannsthal's comedies is *Der Unbestechliche* (1923) which stands in the tradition of Mozart's *Marriage of Figaro* and Molière's schools of manners. Once the Baroness has re-engaged Theodor as head butler, social hierarchy in her son's house is but a formality. Theodor arranges the lives and loves of all who enter with a flair and satirical attitude towards class distinctions that split open the false values of a modern leisured society. Its implications are not so searching as those of *Der Schwierige*, but it reveals a touch of humour which became more and more rare in Hofmannsthal's works after the war.

Hofmannsthal's final great work *Der Turm* (1924 and 1927) signifies the climax of his works and the prospect of European civilization falling into a disaster far greater than that of the first world war. He had experimented with the material, taken from Calderon, from as early as 1900, but found that the situations into which he had placed his characters were too full of problems and associative values for even dramatic form to hold them. Hofmannsthal either gave his characters too much insight into themselves, or analysed them to the core of their being, so that some supernatural force rather than the characters themselves appears to be responsible for their actions. Actions for his characters involve the sacrifice of themselves to other people, or to a fate formed by some allomatic element. Each individual action is seen to be the re-enacting of a myth, so that human life can become an allegory of human existence. It was this that attracted Hofmannsthal to the plays of Calderon, and it is as an allegorical figure that Prince Sigismund in *Der Turm* is to be interpreted. One of the fundamental beliefs in Hofmannsthal's works, which is worked out in its final form in *Das Salzburger Grosse Welttheater* and *Der Turm*, is that man has the power in his actions to lower himself to the status of a beast or raise himself to immortality—he can develop the myth at his will. Hofmannsthal seeks for the most basic motives in man, and tries to see how these fit into the hierarchy of the universe. *Der Turm* shows many of the problems taken out of the timeless world of *Das Salzburger Grosse Welttheater* or the Märchen world of *Die Frau ohne Schatten* set in a political situation. Prince Sigismund's father, King of Poland, learns from an oracle that his son will one day seize the throne by force, and therefore has him imprisoned, so that Sigismund is brought up in complete ignorance of his royal birth. After a complicated court intrigue, Sigismund is brought to the palace, where by drinking a potion he is made to forget his wretched upbringing. He threatens his father, however, and has to be taken back to the tower dungeon. He is made to forget all that has happened by drinking a second potion. Later he comes back to power and meets his death by stabbing by a gypsy woman, and his throne is taken by a child King. Hofmannsthal later changed this to him being shot by Olivier, one of the former guards over him while in the dungeon, and there is no heir to the throne to take his place. Hofmannsthal challenges Western civilization in *Der Turm* to examine its conscience. He attacks the self-sufficient egoist's attitude towards suffering as a punishment, and would set up in its place an attitude towards suffering as atonement. Atonement was the motive for Greek communal sacrifices; and Hofmannsthal finds that Christianity has developed a voice of resignation; it has turned back along the road described in Goethe's conversation with Eckermann of 11 March 1832:

> "Auch werden wir alle nach und nach aus einem Christentum des Worts und Glaubens immer mehr zu einem Christentum der Gesinnung und Tat kommen." [16]

But *Der Turm* has many interwoven themes: those of the self and the world, dream and action, the individual and the state, power and anarchy, communication and isolation, destruction of order, and disunity of the state within itself and man within himself. Act I shows Sigismund still in a pure state of Präexistenz, as if he was not yet born, unconscious of his human capabilities, little more than a beast. With the drink in Act II he awakens to self-consciousness and recognition of other people, to his own mortality and to God. Act III shows Sigismund taking on his fate and guilt as a man and as a role in the state. We are shown that he is fated to destroy the old order so as to establish the new, and from this evil will come good. The fourth Act brings Sigismund back to the tower prison—the prison of himself, where he finds meaning only in his inner life. His encounter with the outside world has brought him wisdom and made him master of himself. Sigismund is happy in peaceful contemplation of the microcosm inside him. Act V shows Sigismund's second acceptance of the outside world, and he returns to power at the head of his people. He rules through power, no longer believing in it, and goes to war to bring others peace. He sacrifices his belief in peace as atonement for his years of silent passivity. In the first version, after Sigismund's death the appearance of the child King brings hope that a new order will replace Sigismund's, but in the second version Sigismund's murder leaves the whole question of succession open.

He is killed by a shot of discontent, probably from the revolver of Gefreite Olivier, symbol of a menacing future order, whose analogy in actual political history is only too clear. Sigismund's last words in the second version of *Der Turm* are a cry of despair, the cry of a leader of an order based on humanity and belief in action and sacrifice for atonement. Like his creator, whose growing despair for Europe was deepened by the belief that he went unheard and unread, Sigismund calls to his doctor and to his tutor:

"Gebet Zeugnis, ich war da, wenngleich mich niemand gekannt hat." [17]

It has been impossible to give an account of the complex material in the opera and Märchen *Die Frau ohne Schatten*, whose themes and motifs come from both oriental and European folklore and works such as Novalis's *Heinrich von Ofterdingen*. As a meeting place for symbolic and moral themes, the work is central to an understanding of Hofmannsthal's creative activity, and is another example together with *Andreas* and *Der Turm* of a work whose ideas overreach the limits of literary form. Nor is it possible to do more than mention Hofmannsthal's debt to Goethe, Grillparzer and Novalis among others. Nor has it been possible to examine the effect on Hofmannsthal of his experience of Greece, which he visited in 1908, whose light and landscape, the cradle of European civilization, were full of significance to him. To discuss his friendships with Rudolf Borchardt, Rudolf Alexander Schröder, Eberhard von Bodenhausen and Carl J. Burckhardt would require a separate essay. Research into his life and works is growing in volume every year, but Hofmannsthal remains for the reading public the author of *Jedermann* and of a few lyrical poems, and librettist to Richard Strauss's *Der Rosenkavalier*. He died two days after his son's suicide in July 1929 at his home in Rodaun a greatly loved but little known man. There is no formula to sum up the complexity of his personality, but two facets of it stand out. First is his extraordinary sensitivity to natural experiences, to human contacts and to artistic and literary expression of all kinds. Second is the honesty of his mind and the way in which he continually set it against the great problems which it met, both personal and universal.

The standard edition of Hofmannsthal's works is that in fifteen volumes edited by Herbert Steiner, who, with access to Hofmannsthal's Nachlass in Harvard University, is accepted as the doyen of Hofmannsthal studies. There is, however, no critical edition of his works, and the select bibliography below includes details of those cheap and other editions which have recently appeared. The bibliography also lists introductory critical works on Hofmannsthal.

Hofmannsthal—eine Bibliographie 1890–1960, which is awaiting publication, brings up to date and extends all previous Hofmannsthal bibliographies both of his published works and critical works on these.

TRANSLATIONS

1. As my life was dead, may you be my life o Death! What compel sme, who do not know both, to call you "Death" and that "Life"? Into one hour you can compress life.

2. But what are palaces and poems: a dreamlike phantasy of reality! The real encloses no patterned web: to lead on the whole dance, the real dance, do you understand this office? Here is a way, it carries me lighter than dream would. I slip right to the sea. . . . Bacchus, Bacchus, someone caught you too and bound you firmly, but not for long.

3. The lover of supreme beauty, which he had already seen, believing it to be the image of that which he had not seen, now desired to enjoy it in its pristine form.

4. Integration with life. Penetration out of "Pre-existence" into "Existence" . . . into Being.

5. Each of them imbibed with a drop of my blood, they dance before me like dismal gnats by a dark wall, on which the bright sun of happy days no longer lies.

6. It was much more and much less than compassion: a dreadful sharing, a flowing over into those creatures or a feeling that a fluid of life and of death, of dream and waking for one moment has flowed over into them—but from where?

7. In these moments a meaningless creature, a dog, a rat, a beetle, a crooked apple-tree, a cart-track winding over the hill, a stone overgrown with moss, means more to me than the most beautiful, most responsive lover of the most ecstatic night has ever meant. . . . It is then as if my body were formed of pure ciphers, which reveal all to me. Then it is as if we could step into a new susceptibly aware relationship to the whole of existence, if only we began to think with the heart.

8. The process of which I speak, is nothing other than a conservative revolution of an extent, the like of which European history does not know. Its aim is form, a new German reality, in which the whole nation may be able to take part.

9. Two antinomies were to be solved: that of relative and permanent time—and that of loneliness and sociability.

10. That from which our soul draws nourishment is the poem, in which, as in the wind on a summer evening that drifts over the freshly mown meadows, wafts to us a breath together of death and life, an apprehension of the fullness of life, a dread of decaying, a now, a here and at the same time a beyond, a terrible beyond. Every complete poem is simultaneously premonition and presence, longing and fulfilment.

11. The lassitude of long forgotten peoples I cannot throw off from my eyelids, nor keep away from my shaken soul the mute downfall of faraway stars. Many fates are woven close to mine, existence gambols in and out among them, and my lot is more than life's slender flame or constricted tune.

12. Methinks it is not the embrace, but the encounter which is the actual decisive erotic dalliance. There is no moment when the sensual is so soulful, the soulful so sensual, as in the encounter. Here all is possible, all in flux, all unattached. Here is an attraction to one another still without urgent desire, an artless intermingling of trust and modesty. Here is the timidity of the deer, soaring power of the bird, torpor of the beast, purity of the angel, the divine. A greeting is something boundless . . . This somewhere, this uncertainty and yet passionately hoping desire, this calling of the unknown to her that is unknown is what is so potent. The encounter promises more than the embrace can hold. It appears, if I may say so, to belong to a higher order of things, to that according to which the stars are moved, and thoughts generate one another.

13. No one is fundamentally less a psychologist than the writer of Novellen. He considers the characters as representing the universal and the situation as the particular event.

14. It is the myth of our European existence, the creation of our spiritual world (without which there can be no religious world), the setting of cosmos against chaos, and it includes the hero and the martyr, order and change, harmony and poetic aspiration.

15. The introduction of musical/theatrical Festivals in Salzburg means breathing new life into what was originally alive; . . . it means giving encouragement to the original impetus of life in the Bavarian-Austrian race, and helping this people find the way back to its true spiritual expression.

16. And we shall all gradually advance from a Christianity of words and of faith to a Christianity of intention and action.

17. Bear witness that I was there, even though no one recognized me.

BIBLIOGRAPHY

HUGO VON HOFMANNSTHAL. *Gesammelte Werke in Einzelausgaben* (15 vols.), Hsg. von Herbert Steiner. Fischer Verlag, Stockholm and Frankfurt/Main. 1946–59.

Ausgewählte Werke in zwei Bänden. Hsg. von Rudolf Hirsch. Fischer Verlag, Frankfurt/Main. 1957.

Festspiele in Salzburg. Bermann-Fischer Verlag, Vienna, 1938.

Der Schwierige/Der Unbestechliche. Fischerbücherei (233).

Fischer Schulausgaben: *Das Bergwerk zu Falun, Jedermann, Der Turm.*

Inselbücherei: *Der Tod des Tizian, Der Tor und der Tod, Das kleine Welttheater, Alkestis, Reden und Aufsätze, Gedichte, Das Salzburger Grosse Welttheater.*

Wege und Begegnungen. Nachwort von W. Brecht. Reclam (7171)

Komödie. Einleitung von J. Nadler. Stiasny Bücherei, Graz, 1960.

Andreas. Bibliothek des 100 Bücher. Y. Fischer Verlag, 1961.

Der Tor und der Tod. Foreword by M. E. Gilbert. Blackwell, Oxford, 1942.

Selected Essays. Foreword by M. E. Gilbert. Blackwell, Oxford, 1955.

Jedermann. Foreword by M. Jacobs. Nelson, London, 1952.

Selected Prose. Translated by M. Hottinger and T. and J. Stern. Foreword by H. Broch. Routledge & Kegan Paul, London, 1952.

Briefe 1890–1901. Fischer Verlag, Berlin, 1935.

Briefe 1900–9. Bermann-Fischer Verlag, Vienna, 1937.

RICHARD STRAUSS/HUGO VON HOFMANNSTHAL: Briefwechsel. Hsg. von F. and A. Strauss, bearbeitet von W. Schuh. Gesamtausgabe, Atlantis Verlag, Zürich, 1952.

Briefwechsel zwischen GEORGE und HOFMANNSTHAL. Hsg. von R. Boehringer.
2. ergänzte Ausgabe, Düsseldorf, 1953.

HUGO VON HOFMANNSTHAL/EBERHARD VON BODENHAUSEN: Briefe der Freundschaft. Hsg. von D. von Bodenhausen. E. Diederichs Verlag, Berlin, 1953.

HUGO VON HOFMANNSTHAL/RUDOLF BORCHARDT: Briefwechsel. Hsg. von M. L. Borchardt und Herbert Steiner. Fischer Verlag, Frankfurt/Main, 1954.

HUGO VON HOFMANNSTHAL/CARL J. BURCKHARDT: Briefwechsel. Hsg. von C. J. Burckhardt. Fischer Verlag, Frankfurt/Main, 1956.

ALEWYN, R. Versuch über Hofmannsthal. Kleine Vandenhoeck Reihe Nr. 17. Vandenhoeck und Ruprecht, Göttingen, 1958.

BIANQUIS, G. La Poésie autrichienne de Hofmannsthal à Rilke (pp. 75–195) Les Presses Universitaires de France, Paris, 1926.

BRECHT, W. Grundlinie im Werke Hugo von Hofmannsthals. *Euphorion*, Ergänzungsheft 16, 1923.

CURTIUS, E. R. Hofmannsthal, George und Calderón. In *Kritische Essays zur Europäischen Literatur*. Francke Verlag, Bern, 1950.

FIECHTNER, H. A. Hugo von Hofmannsthal—Die Gestalt des Dichters im Spiegel der Freunde. Humboldt Verlag, Vienna, 1949.

GRENZMANN, W. Hugo von Hofmannsthal und seine Freunde. In *Deutsche Dichtung der Gegenwart*. Menck Verlag, Frankfurt/Main, 1953.

HAMMELMANN, H. Hofmannsthal. Studies in Modern European Literature and Thought. Bowes & Bowes, London, 1957.

HEDERER, E. Hugo von Hofmannsthal. Fischer Verlag, Frankfurt/Main, 1960.

KEITH-SMITH, B. Hugo von Hofmannsthal-eine Bibliographie 1890–1960.

NAEF, K. J. Hugo von Hofmannsthal Wesen und Werk. Niehans Verlag, Zürich, 1938.